THE CIRCUS IN AMERICA

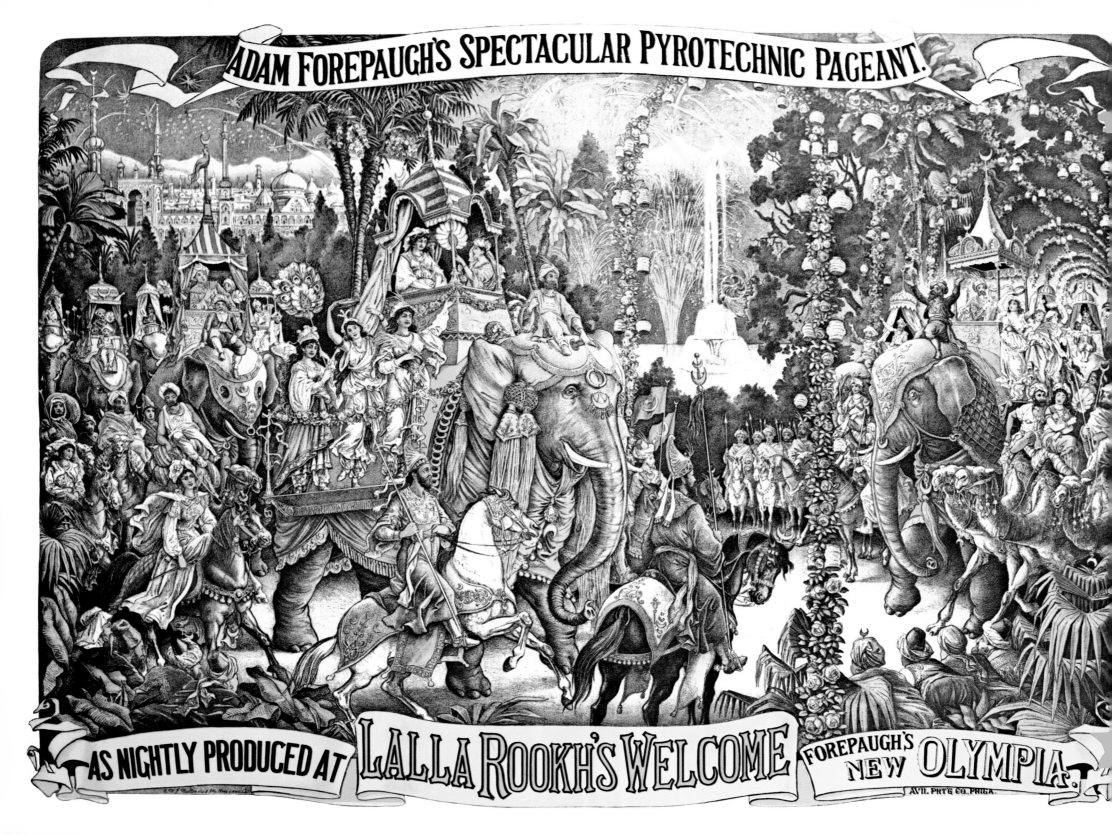

THE CIRCUS IN AMERICA

by Charles Philip Fox and Tom Parkinson

HENNESSEY + INGALLS SANTA MONICA 2002

Originally published by Country Beautiful, Waukesha, Wisconsin, a division of Flick-Reedy Educational Enterprises, Inc., 1969.

Reprinted with permission, 2002, by

Hennessey + Ingalls
1254 3rd Street Promenade
Santa Monica CA 90401

Printed in China

ISBN: 0-940512-33-5

The publisher and authors wish to express deep appreciation to the following sources for providing the illustrative material for this book:
> *Lithographs:* Jos. Schlitz Brewing Co. Collection; Circus World Museum Collection, Baraboo, Wisconsin.
> *Original Art:* George F. Getz., Jr., and Roderick W. McKinnon Collection at the Circus World Museum.
> *Photographs:* Roy Trexler, Steve Albasing, Harry Atwell, Harry Simpson, William Green, Richard Conover, Robert Higgins (through the courtesy of the Circus World Museum.) Douglas C. Green.

Ringling Bros. and Barnum & Bailey © THE GREATEST SHOW ON EARTH © has given the publisher permission to reproduce images from the Ringling Bros. and the Barnum & Bailey circuses.

The publisher thanks The Wisconsin Historical Society's Circus World Museum, Baraboo, Wisconsin, for their help and cooperation in the loan of the original film for this publication.

Library of Congress Cataloging-in-Publication Data

Fox, Charles Philip, 1913-
  The circus in America / by Charles Philip Fox and Tom Parkinson
    p. cm.
  Originally published: Waukesha, Wis.: Country Beautiful, 1969.
  Includes bibliographic references and index.
  ISBN 0-940512-33-5 (hb)
  1. Circus—United States. I. Parkinson, Tom, 1921- II. Title.

GV1803 .F6 2002
791.3'0973—dc21

                                                    2002017206

Frontispiece: Forepaugh's Great Show in 1881

Contents

Part III
THE WONDROUS ONE-DAY STAND

Part IV
THE BIG SHOW UNDER THE BIG TOP

Part I
THE LURE AND THE LORE

1-The Essence of the Circus

Across this land the circus has moved for two centuries as a popular amusement institution, creating its own unique phase of the national heritage and leaving behind a tradition of wholesome entertainment.

It has reached into every byway and crossroad of this country, playing to more communities than the movies. Its beginnings go back to Colonial and Federal periods, making it as long-lived as the American theater. Its art forms are as demanding as those of the ballet and the opera. Its appeal is as universal as band concerts, as basic as baseball, so ageless it attracts grandparents and grandchildren alike.

Despite antecedents in Europe and the constant recruitment of foreign performers, the circus in the form that we know it is a truly American development. Circuses of Europe, Asia, Africa and South America are much like each other; those of North America are unique in their traditions and methods.

The circus occupies a warm spot in the heart of America. It is a favored institution, a part of the national lore, a part of our patriotism. And what is this thing that we accept so readily and yet know so little about?

Grandparents vie for the privilege of taking children to the circus. Parents debate about whether their first-born is old enough to go — a status reached just before the age for electric trains. Today's children know about the circus even if they live in a city no longer reached by a tented show; they know about clowns and elephants and riders.

But for all the accent on children, the circus is for every age — as the Ringling Bros. and Barnum & Bailey announcer says, "children of all ages."

The American circus is a big and blaring thing — bigger and better every year, three rings, more elephants, more horses, more people. In contrast, European circuses emphasize the quality of a performer's art; here the public does not really know the difference between a well-turned pirouette and a poor one. It will applaud a pretty trick sooner than a difficult one. But no matter. American circuses benefit from a marvelous combination of pageantry and promotion. The hoopla of press agentry and of the show itself adds to the enjoyment of a circus, and a spectacle's pageantry adds that much more in excitement and action and romance.

Like America itself, the circus has developed a colorful past described in half-legend, half-fact. President George Washington attended the first full circus in this country and swapped horses with the operator. Circus clown Dan Rice campaigned for Zachary Taylor and was a favorite of Abraham Lincoln. Buffalo Bill was a pal of many cowboy-cavalrymen in Theodore Roosevelt's Rough Riders, and later Cody and Teddy figured in the founding of the Boy Scouts of America.

Opposite: The early circus was frequently the only harbinger of the cultures and traditions of strange, far-off lands. {c. 1930}

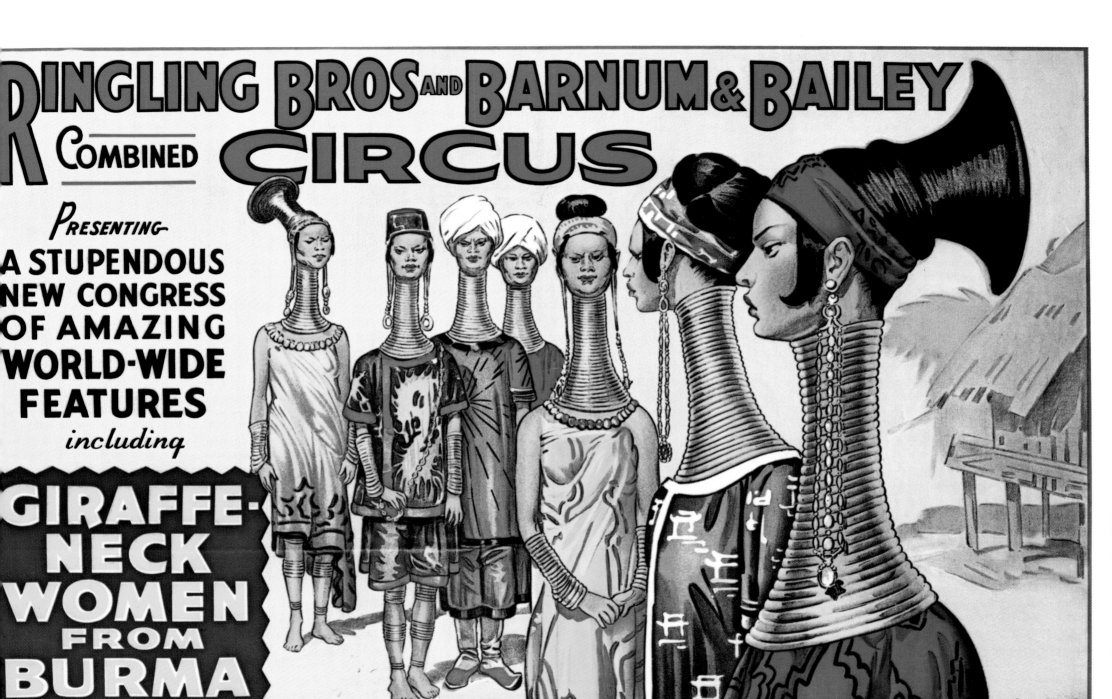

Circus lore has it that a rare birth of an elephant in captivity brought Barnum and Bailey together. Barnum offered to buy the baby elephant but Bailey declined and reproduced the telegram on posters that proclaimed "Here is what Barnum thinks of our elephant!" Barnum concluded that this was a rival he would have to join, according to the legend, which in this case contains a high percentage of truth.

Another tale is that the famous elephant Jumbo died in a vain effort to protect a baby elephant from injury. They faced an onrushing locomotive and the biggest elephant stood firm to protect his infant companion. Again, there is both fact and fiction.

Circus lore tells of the famous love affair of its two most popular and able stars of their era, Lillian Leitzel, petite aerialist, and Alfredo Codona, champion of the flying trapeze. They were an ideal romantic couple in the eyes of the public and circus people as well. Their marriage was acclaimed by their fans. But tragedy stalked their way as it would in a melodramatic novel. She fell to her death and he mourned to the end — an end that he brought about with

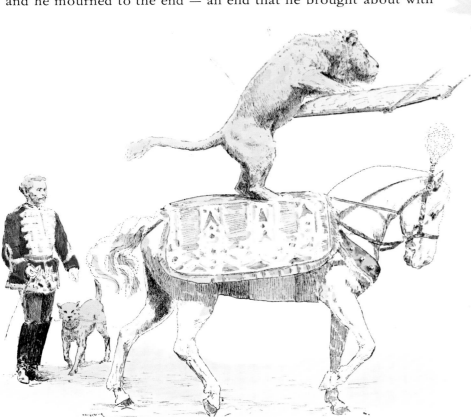

Opposite page: A live marionette with his musical mimicry {upper right}, the elephants' amusing "London Bridge" routine {upper left}, a graceful dressage act complete with doves {bottom}. Left: The unique combination of horse and lion; above: the fearlessness of the lady lion tamer, create that aura of timelessness, that special magic which lures young and old again and again to the circus.

13

bullets for his second wife and himself.

Even in the space age, the age-old and ageless circus continues to weave its magic over the country. In tents and in arenas it performs as always — as it has despite wars and epidemics and depressions and challenges from rivals for public patronage.

Its heritage is told by the roster of its great names. Barnum, Ringling, Bailey, Forepaugh, Sells, Hagenbeck, Floto, Robinson and a hundred more names have been painted on circus wagons and blazoned on millions of circus posters.

Those posters also carried the names of the great performers, the outstanding stars and features of the circus. That roster includes Van Amburgh, the lion king; Levi North, the star rider; Jumbo and Dan Rice.

In a more recent era there were Clyde Beatty, Emmett Kelly, Poodles Hanneford and the Hanneford Family, Codona, Leitzel, the Great Wallendas, Hugo and Mario Zacchini, Felix Adler, Lucio Cristiani and the Cristiani Family, Terrell Jacobs, May Wirth, Mabel Stark, Merle Evans, the Flying Concellos and many more.

These were and are the brave and skilled artists in a business of braggadocio and bravado, which makes it the more remarkable that they retained their own given names. Clyde and Emmett and Mabel and Merle are not the glamorous names of the movie star variety, but great circus performers made them great names.

There have been super features such as the Royal Burmese Giraffe Neck Women, the Ubangi Savages, Gargantua the Great, Tusko the mighty outlaw elephant, Goliath the sea elephant and the best slogan in the history of advertising, "The Greatest Show on Earth."

On the opposite side there have been the countless, faceless thousands who have passed in and out of the circus tradition as workingmen or minor functionaries. Their efforts and their

Above: Because this clown's makeup extended to his chest, he was dubbed "Chesty" by his friends.

Right: A Dailey Bros. clown carefully applies his funny face in Clown Alley, where all the trunks of the clowns are lined up.

Opposite: Wild West shows brought a taste of the frontier to the Eastern towners. {1916}

14

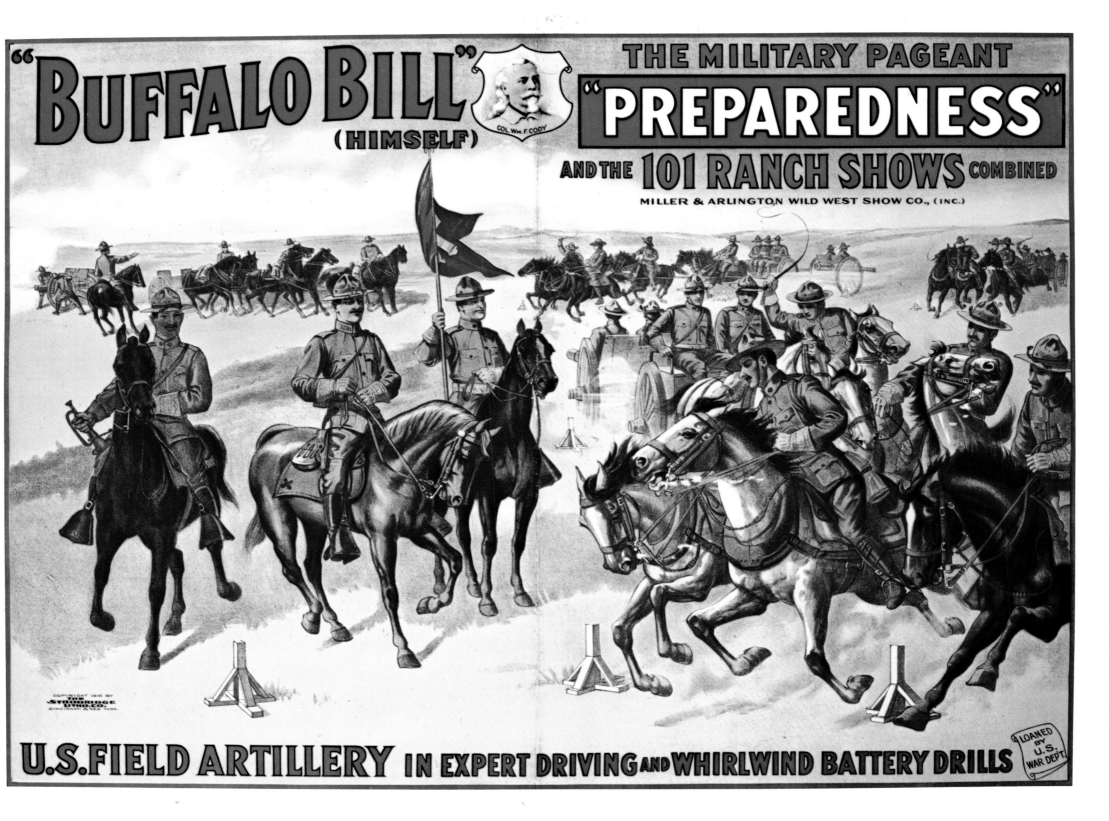

The tempestuous romance between Lillian Leitzel {left} and Alfredo Codona {right} ended tragically when Miss Leitzel fell to her death.

loyalties to a show and to a tradition have kept the circus going in fair weather and mud, in rich times and in those years when the circus could feed them and house them but could not pay them.

Between were the many performers — able and loyal — together with skilled bosses, agents and staff men who served as boss canvasmen, general agents, bandmasters, cookhouse stewards, trainmasters, elephant superintendents and more.

From the lonely advance man, out ahead of the show and lost in a world that cannot speak his show language or share his interests, to the family of bareback riders, reigning supreme at the peak of the circus social structure, troupers always have been positive that their lot was the best possible calling. They are spared that horrible fate of being a yokel, a rube, a towner. They are circus people, with it and for it. It is a high state and a place for pride.

Town children know this, and enough of them have run away from home to populate a hundred circuses. Sometimes it is more

difficult for the community of adults to see the circus in quite the same way. Then they listen for a moment to the child still in each of them and agree that the circus is a marvelous institution.

The circus seen for the first time is a tremendous experience. But seen time and time again and then enjoyed yet another time, it becomes a vehicle for reviving aging memories and excitements. It begins as a novelty and comes back as nostalgia.

For children the most appealing novelty of the moment may be the candy butcher who hawks cold drinks. That turn of events often perturbs adults, but the circus is many things to many people, and why shouldn't the youngster be intrigued by the unusual vendors as well as by the unusual trainer?

Cartoonists usually are astute observers of the current scene and chroniclers of mankind. So it is not surprising that they have incorporated the circus into their repertoire along with the woman driver, the inveterate shopper, the drugstore cowboy and the

An inherent part of any circus is the skill of the dainty equestrienne. {1894}

Ringling's famous bandmaster, Merle Evans, sustains the fast tempo of the show. His band plays for each act and can swiftly adapt from the pace of the dancing horse to that of the flying trapeze.

precocious kid. Every few months some cartoonist composes a new line for the standard drawing of a trapeze artist who is out in the air and discovers that he has no bar to clutch. Cartoonists love the weight lifter, the human cannonball and the circus billposter. There have been scores of funny drawings about the trainer whose head is in the lion's mouth.

The circus affords amazing entertainment, yet its greatest appeal always has been in its transient ways — here today, gone tomorrow, out of the blue and off to nowhere. It traveled widely when few others could tell of far-off places. It reached out toward the frontier when that was the Alleghenies and when it was the Mississippi and still when it was the Rockies and the Pacific.

Into rural areas of drab appearance where inhabitants led a dull, work-a-day existence, the circus sent its brilliant posters to enliven the scene. And then came the show itself, riding fine steeds and gilded carriages, wearing red uniforms and silken gowns, and performing astounding tricks amid exotic surroundings. What was true in the past remains the case today.

The circus is storybooks and fairy tales coming alive with elephants and Arabians, Hungarians and cowboys, tigers and camels, Chinese jugglers and Japanese acrobats, clowns and pretty riders and handsome aerialists. In its earlier times the circus was the only harbinger of such far-flung wonders, and even in current seasons it carries on in this role, sometimes becoming the only factor by which a placid home town becomes a veritable Babel of foreign tongues and the stopping place of a wonder world.

On further examination, the circus as an institution observes two postures. On the one hand, it makes a bow toward the light and cute world of monkeys and clowns, balloons and spangles. Elephants are Dumbo, clowns are Bozo and the lion trainer is Bosco. Walt Disney and before him Tony Sarg created this kind of fairy tale approach that the public thinks it also sees and likes in circuses. In another age the Brothers Grimm might have had Grimm Bros. Circus. Fairy tales and circuses have something in common in the opinion of the public. Many circuses used fairy tales as themes for spectacles. And P. T. Barnum pirated a name from a fairy tale to give to a midget. Now Tom Thumb is better known as Barnum's midget than as the character in a fairy tale, just as Disney took over Snow White and Black Beauty.

Somewhere in the circus appeal there is a fairy tale touch. But for some it is difficult to see and for others a little goes a long way.

In its other posture, the circus takes itself quite seriously. This is the side of the Royal Bengal tigers, the daring high wire act, the drum rolls and the Greatest Show on Earth.

It takes both aspects to make a circus, but the latter is probably

Right: The pachyderm needs only a generous supply of cold water to activate his built-in air conditioning system.

Below: The Clyde Beatty-Cole Bros. elephants do not seem to mind the weight of their comrades as they perform the long mount.

the greatest factor. The superlatives count. Let the press agents declaim "positively the world's most amazing assemblage of aerial artists." Let the sideshow talker exclaim that he is showing the "world's strangest people, alive and amazing." Let the equestrian director create five thousand cases of goose bumps when he announces the sublime pageant, "The Durbar of Delhi."

For pomp and pageantry are among the greatest assets of the circus, and others are surprise and excitement. If the impact is greatest on a child or if it is merely that one feels it first as a child, it nevertheless continues into adulthood. If one thrills, not as the wide-eyed innocent, but as the connoisseur of triple somersaults, he still relies upon the circus to take itself seriously. Attempts at comedy lion acts have never done well, for the king of beasts is essentially a thing of dignity. Ultimately, this is also true of the circus itself, and all true circus people realize it.

The attitude of a circus man is not unlike that of his townsfolk counterpart. Each may develop an outer shell of indifference or cynicism, but underneath there is a strong emotional attachment. If the trouper's façade is tougher, it is because his case of circus fever is more virulent.

The most unemotional troupers will state that they are with the show to make a living, to make money. Yet when the mainstream is tapped there is a deluge of sentiment after all. Most of them will say eventually that they joined the circus so they "could hear the band play." In an age of electric organs and few real bands, it may become difficult to recruit for tomorrow's circuses. But meanwhile, circus people are with it "to hear the band play" — and they mean for its adventure, its pageantry, its touch of never-never land.

Above: Surprisingly, children were seldom frightened by the huge elephants and waited impatiently near the rails for their arrival.

Left: The stringer wagon moves slowly towards the Brooklyn circus grounds in this 1938 photo. An eight-horse team pulled the heavily loaded wagon.

*A spectacle featuring Oriental splendor
inspired wonder even in city folk.*

2-Folklore and Lingo

Two centuries of circusing have given rise to a heritage and a culture, a lore that only troupers can share to the fullest. It is known to the man who has "been with them all — from Mollie to Jim," meaning the little Mollie Bailey Circus and James A. Bailey's giant Barnum & Bailey show.

It has developed nicknames for some of the more prominent outfits, among them the John Show for John Robinson, the White Show for the white-painted Sells-Floto, the Two Bills Show for Buffalo Bill & Pawnee Bill Combined, the Hog Show for the Mighty Haag Circus — and much more recently "Benny Bros." for the King Bros. Circus under the ownership of Benny Cristiani.

Troupers once referred to Ringling-Barnum as "Wait Bros." because of the big posters exclaiming "Wait for the Big Show" that it used against competitors. It was also known as Big Bertha when memory still was strong of Germany's World War I giant cannon of the same name and the Barnum and Ringling shows had just combined. Now it is known usually as the Big One. Because of its ethics and attitude toward the public, Ringling Bros. Circus was known among rival circus men as a Sunday School show and as Ding-A-Ling Bros.

Although Barnum had little to do with the show and troupers held Bailey in higher esteem, the Barnum & Bailey Circus was abbreviated in conversation to the Barnum show. And Carl Hagenbeck never got much of a nod from circus troupers; they called Hagenbeck-Wallace just the Wallace show. Sells-Floto was referred to as the Floto show, and Miller Bros. 101 Ranch Wild West became merely the Ranch show.

Circuses of the American Circus Corporation were known as the Peru Shows because they wintered at Peru, Indiana, and they were owned by the Corporation, in the parlance of circus people. Later another set of shows was identified as the Hugo Shows; Kelly-Miller, Cole & Walters and Carson & Barnes came out of Hugo, Oklahoma.

Among the literally hundreds of circuses that traveled this country, some were low-grass shows and some were high-grass shows. It all had to do with the lots and the towns that they played. Bigger shows and even the smaller ones that played more sophisticated communities found the grass and weeds were cut — thus, low-grass shows. "Head for the smokestacks," was their agent's routing policy.

Then there were the high-grass shows, playing the back hills, the small towns, the crossroads.

Never was this pointed up better than when circus business had to contend with the problem of two show owners with the same name — William P. Campbell and William P. Campbell.

One became known as High Grass Campbell, operating out of Oklahoma with the miniscule Campbell's Overland Circus and later selling a two-car railroad show to the King brothers. The other, naturally enough, was Low Grass Campbell, who took a separate little Campbell Bros. Circus out of Evansville, Wisconsin. High Grass claimed relationship with the Nebraska Campbells who had the big Campbell Bros. Railroad Circus. Low Grass married a member of the Gollmar circus family and was associated with the circuses of Popcorn George Hall.

They did not leave well enough alone. In 1920 Fred Bailey Hutchinson and High Grass Campbell framed the Campbell, Bailey & Hutchinson Circus, and for 1922 they took in another

Opposite: Exotic educational features were the most popular sideshow attractions. {1933}

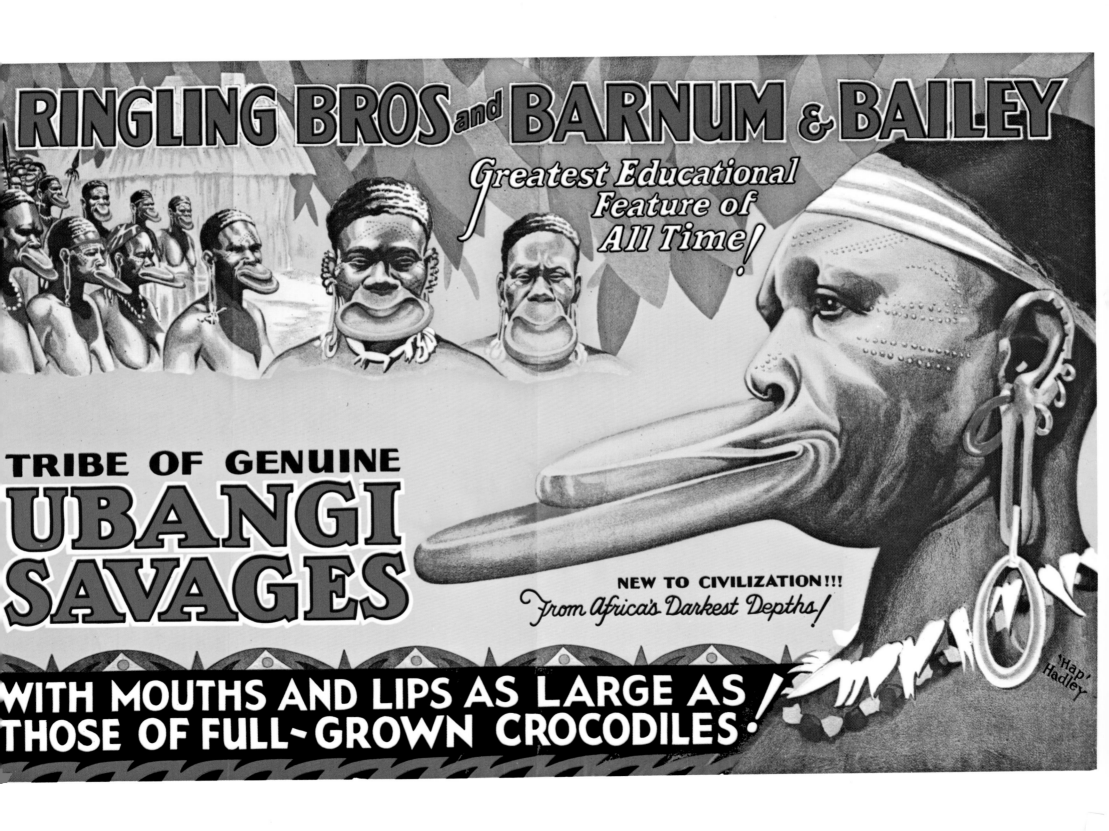

The center poles have been positioned and, as the quarterpole wagon lumbers off, the men in back unroll the big white canvas.

partner — William P. Campbell. Thus both High Grass and Low Grass were on the same circus as co-owners.

People in this branch of show business were categorized according to their affiliations and allegiances. Some were Ringling people, some were Corporation people, and usually one was not able to switch from one camp to another. There were mud show people and rail show people. Western shows and Eastern shows operated differently and with different people. Only in most recent times has there been much exchange of staff people and performers between the Western shows as epitomized by Kelly-Miller and the Eastern shows such as King Bros., Hunt Bros. and Mills Bros. — smokestack shows.

Trade papers — mainly *The New York Clipper* (1856-1926) and *The Billboard* (1894-1960) — carried the advertisements of circus employees and employers. There were the springtime ads that began "Call! Call! Call!" and announced the dates when contracted people were to report to a given circus to start the season. When the show was ready to take on a working crew at winter quarters, its advertisement said, "Cookhouse now open." Often enough there were vacancies; the resulting want ad would say that "due to disappointment" the circus could use a boss hostler or twenty-four-hour man or "family act doing two or more." The troupes that could do at least two kinds of acts were more desirable than those which could make only one appearance in the ring. Another explanation for an ad read "due to enlargement"; one never admitted, of course, that the previous employees might have quit in

anger or that working conditions might be less than congenial. Even so, circus people knew the reputation of each show and could decide readily whether they were interested in a particular job.

The show advised those who replied to the ad to "State lowest salary in first letter" — no use in stalling or negotiating. If it happened to be rather late in the season, the performers might not think it worthwhile to join out for a few weeks only to have the show close and go to winter quarters. So the ads promised "long season South." The circus owner might list a few names in his want ad, either seeking those specific people or indicating the caliber of employees he wanted. "Joe Scott come on; Wylie Campbell where are you?" the ad might read. The Capell Bros. Circus, once disenchanted with a certain legal adjuster, reversed the approach. Its ad said, "Due to disappointment, want legal adjuster; Bill Williams stay where you are." That was a little more direct than usual. Most circuses just signed off with "Consider silence a polite negative." Thus there was no need to acknowledge all of the mail. The performer whose application got that polite negative would then run an ad stating that he was "At Liberty."

The circus has never developed its own equivalent of Paul Bunyan. In its world of superlatives there was no place for a mythical character who could outdo even the greatest acrobat or the world's best juggler or the only human ever to accomplish a triple somersault. But the reverse did come into play: circus people laughed at the plight of a make-believe show that was even worse than the one they were with. It had more rain and mud, skinnier horses, fewer elephants and fewer paydays. This was the Won, Horse & Upp Circus, the literary creation of a press agent, Starr DeBelle, and described in a weekly column of *The Billboard*. It was especially popular in seasons when business was poor. Troupers gained some satisfaction out of reading about something even tougher than their own situation.

One non-existent circus comes in for extensive mention when circus people are spinning yarns. That is the Windy Van Hooten Circus. This one existed only in the collective memory of old circus men. It never really trouped. The Van Hooten show was just mighty handy to mention when no other show would do. If a trouper's story of the old days became too much to swallow, his listeners would decide the episode had taken place on the Windy Van Hooten show. That was the home of all the tall tales. And of course it was great sport to tell some fantastic story to a towner and, in the presence of other circus people, declare to him that it all took place on the Windy Van Hooten Circus.

24

Top: The big tent is up and soon over 12,000 people will crowd inside for an afternoon of enthralling entertainment.

Above: A tandem team trots nimbly through a high-grass town in a 1910 Yankee Robinson parade. Circus date sheets are prominently posted on the building at left.

Right: Sixteen camels pulling a bandwagon is a rare spectacle in any parade for the animal is usually considered too temperamental to train.

The Barnum & Bailey Greatest Show on Earth

SPLENDIDE REPRODUCTION DES COURSES IMPÉRIALES DE L'ANCIENNE ROME COURSES DE CHARIOTS À 4 CHEVAUX ÉLECTRIFIANT LES SPECTATEURS.

L'INSTITUT DE DIVERTISSEMENT LE PLUS GRAND ET LE PLUS MAGNIFIQUE DU MONDE.

For more down-to-earth conversation, show people gathered around the pad room or pie car to "cut up jackpots." In this verbal sport they would recount the gossip, rumors and legends of their craft. They might recall again how Emmett Kelly came to switch from a double traps act to clowning or how Arky Scott handled an outlaw elephant on Lee Bros. Circus, how Dailey Bros. Circus outwitted the railroaders at Ashland, and did you know that Camel Dutch Narfski came over with the Hagenbeck show for the St. Louis World's Fair?

There were apocryphal circus stories. In one, a ticket seller had a pet dog and gave it a bone each day, whereupon the dog dug a hole to bury it under the ticket wagon. In a day or so the dog would go back to the ticket wagon and dig, dig, dig, but never find those bones. Of course, the show had moved, so it was the same ticket wagon but a different lot. The story has been told for fact a thousand times. Occasionally, it was a stake and chain wagon in place of a ticket wagon, but the search for the bone was equally fruitless.

In another story, business had been weak and finally the show had to close. "Line up alphabetically," the owner said to the performers. "Alphabetically. We'll pay you off in that order." And so it was done, or rather begun. Because by the time they reached mid-alphabet the money had run out. Zeno, the great cannonball juggler, was out of luck and had no winter bankroll. By the next spring the show was in better shape and he rejoined. The owner saw him coming and went across the lot to meet him. "Well, Zeno, it's good to have you back! It's going to be a great season." The performer replied, "What do you mean Zeno? My name is Ajax."

Winter money was a problem for a performer with the Great Wallace Show one time. Uncle Ben Wallace announced suddenly that the show would close three weeks earlier than anticipated. The wire walker had been playing to a streak of bad luck in the nightly game at the pie car and had no cash. He was counting on the final three weeks' pay as transportation home at the end of the season and as a reserve to tide him over until he could get winter work. He went to Wallace to complain and asked, "How will I ever get home?" The governor, as every circus owner was called, asked what the man did for the show and heard the distressed man say he was a wire walker.

Wallace pointed to the top of a nearby telegraph pole and said "Western Union goes all over the United States. Those wires are strung to every town you can think of. So as a wire walker you will have no problem getting home."

Above: Fred Bradna and his wife Ella pose near the Ringling-Barnum tent. Bradna, always impeccably dressed, was dean of all equestrian directors.

Opposite: In 1900 Barnum & Bailey began a successful three-year tour of Europe. {1902}

27

AL.G. BARNES CIRCUS

WITH
TWO NEWLY ADDED
· SPECTACLES ·

THE PAGEANT
OF GOLD
AND

THE GORGEOUS
PROCESSIONAL
FIESTA
OF ALL
THE CHARM. ROMANCE
AND GAIETY OF
OLD SPAIN

The true spectacle eventually evolved into a "Gorgeous Processional" around the track.

Pretty girls, horses and clowns are some of the ingredients which comprise that one-of-a-kind entity — the circus.

On the Wallace show, ticket sellers had to put up the sidewall on the big top. Eddie Dowling, boss ticket seller, excused Brandy Johnson from that onerous duty. Instead, Brandy's task was to bring Eddie the boutonniere that he wore in his lapel each day. It was a stylish extravagance that he liked. One day's flower was quite withered and Dowling asked why. "Eddie," said Johnson, "there hasn't been a person buried in this town's cemetery for six weeks." The next day he was back on the sidewall detail.

Cutting corners on the job was also the problem for a girl with the Ringling-Barnum Circus while the demanding Fred Bradna was equestrian director. Jimmie Reynolds was boss elephant man at the time and had his charges at the back door ready for their entrance in an important spectacle. The girl was to ride in the howdah on the leading elephant, but she was late and Reynolds waited. Bradna cut loose with one of his Prussian cavalry tirades that made even an

elephant boss cringe. The girl was late another day and a third time.

Reynolds had taken as much of Bradna's scolding as he could, so he turned to his elephant hands. The nearest one was Nine Blankets — unshaven, unwashed and clad in a crummy uniform that had seen a whole season's service without respite. Nine Blankets climbed into the beautiful silken howdah, parted the plush curtains and smiled toothlessly to the audience as the elephants entered on time. When the impeccable Bradna saw this outrage, his temperature and his top hat went straight up. Jimmie explained that the girl was late again and rather than be late he drafted Nine Blankets. A new girl was on time thereafter.

Bradna also figured in a recollection of Tuffy Genders, now general manager of Ringling-Barnum and earlier a star of the flying trapeze. The show took a winter unit to pre-Castro Havana and Bradna was in charge. Business was not up to par so Bradna urged that the performance be strengthened. He sent a hurry-up call to Genders, then relaxing in Florida. A month had passed since the regular season ended and the flying act was out of shape. On arrival in Havana, they set up the rigging and went right into the act without practice. The rigging and net were directly over the spot where Bradna stood. They began with some simple routines, but they were not coordinated and their hands were slipping. Bradna, in top hat and red coat, was nervous under them. In a loud voice he called out. "Don't fall down here, you blankety-blanks. Don't you fall down here!"

It was another Ringling story that Red Sonnenberg recounted. In 1956 the Teamsters' Union was picketing Madison Square Garden in an effort to force the circus into the union. On the day before the opening, a semitrailer truck pulled up to the Garden with a load of souvenir program booklets. It was Red's job to sell these at performances. Circus brass were worried about how the books could be unloaded and brought in past the pickets. Sonnenberg realized that the pickets were professionals paid for that work and they had no real interest in the union problem at hand. "Let me handle it," he said.

Going to the picket line, Red asked them if they wanted to earn a few extra dollars. They all nodded. So they rested their picket signs against the building and proceeded to carry the circus programs from the truck into the Garden. When the truck was unloaded, Red paid each of them $4. The truck drove off and the pickets gathered

An electric atmosphere pervades the big top as the grand finale nears.

up their signs and started parading around the Garden again.

Circuses issue route cards which list the towns to be played for the next two or three weeks. Then employees can tell relatives where they will be playing. The usual pattern is for the circus to play a different town on each of six days of the week. Sunday often is a day off, and opposite it on the route card is the explanation, "en route." John Herriott tells the story of "a Simple Simon sort of fellow" who joined Mills Bros. Circus. He was the kind of individual who always tried to seem important, and on the day in question he got into a conversation with Herriott about the route. The newcomer said it seemed strange to him that the show would be traveling in circles for so long. Circles? asked John. Why did he say that? "Well, the route card shows it. Each week it plays these different towns, but every Sunday it circles back and plays En Route again."

On a circus the rest room facilities, never very elaborate, are known as the donnikers. Explanations for the origins of this term are lacking; it is simply one of those specialized terms that develops in any group. Since the public has no idea what a donniker is, circus people are not above having a little joke. There has been talk of a Donniker Bros. Circus and there actually was a show called Don E. Kerr Circus. The Ringling-Barnum tented circus devised two huge wagons that served as rest rooms as neat and serviceable as any traveling aggregation could hope for. These wagons eventually went to the Circus World Museum in Baraboo, Wisconsin. The museum's circus train had arrived in Milwaukee for its annual Fourth of July Circus Parade. Deacon Blanchfield had just dropped off of the coaches and was walking alongside the flat car holding the Ringling rest room wagons when a lady stepped out of the crowd and called to him.

"Mister, what do you keep in those wagons?" she asked.

Never breaking stride and without looking up, Deacon said, "Madam, we keep our ferocious donnikers in those wagons."

These are the tales that circus people recount. Some are worth a laugh. All help to pass the idle time until the next performance or until it is spring and time to start another season, another tour, with another circus.

Opposite: The lion trainer will never compromise the dignity of the king of beasts.

3-Pages from Life on a Circus

A reflection of life on a circus and of the spirit around a particular circus is illustrated and preserved by a show's annual route book. Not so individual and intimate as a diary, not so deadly as a college yearbook, the circus route book records the staff, program and route of the show as well as the principal events along the way.

The earliest route book still in existence is the 1835 issue for the Zoological Institute, and a couple of hundred have been published since then. They come in all sizes and shapes. Some shows put out a series of annual books; others merely print a book for one big season. Some are modest folders; some are elaborate slick-paper books. Some have pages die-cut to the shape of animal heads and some are bound with red ribbons.

Unfailingly, route books praise the show and its management. Business is always great, decisions are always profound. Accidents, bad weather and muddy lots are recorded. But shortcomings of the show or peccadillos of the owners are never apparent.

In reporting the "biggest show and best season" ever, the 1892 route book of Ringling Bros. World's Greatest Show was typical. Its author and compiler was a juggler, O. H. Kurtz, who began his account with a few kind words about the management:

> Among the nobler managers of America, who have sought to make the current amusement era an "age of better metal," the Ringling quintette stands proudly eminent, poised upon five of the highest peaks that are known to the circus world. They are now in the full flush of fame and fortune. Great glorious gains and rousing round receipts have heaped their coffers full. With lucky stars on foreheads sound in judgement, they still aspire to "grow from more to more." To see them plumed with victory is pleasant, for their record is white as linen. They treat the public as friends and the level scales of justice hang over all their doings. They have never stooped to questionable methods. They have always believed that being sharp is all right and being sharpers all wrong. With banners of victory flying and bugles of triumph blowing, their show has closed the eventful season of 1892. It has scored a tremendous business all along the line, from the time the first drum taps sounded, clear down to the closing stand.

Perhaps the juggler was assisted just a mite in that composition by the show's press agents.

"As the hand's five fingers of different length when bent are seen to meet equally," he wrote, "so the five Ringlings, bent to their work, have one common stature and merge to one common harmony."

The Ringling brothers all were on the show at that early time. Al, Charles, Alf T., Otto and John were listed as proprietors and managers. Then each was listed in his special assignment. Otto Ringling was superintendent of tickets and show treasurer. Charles was general advertising agent; John, router and railroad contractor. Alf T. was manager of the sideshow. Al Ringling was boss of all the performers and director of the performance, tasks expressed in the title of equestrian director. His name also was given as starter of the races and as "ghost," the latter indicating it was he who gave

Opposite: No one can possibly forget when the show is coming since the date is always placed even more prominently than the name of the circus. {1938}

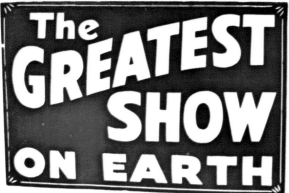

OFFICIAL
ROUTE BOOK
OF
RINGLING BROTHERS'
World's Greatest Railroad Shows.

SEASON OF 1892.

ISSUED BY AUTHORITY OF THE RINGLING BROS.

COMPILED BY O. H. KURTZ.

BUFFALO:
THE COURIER COMPANY, SHOW PRINTERS.
1892.

The official route book of each season of circusing was liberally sprinkled with plaudits for the owners. Amusing misadventures were recounted, and a variety of advertisements rounded out the record.

Monday, May 30th.   **Holton, Kan**

C., R. I. & P., 158 miles. Pop. 2,727. City Hotel, very nice. Fine business. Steve Scaggs, holding a "box seat," fal through it to the pavement. Fronting hotel, West Indi Museum, combined with five-cent alligator show. "They'r alive, alive, and ready to jump out of the wagon." Five-ce glass man sells lemonade red enough to dye your tight. Heavy night rain ; one show. At a K. P. meeting some o the boys sup too much flavoring extract.

Tuesday, May 31st.   **Pawnee, Neb**

C., R. I. & P., 71 miles. Pop. 1,550. Exchange Hotel. Ha a one-lunged engine that frequently stopped to take breath, o went ahead to give first section an elephant push up-hil Cow-catcher needed on rear of the train, so a vicious co couldn't walk on and bite the passengers. Arrived 12 M. Har rain ; swamped lot. Show postponed till October 7th. Als missed by Sells Brothers, June 3, 1891. Month's run 1,84 miles.

the performers their pay envelopes.

While five Ringling brothers owned the show there were seven in the family and on the circus. A. G. Ringling was manager of the Number 1 Advertising Car and Henry Ringling was principal door tender and superintendent of the concert.

In listing the circus personnel, the route book revealed the great range of tasks and skills required by a big circus plus the huge number of people necessary to its operation.

The four advertising cars were listed by name — the Cannon Ball, the Thunder Bird, the Battle Bolt and the War Eagle, all carrying a belligerent tone in keeping with their duties of crushing the billposting forces from any rival shows that crossed their path. Exactly seventy men lived aboard these cars and put up the show's billing in each town. Among them were those who posted lithographs in store windows; programmers, who distributed heralds, sometimes hiring boys to take them door-to-door; and billposters, those who pasted bills on the sides of barns and fences and any place else that they could get away with.

Ringling Bros.' train, according to route book statistics, numbered thirty-two cars. The year before there had been twenty-two cars, indicating great growth. Specialists included the chief car inspector, a man in charge of torches that lighted the area during loading at night, and six polers, whose dangerous task it was to guide the wagons along the flat cars. The show train included fifteen flat cars, eight cars for horses and elephants. The train's five coaches included the "Caledonia," the Ringlings' private car. There was a porter for each of the cars, which a circus always called coaches even though they were sleepers.

More strange occupations turned up in the mechanical department, as listed in the route book. Master mechanic, carpenter and blacksmith could be anticipated, but the "carver and decorator" and the "designer and painter" remind one that a circus had ornate wood carvings plus numerous scenic paintings on the parade wagons as well as on sideshow banners and in the equipment used in the show's spectacle. Others in this department were the buggy man and the oiler — let there be no squeaking wheels!

In the canvas department John H. Snellen is listed as general superintendent, a fanciful way of referring to "Happy Jack," the boss canvasman. Working for him were three assistants and fifty-six big top men.

The seating department lists specialists that include those responsible for back leveling, second-sized jacks, third-sized jacks, toe jacks, toe leveling, toe pin drivers, stringer setters, plank leveling, second planking-up.

Thirty-one men staffed the seat department. Another twenty-nine men worked on the menagerie tent, which the Ringling route book called the "oblong." Ten men handled sideshow canvas.

Specialists certain to be found only on a circus were the ring makers; Ringling Bros. had a man in charge and three workers, one to make each ring each day. Three more were in charge of preparing the hippodrome track and two put up the guard ropes in front of the seats.

This route book, eager to list as many names as possible, named stake puller crew members, and those in charge of the various stake and chain wagons, rope wagon and canvas wagons. It even named those in charge of flying six flags on the big top, seven on the menagerie tent and two on the sideshow canvas. Joe Smith was the sailmaker, who kept the acres of canvas in good repair.

And the route book describes those tents in detail. The big top was a 180-foot round top with four 50-foot middle pieces — or 180 by 380 feet. The "oblong" was 80 by 280 and the dressing tent was 70 by 100. Other tops included the 80 by 120 sideshow, six 70 by 40 horse tents, two 70 by 40 dining tents and a 50-foot round wardrobe tent.

The chandelier department reported consuming three and a half barrels of gasoline and twenty-five gallons of coal oil nightly for eighteen big top lights, twelve menagerie lights, four side lights, nine beacons, seventy-nine torches and twelve lanterns.

Ringling's menagerie listed twenty-five cage wagons, ranging from little cross cages to the big Cage 42 with the Giant White Nile hippopotamus. Specific men were assigned to care for animals in each category. One had the birds, bears and monkeys, and another had the gnu, ibex, zebras and antelope, while a third had four cages of lions.

Suprisingly the elephant department lists only two men to care for the six elephants — Babe, Jules, Fanny, Zip, Queen and Lou. Two more men were in charge of the camels.

Superintendent of the ring stock was the dapper and distinguished Rhoda Royal — "mister" despite his first name, and one of the typically striking horsemen in circusdom. Working under him were the private grooms (for bareback riders who brought their own horses), stallion grooms, ring stock grooms, hippodrome stock men, pony boys and jockeys. Royal later would expand his career to become a circus owner but with less success

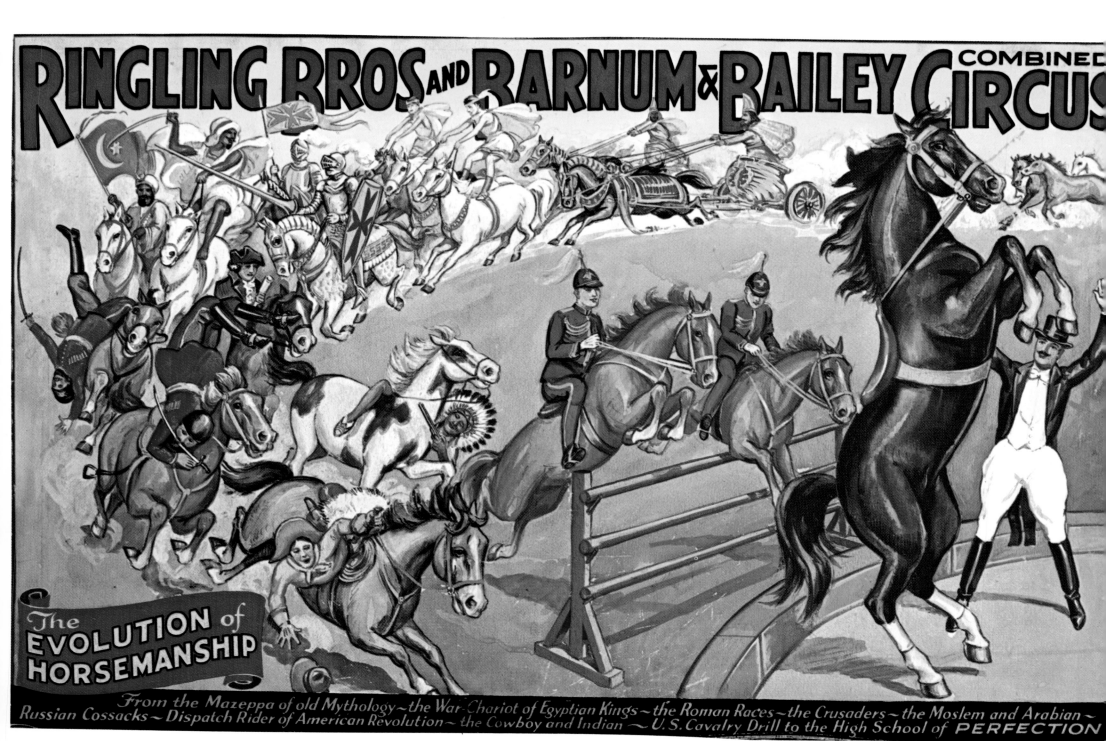

than he enjoyed as ring stock boss and performing horseman.

A fixture around the Ringling Bros. show for many seasons was Spencer Alexander, of Delavan, Wisconsin — who was known far and wide as Delavan — the boss hostler, or superintendent of baggage stock. The compiler of the route book listed him no less than five times, twice as Spencer Delavan and three times as Delavan Alexander — twice as superintendent of baggage stock, once as the veterinarian surgeon, again as surgeon of the Hotel de Hoss, and finally as "sole superintendent of the horse tents."

Working for Delavan were several specialists peculiar to a circus in the horse and buggy days. There was a blacksmith and a harness maker, a wagon repairer and a wagon greaser, a forage master and a master of trappings. Elite of the baggage stock department were the four drivers of eight-horse teams, followed by the five six-horse drivers. The show carried twenty-one four-horse teams and drivers and three pull-up drivers for work at the trains.

The route book author pointed out that the eight-up hitches were on the big bandwagon, Moscow Bell Chariot, hippo den and second bandwagon in the parade. Six-horse teams were assigned to the Number 3 bandwagon, Organ tableau, Continental band-wagon, Neptune tableau and St. George tableau.

For the circus dining department there were the usual categories of steward, chief cook, second cook, pastry cook, pantry man and purchasing agent. But there also were the camp fire men, wood-chopper, water boys, pan washer, oil stove man and laundry man. The route book lists two dining tents. One was called the Oriental Dining Pavilion No. 1 and the other was Occidental Dining Pavilion No. 2. Although there were nine performers in the Mikado's Troupe of Royal Japanese for the performance, that hardly warrants fifty percent of the dining facilities. More likely, the dining tents, despite their names, were for performers and bosses in one case and workingmen in the other.

At the sideshow, the route book writer found Lou F. Nichols as the "enthusiastic orator," to ballyhoo the attractions outside and describe them inside the tent. Also listed were four solicitors, not English lawyers but rather the ticket sellers who worked in the box-like stands outside the sideshow.

The sideshow had a fine list of attractions: Miss Ida Williams, the mastodonic fashion plate; Harry Nelson, the living skeleton dude; the Colossal Mexican Giant and the Arkansas Boy Giant; the Lilliputian Princess and the King of Dwarfs; the Wonderful Tattooed Man; and a snake enchantress, among others. There was a nine-man sideshow band.

Above: When the circus came to town, large, colorful circus bills were posted on every available inch of space in the surrounding area.

Opposite: This act was a favorite in the horse-and-buggy days for the horse was familiar to everyone including children.

37

In that era the aftershow was not yet a Wild West show but was, indeed, a concert — a term that continued long after the nature of this show changed on all circuses. But for 1892 the Ringling Bros.' concert included performers in vaudeville style who did a "biddy turn, seriocomic bit, amusing sketch, Italian music act, a scientific sparring exhibition [boxing!], a skirt dance, Irish turn and a black-face song and dance act."

Makeup of various bands for the circus performance and parade duty was important to the circus. First, there was William F. Weldon, musical director, and his Ringling Brothers' Grand Military Band of twenty-one pieces. They all played together for the main performances. But for parade time, some were assigned to each of the bandwagons, and their number was augmented by the addition of other performers or staff people who could play instruments as well. Thus in parade the Number 1 Band had thirteen pieces riding the biggest bandwagon, "the largest, grandest and costliest chariot ever brought to America, carved with many monster forms of unicorn, griffin, and gorgeous with a shining multitude of leaping, creeping, rampant and crouching lions." On board the second bandwagon — "a canopied chariot of richly beautiful pattern, with a blazing design of two golden lions wreathed with silver serpents" — were ten musicians. Eight men rode the parade as Band No. 3, on the Neptune wagon, while a fifer and three drummers rode the Continental bandwagon as a Revolutionary army field band. Finally, two men were instrumentalists for the Bells of Moscow feature, which was pulled by the Giant Highway Locomotive Hercules, a steam traction engine manned by an engineer and fireman.

Ladies were definitely in the minority on this circus. One was listed in the wardrobe department, four were sideshow attractions, and thirteen were named as big show performers. Undoubtedly, there were a few others, including wives of the Ringling brothers, but their number was small.

The "lady artists" were listed for principal bareback act, which was the Lady Principal Act; Beautiful Manege Act, riding gaited horses; a lady jockey rider; perch and impalement acts; impalement and musical acts; slack wire act; fancy skating act; Japanese rope act; and Japanese Ladder of Swords.

The "gentlemen artists" included Charles W. Fish, champion principal bareback trick act; Mike Rooney, jockey and principal somersault acts; Will Marks, principal bareback and carrying acts; Charles Reed, grand carrying acts; Charles O'Dell, five-horse tandem and four-horse acts.

Others included the principal leaper, Dan O'Brien, plus sixteen others who appeared in The Leaps in addition to their own featured acts. It was long a standard procedure in circuses that any performer was expected to appear also in The Leaps.

Other categories of performers were bars and brothers act, perch and brothers act, perch and impalement acts, impalement and musical acts, each illustrating that often performers did more than one act. Advertisements for performers usually sought those "doing two or more."

This season of 1892 the Ringling show had a two-man flying return act, the Vernon Brothers, plus a chair-balancing trapeze act, a double traps act, a tutor of wise donkeys, an exponent of toss juggling, and a skatorial artist.

There were nine clowns on the show, chief among them Lew Sunlin, a talking clown; Jules Turnour, a general clown; a German immigrant clown; and the King of the Dudes.

Races were a major part of any circus performance in the 1890's and usually they comprised the finale and came in considerable numbers. The Ringling Bros. outfit was no exception. This season the route book spoke of chariot races, Roman standing riders, lady jockeys, gentlemen jockeys, runners, tandem riders, clown sulky race riders, sack race participants, wheelbarrow racers, camel race riders and elephant race riders.

This performance opened with one of the Ringlings' most pretentious grand spectacles — "Caesar's Triumphal Entry into Rome." The route book recalled it as "Huge sights of joy and victory."

At the blare of trumpets and the blast of bugles, [it said], a tremendous outpouring and outspreading of a vast bannered army and motley throng of mailed marching warriors, gladiators, charioteers, steel-clad knights, royal grandees, mounted cavaliers and ladies, helmeted spearmen, civilians, squires, pontifical high priests and wandering Jews, actors courting the dramatic muse, Moors and Mamelukes, Bedouins of the desert, outlaws booted and spurred, Grand Turks, nobles, vestals, senators, greybeards, orators, Barbarians, captives, travelers, wayfarers, ambassadors, dames

Opposite: Many problems were involved in transporting a complete menagerie of undomesticated animals from town to town. {1895}

The Barnum & Bailey Greatest Show on Earth

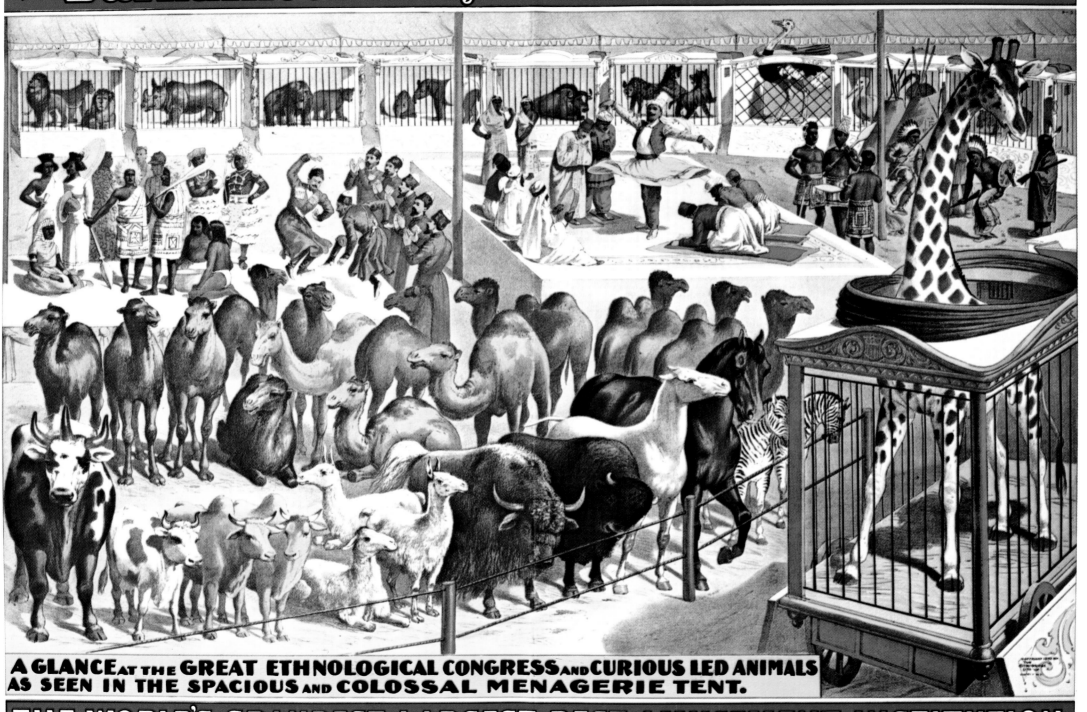

A GLANCE AT THE GREAT ETHNOLOGICAL CONGRESS AND CURIOUS LED ANIMALS AS SEEN IN THE SPACIOUS AND COLOSSAL MENAGERIE TENT.

THE WORLD'S GRANDEST, LARGEST, BEST, AMUSEMENT INSTITUTION.

Circus personalities behind the scenes were often as colorful as the superstars. Boss canvasman Jimmie Whalen {above right} directed the tent raising operation {above left} for the Ringling-Barnum show in an era when the circus needed a ten-acre lot to set up. Waxie {below right}, who was blind, was expert harness maker and repairman. The rigors of circus trouping never dampened the pride and loyalty of the roustabouts {below left} who performed such arduous tasks as pulling up the five-foot tent stakes after the show.

STAKE PULLERS RINGLING CIRCUS 1913 HECK PHOTO

Men like Tom Lynch {above right} moved the circus swiftly on or off the lot regardless of its condition. Boss hostler Lynch could deftly handle the lines of any draft horse team {above left}. The Percherons {left} were most frequently used as baggage stock.

41

of the harem, turbaned Arabs on camels, Nubians bearing gifts, slaves bearing incense, chariots of conquest, huge herds of swaying elephants, prancing war horses, wild beasts, runners, couriers, pages. . . .

Display 4 was the Grand Leaping Tournament and next was an array of Japanese stunts. Sixth were the Lady Principal riders, followed by head balancing, hat spinning and a brothers act, then trick ponies, a clown and performing donkeys. Charles Fish, the rider, was in the tenth display. Twelfth brought the Japanese acrobats back.

There were trained horses, fine riders, Mexican perch performers, a roller skating turn, and more jugglers and acrobats. The Japanese gave twin high wire acts. Late in the show came the featured flying return act.

The big performance was strong on riders, as would be expected in the early 1890's. The flying act was something of a rarity then. But the show also was notable for what it did not include. There was no wild animal act — enough that there were lions in the menagerie. And there were no displays featuring trained performing elephants. The show's six elephants made up those "huge herds of swaying elephants" in the spectacle. They were also back for The Leaps and there were three of them in the final races. But nowhere did the Ringlings then have a military drill or tableau act by the elephants.

A feature of this and most major route books was the day-by-day account of the season. This diary opened with an accolade for Baraboo, the winter quarters town. The show opened there on April 30, with this notation:

> "To your tents, O Israel!" cried the ancient Hebrews, and with similar impulse the clans of the Ringlings blew in on four winds to Baraboo, awaiting the grand spring opening. Many of the old familiar faces, while many new ones also arrest attention, like a strange face in perdition.
>
> Everything from hoof to helmet, new. Brand new snow-white canvas. New chariots, bright as a gold piece, and wardrobe new fangled and spangled. The five Ringlings come up smiling, with that look on their face which sporting men describe as the "air of the winners."

> "The elephant now goes 'round; the band
>   begins to play,
> "The boys around the monkey's cage
>   had better keep away."

The season was on.

At Baraboo, that first day the show ran smoothly "to the tune of Al Ringling's whistle." Despite heavy rain a big crowd attended, "and all wish the circus bon voyage and a happy return in the fall to its countless friends in Baraboo," said the route book.

Sunday, May 1, brought the show's first move. The chronicler said, "Late leaving the lot last night. The first day's capering on the pine-scented sawdust leaves all the actors too stiff to fall down or get up."

The first few entries were typical of the entire season's diary:

Monday, May 2nd, Madison, Wis.

C&NW railroad, 37 miles. Population 13,426. Capitol Hotel [where performers stayed]. Barbaric weather, but record-breaking business. Here poor Bob Memhard, our friend of last season, lies turned to pathetic dust . . . .

Tuesday, May 3rd, Monroe, Wis.

Ill. Central, 37 miles. Population 3,768. Ludlow Hotel. Bottomless roads and juicy mud. No show. The sinking fairgrounds lot abandoned after pitching tents. Dan O'Brien's new $5 silk umbrella blown to ribs and ribbons. Grandstand gallery roars as Dan gets soaking wet. Left 9 p.m. The show had also been stuck here in 1890.

Wednesday, May 4th, Savanna, Ill.

IC and CMStP, 62 miles. Pop. 3,097. Occidental Hotel, run by Mr. Booz, but no booze sold. Special train between hotel and lot two miles apart. Men rained out of work until morning. Left May 5th, afternoon, missing that day's stand.

Thursday, May 5th, Maquoketa, Iowa.

CM&StP. 42 miles. Pop. 3,077. As per item preceeding, this town was left out cold. We jumped

Opposite: A patient trainer could teach his dogs a variety of outlandish stunts. {1932}

Pat Valdo has been with Ringling-Barnum for over forty years. He started as a clown and recently retired as Personnel Director for that circus.

it altogether, with two somersaults. [The town was also] missed by Cook & Whitby on account of an accident following July 10.

Friday, May 6th, Anamosa, Iowa.

CM&StP. 89 miles from Savanna, 50 miles from Maquoketa. Pop. 2,078. Kinert Hotel and Wallace Restaurant. Clear weather. Elegant business. Hippodrome steed falls dead. Impalement act billed as "implement" act. Major Winnar, renowned dwarf, visited. After show, Anamosa and Rock City toughs, full of fighting whiskey, had a grand battle royal. One Irishman got his face pounded off, but denied that he hollered "enough."

After Saturday at Sigourney, Iowa, the show made a long Sunday run to Kansas City and arrived there in time for a late dinner on a rainy evening. The tuba player quit.

"Old side whiskers fights us here," wrote Kurtz, "and we see many vivid pictures of canvasmen in Columbus clothes discovering America." That is a reference in the veiled vernacular of a route book to an opposition battle. "Old side whiskers" refers to James A. Bailey of Barnum & Bailey, which also had advertised heavily in Kansas City in opposition to Ringling Bros. The Barnum show that year featured a spectacle called "Columbus and the Discovery of America" — thus the opponents' reference to "canvasmen in Columbus clothes."

On Monday, May 9th, the Ringling show paraded and performed in Kansas City. The route book recounts that the parade was a gigantic success and that business was equally great.

"Here opposition shakes its horns in vain. The Ringlings have out paper enough to bill the walls of China and, dazzled by the glory of our circus, the folks refuse to wait for Jumbo's skeleton." — another sly reference to the Barnum show which formerly had exhibited the skeleton of Jumbo, the elephant.

At Ottawa, Kansas, there was a fight between a youthful rider and a Japanese boy. "The red paint gang, who missed the train while tasting the roses and raptures of Kansas City joy, made parade on the 'implement train,' not very velvet riding." Diamond Dick was a visitor on the lot, wearing "good rags, white slouch hat and cream overcoat, Wild Bill hair the length of a lion's mane, and a flash of white diamonds with glittering frozen fire. Profound impression on Kurtz who also wears long hair to keep the flies off him while juggling," Kurtz wrote.

Left: The Lady Principal Act attracted many who delighted in the graceful ballet poses and pirouettes of these riders. Above: Oriental performers figured prominently in the acrobatic and aerial acts of almost every circus. {1916}

At Topeka there was "incessant rain. No Parade. Impossible to show." The Ringling people stayed at the hotel operated by Ad Sells of the Sells Bros. Circus family. Ringling had used 24,000 sheets of billing paper against Barnum & Bailey's efforts there. Sells Bros. also was coming in June.

Circus troupers, having been stranded or left unpaid from time to time, were not always emotionally secure, so the continued rain and loss of performances might have caused some concern on other shows than this. But the route book writer assures all that the mighty Ringlings can cover their costs: "Money sacks as fat as Boss Tweed's settle all bills in full."

At Junction City a performer, Molly Regan, was thrown by a falling horse and just missed striking a quarter pole. The weather was bad there and at Clay Centre, where a performer, making "a betting proposition, throws $500 on his trunk to back it. The walls of the dressing room shiver" at such a sight. On Sunday the people arrived at the appointed hotel in Beloit, Kansas, only to be told they were not expected until the next day, when the performances were to be given. So breakfast was served late and in sections. Skies were clear on this Sunday off. For the Monday show there was "magnificent packed and jammed business." After the night crowd was in the tent a heavy rain storm broke, soaking all of the wardrobe. Some men were hurt in dropping the canvas later, and a horse died.

On May 17, the show was to play Washington, Kansas, but never got there. Instead, near Concordia, the first section roared over a trestle that was weakened by storm waters and now gave way:

> At 2:45 a.m. an appalling crash awoke train section No. 1. In an instant all was excitement and "confusion worse confounded." Pouring out into the night, our men perceived by the flickering light of lanterns a chaos of wrecked cars, some crushed to utter kindling wood and others hurled headlong or sidelong into a lake of mad waters that held both sides of the track, and whose undermining power had wrecked a trestle and train.

Two men were killed — "nothing but broken skull and oozing brains" — and twenty-six horses died outright while others had to be shot. One of the dead men had just sold a farm and was traveling west with the circus in search of a new place to settle his family.

This fearless snake charmer actually has little reason to worry. The big snakes, when well fed, are sluggish and not dangerous.

Opposite: Every season's show was "new," offering more thrills than before. {1909}

Above: This 1916 photo shows Robert Ringling {right} with the Bartiks, producers of the Big Show's spectacles. Ringling was elected president of the outfit in 1943.

Right: The children would cheer their favorites on as the horses thundered by in the Roman standing races.

Left: In spite of the bottle he holds, this Dailey Bros. artist displays the intense concentration necessary for his high wire act.

Below left: Nine horses at full gallop practice for the hippodrome races, a feature unique to the circus.

Below right: The unicyclist uses an umbrella to maintain a delicate balance on the tight wire.

The circus missed one day and appeared the next at Concordia, but because of a high lot and fearful winds the big top was not put up; instead one performance was given with sidewalls of tents alone. A leaflet was circulated with an offer to buy fifty horses. People at Abilene were surprised the circus arrived because they had heard exaggerated reports of the train wreck.

At Abilene the author wrote that "the spectre that made Hamlet's fright-wig rise here walks his sheeted round, first time." In other words "the ghost walked" — it was payday. This was some three weeks after the opening, but circuses customarily held back the pay for the first two weeks or so, a device to encourage employees to stay for the full season. If they lasted that long, the show paid the holdback at the closing day. It gave the less thrifty a stake with which to buy a ticket home.

But in circus parlance payday was the occasion for the ghost to walk. Each payday the route compiler found some new and fancy way to say the same thing, that the ghost walked.

So went the eventful tour day after day. There were more days of rain and mud. While the mayor of Wichita was at the show, thieves stole the silver from his home, but it was recovered. The show train moved through the Cherokee Strip into Oklahoma and cowboys rode alongside firing salutes. There were coyotes and prairie dogs and Indians. At Oklahoma City a sharper turned up with a little roller machine that turned plain paper into $5 bills. A new cookhouse employee lost a foot under the train and the next day a railroad fireman fell between the cars to his death. A circus man was bitten by a hyena and "it took four men to hold him in his spasms of nervous agony." Business was especially big at Guthrie, the capital of Oklahoma Territory.

They complained about the "one-lunged engine" that struggled to move the second section into Pawnee, Nebraska, then hard rain prevented giving performances. A poler's leg was broken while he was bringing the ticket wagon down the runs at Fairbury. Madame Sunlin's manège horse died.

The Ringling train passed that of the Cook & Whitby show. Again the Barnum & Bailey Show advertised it was "coming soon" though it meant, not June, but September. Sioux Falls, South Dakota, is described as the "divorce city," apparently an early day Reno. A hundred Indians visited the show at Yankton.

The audience numbered 2,500 more than the population of the county at Madison, South Dakota. That is where the kangaroo cage broke open and its contents went "wildly hop-step-jumping over the sea of plains" and where the Arkansas Boy Giant declared he was going to leave for home, and where a canvasman was ridden off the show on a rail.

There was always some sort of action: That kangaroo was recaptured but it died. Blanche Reed got the measles so Mike Rooney donned a wig and dress to take her place in the Lady Principal Act. The lady target for the knife thrower in an impalement act was ill, so a substitute was necessary. At Duluth a lion tore up a man's arm and it had to be amputated.

Three pickpockets were arrested at Ashland, Wisconsin, and three more two days later, results of Ringling vigilance against such trailers.

Still the rigors of circus trouping persisted. "Some canvasmen plant a beer keg on a stump in a lonely hollow and drain it to the dregs . . . . Sandy lot, long way out . . . . Parade caught in rain . . . . Two center poles broken . . . . May Reed fell, not badly hurt. Toyo cuts head on trunk. Bad runaway in the morning . . . . Train stalled on steep grade . . . . A trainman was run over by the tiger den . . . . Big business . . . . Grandest lot of the season . . ." And finally: "Well, boys, I guess we will wind up the show tomorrow, and send it home for a rest, as it's made enough money for one season. If the Great White Nile hippopotamus was to bite the face from Otto Ringling's safe, the floor of the ticket wagon would be swamped with shining gold. He will give us this gold tomorrow."

And indeed they would get their final pay, holdback and perhaps a bonus. More than twenty-five weeks and exactly 11,372 miles after that opening day the circus trains pulled back into Baraboo for the winter.

Opposite: The Big One, as Ringling-Barnum was known among circus people, presented a variety of acts lifted from the pages of world history. {1925}

4-How Troupers See the World

The Ringling Bros. and Barnum & Bailey train was moving slowly across a city street at midnight. A grizzled trouper on the steps of a sleeper called to a towner. "What town is this?" Although this was in 1968, it has always been so with a circus. Geography holds a strange status here.

There are many who join the circus, like the navy, to see the world. They pass through much of it and see very little. Theirs is a world that travels by night and spends its days sequestered in its own excitement on a show grounds that is not much different from yesterday's.

Troupers for the most part see railroad yards or dark highways and pastures or arenas filled with their familiar show property. The use of personal automobiles and daytime jumps between extended indoor runs have lessened the effect somewhat, just as when parades once took troupers downtown. But for the most part, their life is with the show and they rarely find need or time to venture from it to see the distinctive features of the area in which they happen to be for the day. Often a veteran circus trouper has no idea of what town he is in unless he can see its name on a poster.

However, two divergent factors of geography modify this aspect of circus life, this placelessness in eternal travel.

First, one department on the circus knows much about geography, enough to make up for all the others.

Second, the circus superimposes a geography of its own on the maps and over the countryside that it shares with the prosaic world.

That exceptional department is the advance — the contracting, routing and advertising department. This is the staff that decides where the show is to go and then makes all of the arrangements. General agents of circuses are walking encyclopedias of geographical statistics. John Ringling filled this role among the brothers; he knew geographical facts and figures like few men before or since. He entertained fellow passengers on trains by holding his hand out of a window to "sense" their location and then reciting a wealth of localized geographical data. He, like every other good railroad circus agent, knew as much about railroads and the track network as does today's efficient industrial corporation traffic manager. They also know the nature of local industry, timing of paydays, types of crops and their seasons, the recent volume of business and degree of prosperity. All of this and more is needed if the general agent is to make a well-informed decision about where to steer the show. He must determine not only which towns give the best promise of good business but also what time of year is best to play them and whether there are sufficiently good towns on the railroads or highways leading to and from the city in question.

By their constant traveling ahead of the circus, the agents together with their crews of billposters, contracting agents and other advance men come to know a great deal of geography. Each lives by a different measurement. The billposter knows every shed and fence in the nation. With other billposters he can compare the choice "hits" all over the country. The biller knows the principal streets of every city because on them he made his rounds to post the bills. He knows the multitudes of little towns, because he travels to them to paste up the big posters on the sheds and barns and grain elevators. Press agents know primarily the newspapers, but that includes an awareness of their trade territories and the limits of their circulation. The contracting agent knows the merchants and feed dealers, but most of all he knows the show

Opposite: Thrilling scenes from Wild West shows captured the imagination of every child.

53

Above: This fine billing stand was sure to attract the attention of every passerby. Forepaugh, upper left, has been abbreviated to 4 Paw.

Below: Although many troupers joined the circus to see the world, they seldom ventured beyond the familiar show grounds.

grounds in every city. Vacant space may not be geography for the public, but for this agent it is vital. If the traditional circus grounds is not available, he must find a substitute quickly. So he studies the vacant areas in every locality — and hopes there will not be a building boom.

The general agent needs to know the facts about alternative towns and highways or railways. If one town cannot be had or should not be played, what else is within the mileage range? What railroads go there and how much side trackage do they have?

On the matters of hotels and restaurants all of the advance men are experts. No one knows more about these facilities than a circus man. Traveling salesmen are close behind, but usually they operate in a smaller territory. Circus agents can name and classify the hotels in every city. They know the rates and whether reduced prices are permitted to show people. They know the hotel manager, desk clerks and bell captains. It is the same among restaurants. Agents constitute a continuing research and testing service that would be a valuable aid to Duncan Hines.

Advance agents travel on their own, apart from the self-sustaining circus itself. It is they who put prime importance on geography and it is they who see the country.

For those people back on the circus, whereabouts in the usual sense are of minimum importance. After all, that world is inhabited by towners, those non-troupers who do not interest them except as ticket buyers.

But superimposed on the old familiar map is a new geography — that of special importance to circus people.

This includes the location of other circuses, truly a changeable geography. Circus people almost always know where the other shows are playing at a given time. This might be because they have friends or relatives with other shows. It might be because of the competition for towns and a general awareness of routing.

Most of all, there are the towns that hold special significance to circus people. There is little or no similarity between this special geography and that which school children learn. Showmen know that the really important metropolitan centers in this country include Peru, Hugo and Macon.

These are some of the winter quarters towns. Chief among them in recent years has been Sarasota, Florida, home of Ringling-Barnum and many of its people. Other shows and showmen cluster around this focal point.

Now Sarasota has sprouted circus suburbs like DeLand, home of

Precise timing is essential to a perfectly executed act. {1895}

Above: An almost endless task at winter quarters was building
new harness and repairing the old for the horses.

Right: Bridgeport, Connecticut, served as winter quarters
for the huge Barnum & Bailey show.

the Beatty-Cole show, and Venice, new quarters for Ringling-Barnum. Gibsonton, Florida, called "Gibtown," is inhabited largely by circus and carnival people. A giant was its mayor. Numerous other Florida towns have been the off-season base for circuses, but usually not for long enough to establish a definite association. It takes more than a single season to qualify a spot in circus geography.

Earlier, Bridgeport, Connecticut, was important as the home of Barnum & Bailey. A little town in southern Wisconsin holds importance because it is Baraboo, once the home of the Ringling brothers and their circus, as well as the location of a circus wagon factory and quarters of the Gollmar show. Now it is important as the site of the Circus World Museum.

Peru, Indiana, was a major circus center from 1884, when Ben Wallace founded his circus, until the Depression ended Sells-Floto, John Robinson and Hagenbeck-Wallace. More recent seasons have put Hugo on the map — Hugo, Oklahoma, the home of Kelly-Miller Circus and its several outgrowths and subsidiaries. Few cities have had as much association with circuses as Macon, Georgia. This was home for Sun Bros., Sparks Circus, King Bros., and other shows. Mention Macon or Hugo and a circus man knows the geography and who among his friends still lives there. Write to Macon or Peru or Hugo or Sarasota and the post office is familiar with the technique for locating circuses and circus people by mail. On any map of circus geography, these cities would be in the biggest type.

Of perhaps equal importance would be a place called The Garden. It is not far from Bridgeport but a long train ride from Sarasota. In the other world it is called New York, but to circus people little counts there except The Garden — Madison Square Garden in any of its four locations and structures, where the Ringling-Barnum show always plays in the spring.

Its suburbs include Somers, where circus business itself was born in this country. Close to Bridgeport is Hartford, site of the tragic fire. It is a fair jump to Philadelphia, former home of the Adam Forepaugh Circus and O'Brien shows, now the place where carnivals and circuses work together each spring and where circus sideshow business is tremendous.

To the south is Havre de Grace, once the home of Andrew Downie's circuses, and York, the South Carolina town that was winter quarters for Wallace Bros. and Barnett Bros. If a performer comes from York, it is a safe bet that he or his family was with

These show girls are at the Cole Bros. wardrobe department, being fitted for the show-owned costumes they will wear in the elaborate spectacle.

Wallace Bros. Circus twenty-five years ago, and there are several in that category.

Marianna, Florida, and Shreveport, Louisiana, were quarters of the Mighty Haag. Christy Bros. is identified with Beaumont and South Houston, Texas. M. L. Clark operated out of Alexandria, Louisiana. Dailey Bros. Circus established Gonzales, Texas, as a circus city.

Before Hugo mattered much, Oklahoma troupers centered on Ponca City and Marland, both having served as home base for the 101 Ranch Wild West Show. To the northwest lies Denver, original home of Sells-Floto Circus, and west of that is Baldwin Park, California, the Al G. Barnes town.

Back in the Ohio and Mississippi valleys are many circus towns. Sheboygan was home to Seils-Sterling. Robbins Bros. operated out of Granger, Iowa. The many generations of Ortons in circus business called their quarters Ortonville, Iowa. Rolla, Missouri, was headquarters for Russell Bros. Circus. But Missouri's most important city was Lancaster, because that was the location of William P. Hall's used circus farm.

Wisconsin had several circus towns, among them Evansville as home of the Hall and Campbell family shows and Delavan, as a principal circus center before the Civil War. Dozens of circus people lived at Delavan and many shows came and went from there.

In Illinois, Bloomington was the home of most of the world's flying trapeze troupers and its skyline included two buildings where flying rigging was mounted and performers practiced in shifts.

Another Bloomington, this one in Indiana, was winter quarters for Gentry Bros. Dog & Pony Shows, enough to give it a prominent spot on a map for circus geography. Indiana also had Rochester, home of Cole Bros. Circus until it moved to Louisville, and Hammond, scene of the Hagenbeck-Wallace train wreck.

Cincinnati was for decades the home of John Robinson Circus as well as the headquarters for *The Billboard* and several poster printing plants. Other posters came from Erie, Pennsylvania, and Eureka Springs, Arkansas. Columbus, Ohio, gets into the listing as the home of Sells Bros. Circus.

Some towns are smaller than usual and home to smaller shows.

But if show people come from there often enough, the town would be recognizable to others in the business. Such a town is Quenemo, Kansas, put on the map by Bill Newton and his Honest Bill Shows. It is the same story with Von Bros. Circus at Wapwallopen, Pennsylvania.

Towns known for circus troubles include Scranton, Pennsylvania, scene of a strike that closed Ringling, and Tyrone, Pennsylvania, where Walter L. Main Circus had a wreck.

Places almost mythical to circus people, too small to be played by many circuses, too remote to see otherwise, are Ringling, Oklahoma, and Ringling, Montana, both named for John Ringling and associated with his ownership of shortline railroads.

Geography in a class of its own is linked to circuses by contracts to produce Shrine shows. The Polack Bros. Circus plays under Shrine auspices at San Francisco and therefore in circus vernacular it "has" San Francisco. It also has Chattanooga and Richmond and Harlingen and more. The Hamid-Morton Circus has Milwaukee, among others on its route. Clyde Bros. has Chicago and Hubert Castle Circus has Indianapolis. New Orleans is Tom Packs Circus country. For years, Detroit and Cleveland were the sovereign territory of Orrin Davenport, inasmuch as his show played the Shrine dates there.

After the circus becomes his home, a trouper is often known by his home town. Shreveport Ethridge, Delavan Alexander, Kokomo Anders and Pittsburgh Yellow are typical. Charlie Brady's name looks normal enough but he borrowed that last from Brady, Pennsylvania, when he trouped out of there with the Sparks show.

This homeless world with strange geography used its trade papers for forwarding mail to temporary stopping places. Hundreds of performers, staff people and workingmen said "Permanent Address, The Billboard." That magazine published names in a weekly letter list so troupers could send a current forwarding address. *Amusement Business* magazine continues this service.

In this world on the move, geography means everything to the agent and nothing to the confirmed old trouper except "How far is it to the next town?" For all circus people, the map takes on an aspect that no one else would recognize.

Variety has been one of the principal assets of the circus.

Part II

A PAGEANT OF TITLES

1-What's in a Name?

If you are from the middle states you knew the circus as Hagenbeck-Wallace, Cole Bros. and Sells-Floto. If the East was your home you knew Sparks, Downie and Walter L. Main. For Southerners the circus was epitomized by John Robinson, the Mighty Haag and M. L. Clark, while Westerners knew it as Sells-Floto, Al G. Barnes or Norris & Rowe.

If you came from the smaller towns you saw Gentry Bros., Christy Bros., King Bros. Young circus goers have known it as Kelly-Miller, Clyde Beatty, Mills Bros., Hunt Bros. and the Shrine Circus. If one has seen many seasons go by, he recalls Forepaugh-Sells, Buffalo Bill, Sig Sautelle or W.W. Cole. Generations of earlier circus goers saw Van Amburgh, Howes, Sands, Lent and Welch.

Those from nearly everywhere know the biggest circus of all time. If they live in the East they call it Barnum & Bailey, and those west of the Alleghenies call it Ringling Bros., although it has been combined for fifty years as the single, supreme Ringling Bros. and Barnum & Bailey Combined Circus.

The story of the circus is expressed in terms of ornate and unique names — the titles. There have been literally thousands of circus titles. They incorporate in some way nearly every English family name and those of many other origins in Western civilization. Out of this plethora, however, most names that comprise the famous titles are the picturesque and the unique. There was a Jones Bros. Circus of some prominence and it actually was owned by brothers

of that name. But one must probe deeply into circus history to find the ones named Smith and Brown. The names — sometimes strange words — that made circus history were those such as Sells, Main, Forepaugh, Gentry, Floto, Gollmar and Haag.

In its earliest form the circus sometimes carried corporate or institutionalized titles. The most prominent was called the Zoological Institute, a designation selected largely to overcome objections of churchmen to circuses. But institutionalism soon gave way to personalities, and of the latter, circus business had more than its just share. Though there was to be an American Circus Corp., it never billed its shows that way and called them, instead, by names of Robinson, Barnes, Floto and Hagenbeck. No one advertised a General Circus Corp. to go with General Foods, General Electric, General Motors and General Tire. Circuses became established and grew to importance in an era when individual names held prime importance, and no circus man has changed this.

The title of a circus reflected not size or entertainment alone, but exuded the quality of respectability, confidence, honesty and ability attributed to successful tycoons. Most important circus titles were developed in a period when patents and trademarks held special importance in the eyes of Americans. The names of individuals still

Opposite: Shows that combined always implied "bigger and better than ever." {1902}

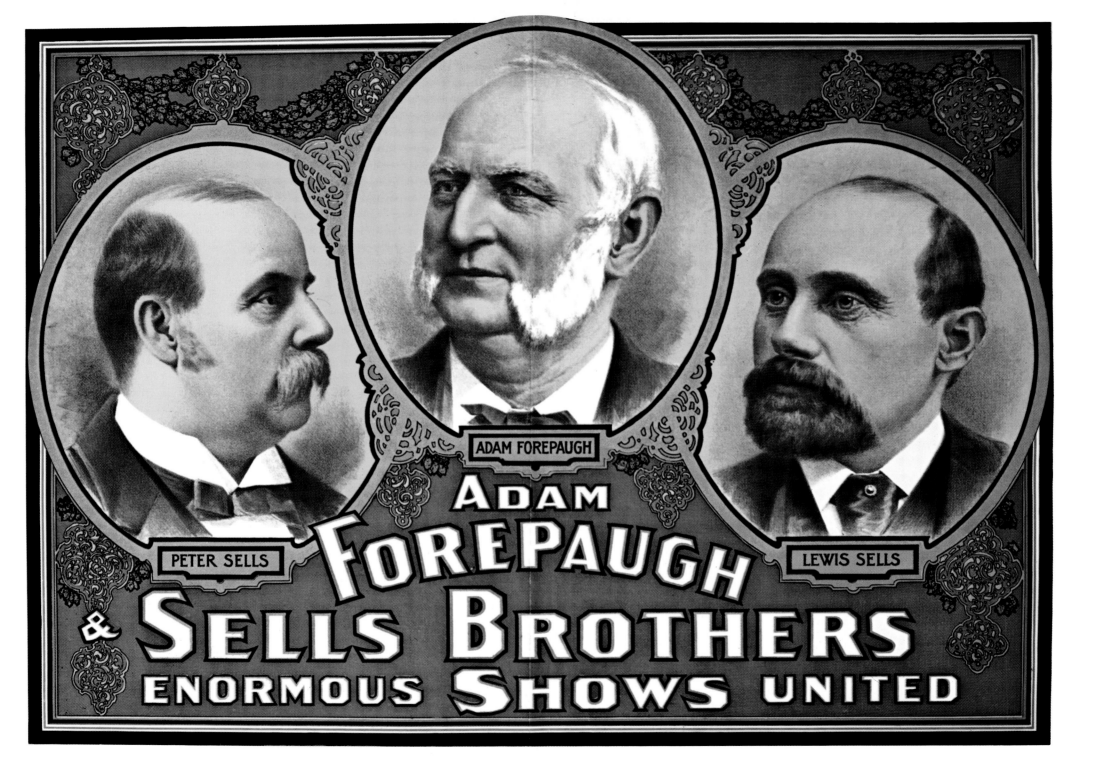

identified most products and trademarks. It was in this climate that a circus thrived under the advertised titles and hard line individualism represented by the showman with the strange name.

Just as patent medicines gave assurance of their integrity by use of the title "Dr." or "Prof.," so the circus gained similar prestige and stature by claiming "Bros." The Ringlings actually were brothers and so were the Sells circus owners. While the name Cole holds a high place in circus history, unrelated individuals built the title and there were no Cole brothers, nor were there any Christy brothers or Robbins brothers. On the other hand, the Miller brothers actually operated the 101 Ranch Real Wild West and there were blood brothers behind such latter-day shows as Hunt Bros., Mills Bros. and King Bros.

Of course, from the very start, circuses declared themselves to be "Gigantic" or "Immense." Later they capitalized on the implications of size in such words as "United" or "Combined." Probably the most common element was "Three-Ring." But surely, next to the name, the most important word in a title was "Railroad." For most of the span of circus history, railroading held a special appeal because it was compatible with the itinerant ways of a circus. For most of the seasons, to say "railroad" was to say "modern," as if one would boast of a jetliner circus today. Ultimately railroad circus meant it was a big show and not to be confused with insignificant wagon shows or truck circuses.

It is in terms of these titles that the circus tells its tale and records its history. They read like the genealogy of kings and the begats of Genesis.

Opposite: Hagenbeck disliked having his name linked to that of Wallace, a showman of low repute. Right: Ringling Bros. adhered to a high ethical standard which earned it the name "Ding-A-Ling Bros." among lesser showmen. {1900}

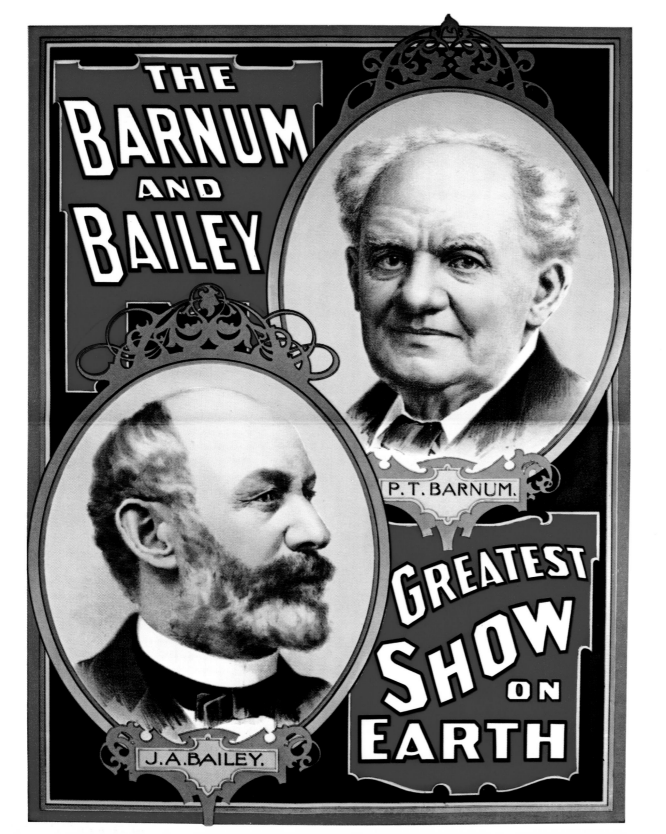

Left: Barnum's flamboyance and Bailey's business acumen combined to produce "The Greatest Show on Earth." {1898} Opposite: Many picturesque titles have appeared for a short time on the circus scene.

2-The Early Decades

It is strange that the circus as we know it is not a much older institution. All of the elements existed long before they were brought together. In the ancient civilizations of Egypt, Cambodia and points between, there were trained animals and acrobats. Romans made much of their similar entertainers at the Coliseum and the Circus Maximus. There were jesters and jugglers in the courts of medieval royalty. Men with trained bears busked at the crossroads and the courtyards throughout the civilized world.

Yet it was not until 1770 that Philip Astley established in the outskirts of London near Westminster Bridge and Sadler's Wells the first version of the circus as we know it today. Some features of that pioneer show have survived the ensuing two hundred seasons.

Astley had been a sergeant-major in the British army, serving in a conscripted regiment of unmilitary shopkeepers and tradesmen — ridiculed as a "regiment of tailors." Yet in battle against the French, this regiment distinguished itself, and Astley was cited for bravery after he captured the enemy's colors. A war hero, he came home and traded upon his cavalry background to become a teacher of riding and a performer of trick riding. He devised a comedy ride that poked fun at his "regiment of tailors" and it became a circus classic that survived in show after show for scores of seasons.

In America all of the elements for a circus existed in the same period. Among them were trick riders named John Sharp, M. F. Foulks and Jacob Bates.

In 1785, Thomas Poole erected manèges at Philadelphia, New York and Boston. Like his British predecessor and the Americans to follow him, Poole performed feats of trick riding as a means of publicizing his availability as a riding instructor for more staid styles of equestrianism. During his stay in each of the cities he offered performances two or three days a week and lessons in ordinary riding every alternate morning for three-week terms. The circus side of the business included a clown, probably some musicians and certainly a fireworks display.

The first of the great titles among American circuses was that of John Bill Ricketts, who arrived in Philadelphia in 1792 and opened a combination of riding academy and circus. His initial programs included not only his trick riding but also a tightrope walker, other riders and a clown. He established a permanent building at Twelfth and Market streets in Philadelphia and opened on April 3, 1793, claiming the first complete circus performance "in all America." President George Washington attended a performance on April 22 and perhaps other times prior to Ricketts' closing in July and moving to New York. Ricketts later built a new circus structure at Philadelphia, accommodating about 1,200 people. He had a similar building in New York and made appearances also at Boston, Salem and other cities in this country in addition to some in Canada. His show thrived and featured historical pantomimes and equestrian dramas as well as various circus acts.

By 1797 a competitor from France, the Lailson Circus, had built a pantheon across the street from Ricketts' circus building in New York. Meanwhile, at Philadelphia, the Presidential term of George

Opposite: America's circus developed from eighteenth-century riding schools. {1891}

The Barnum & Bailey Greatest Show on Earth

P.T. BARNUM

J.A. BAILEY

THE MOST ACCOMPLISHED & DAUNTLESS LADY RIDERS IN A SPIRITED & DASHING ORIGINAL HURDLE RACE, WITH FREE REIN BRAVELY & FEARLESSLY TAKING THE MOST DIFFICULT LEAPS & DANGEROUS OBSTACLES.

THE WORLD'S GRANDEST, LARGEST, BEST, AMUSEMENT INSTITUTION.

Spalding & Rogers was the innovator among major circuses before the Civil War. In 1852, it completed the Floating Palace, a theater barge on which they played the river route. The show was eventually closed down by increased war action.

Washington ended and local merchants honored him with a special program at Ricketts Circus on the night of March 4. Two years later Ricketts' luck had come to an end. First, his New York building burned when fires from the Hell scene of "Don Juan" got away from the attendants. Then his building in Philadelphia burned as well. Ruined, Ricketts performed his trick riding at the Lailson building and elsewhere in order to earn his passage back to England. He sailed for home but the ship was lost at sea.

For nearly twenty years the few circuses made little progress. Year-to-year success in order to stay in business was about as much as the shows could claim, although they were becoming more numerous. Both American and European circuses toured the Eastern seaboard from Florida to the Bay of Fundy.

While all the elements for circus performances had existed a long time and now showmen had brought them together for around twenty seasons, there was one principal oversight — there were no elephants. In 1797 Captain Jacob Crowninshield brought the first elephant to this country. But for another fifteen years this great feature was exhibited on its own, independent of any other organization. Only in 1812 did it make a brief appearance with a circus. It was different with the second elephant. Hackaliah Bailey of Somers, New York, placed his elephant with the Nathan Howes Menagerie.

The tiny little road show that Nathan Howes operated in 1816 looked just like the rest except for the elephant. Yet it was his show which sired nearly every American circus that was to follow. His activities began the great genealogy of titles.

On the roster of the little Howes show was Nathan's brother, Seth B. Howes. He went from that show to others, starting as a rider and general handyman, then becoming assistant manager and in 1840 being selected as manager of the new Mabie Bros. Circus. He was there five years as manager and two more as partner before launching a show of his own. It would be one of the principal titles in American circus history.

Nathan Howes took in as partner an Englishman who had come to this country several years before. He was Aron Turner who, in turn, trained a son-in-law, George F. Bailey, and Bailey would fill a key role in later shows.

Those 1816 profits from the combination of the elephant and Nate Howe's show caught the attention of his neighbors in Putnam and Westchester counties of New York. Menageries were free of the sort of objection churchmen of the time raised against circuses, so

Dan Rice started as a clown with Spalding's American Circus. He rose to national prominence as a commentator of the political scene, was a favorite of Abraham Lincoln and campaigned for Zachary Taylor.

these proper Yankees saw no reason why they should not get into this lucrative game. First came John June, Lewis B. Titus and Caleb Sutton Angevine. They would be joined by other Putnam and Westchester neighbors who came, sometimes as employees and sometimes as partners, in what became a mighty syndicate of shows. June, Titus and Angevine began by purchasing a small menagerie entitled the Zoological Institute. Its name was more impressive than its exhibition, but all that would change. This group was soon joined by others and they organized an increasing number of menageries and later, circuses. This informal alliance of showmen worked closely together, routing their own shows to profitable territory, renting equipment to other newcomers to the circus business and tightly controlling the import and supply of wild animals in this country.

They were not beyond using aggressive tactics. More than one farmer-turned-circus-man rented his equipment from the syndicate only to find that his suppliers then placed a bigger rival show on the same route and eliminated his profits. When his show collapsed it was repossessed by the syndicate who then had not only his purchase money but their wagons and animals as well. When more established showmen got into financial difficulties the syndicate came to their rescue, but thereafter they did as the syndicate directed. One rival show was Raymond & Waring which laid plans for playing the lucrative upstate New York territory, but the syndicate said no. It claimed exclusive rights to the territory and declared, "We put our foot down flat and shall play New York." From that day on they were known as the Flatfoot Party.

Apex of the Flatfoot Party's control came in 1835 when they joined with about 130 other showmen and stockholders to form the Association of the Zoological Institute, a company intended to tighten control of the circus and menagerie business. They spoke of Unit 10 and Unit 15. They assigned territories, consolidated the planning of routes and allotted the feature animals and performers in ways that suited the Flatfoots best. For the Flatfoot Party, made up of those neighbors from Putnam and Westchester counties, continued in firm control. Nathan Howes, Aron Turner, James Raymond — virtually every meaningful name in show business was affiliated with this company and thus was controlled by the powerful Flatfoots.

Such concentration, however, was short-lived because the panic of 1837 struck down the circuses, menageries and men who owned them. The Association of the Zoological Institute fell apart, but the showmen involved quickly regrouped, recovered and resumed their trouping, often with new alliances. The Flatfoot Party continued with two shows, G. C. Quick & Co. Circus as well as June & Co.'s Oriental Circus. Though temporarily on a less pretentious scale, the Flatfoot Party continued its sixty-year domination of the circus business. Rufus Welch, Lewis B. Lent and Richard Sands were among the Flatfoots who rose to prominence in this period.

The first American circus performer to win permanent fame on a national level was Isaac Van Amburgh, a cage boy boosted into national prominence by the thousands of June, Titus & Angevine posters declaring him to be the Lion King. Van Amburgh was, in fact, the first man to develop or revive the trained wild animal act. The Roman toga he wore as costume gave tacit recognition to the ancient combination of lions and gladiators. He also took a text from the Bible for that part of his act in which a lion and a lamb lay down together. Van Amburgh himself made it a trio. He was usually on the Flatfoot flagship, either the Zoological Institute or June, Titus & Angevine Menagerie.

By the end of the 1830's his own name was on the wagons and he was starting a seven-year tour of Europe, but he still was a Flatfoot property. His tour of England was notable for its royal patronage and for the demonstration it provided European showmen about American tenting and one-day stands. For the last half of the 1840's the Van Amburgh menagerie toured the United States, still under the Flatfoot banner. But their twenty-year alliance ended and, starting in 1851, Van Amburgh was with James Raymond, the sometimes rival, sometimes partner of the Flatfoots and now in the competitor side of the cycle. After the death of James Raymond and despite retirement of Van Amburgh, the show continued under a host of varieties in the title, but always stressing the name of Van Amburgh. Soon, it came under the control of its press agent, Hyatt Frost, who operated it through 1883.

Meanwhile, another of those Nathan Howes offshoots was continuing. The Aron Turner Circus was taken over by his son-in-law, George F. Bailey, a nephew of the Bailey who imported the elephant that inspired the Flatfoot's circus activities. As a young man, George F. Bailey induced his father-in-law to give up the rental of menagerie animals from the Flatfoots and buy his own animals. Upon inheriting this circus, Bailey put his own name on it

Opposite: Such familiar names as Jones and Wilson did exist, but circus history was made by strange-sounding titles like Gollmar, Floto and Haag. {1914}

70

and within a decade saw fit to join the current edition of the Flatfoots. As the families involved in that operation moved through echelons and generations, they centered activity on the shows of Sands, Lent and Nathan. They trouped Sands, Nathan & Co. Circus until 1863 and then concentrated all of their operation on the George F. Bailey Circus.

Still another outgrowth of the pioneer Nathan Howes show was the career of his brother, Seth B. Howes. In the 1840's he had been agent and ultimately partner in the Mabie Bros. Circus. But when the Mabies decided to buy land in frontier Wisconsin and stay in that Western country rather than the East, Howes bowed out. Instead, he launched his own circus, initially called Seth B. Howes United States Circus, for 1848 and immediately thereafter. Briefly he was a partner of Lewis B. Lent and P. T. Barnum in a show that featured Tom Thumb. This was a case of a circus man, Howes, capitalizing on the name of a famous person; Barnum was not yet to make more than a temporary foray into circus business. Howes joined with the Flatfoots again to bring from France the Franconi Hippodrome Show, and then for seven years, beginning in 1857, he and a partner had the Howes & Cushing Circus in England. Cushing wearied of the deal and came home, but Seth B. Howes continued with Howes Great American Show. For its return to America this outfit was retitled Howes European Circus, and it was responsible for importing finely and intricately carved parade wagons from England.

By this period, American circuses had developed the parade into something of special interest, but it was the Howes importation of English wagons which introduced really ornate equipment and led to construction of costly and elaborate parade equipment on all major shows thereafter. For a while Howes assigned management of this outfit to his nephew, Egbert, but then he sold the equipment and leased the title to the Flatfoots. In 1870 Howes & Cushing again toured Europe. This time Seth B. came back with a title reading Howes Great London Shows, and he brought more English wagons. Howes then sold the show to James E. Kelley, an old Flatfoot who owned a percentage of the Van Amburgh show at

Pardon A. Older was a partner of Mabie Bros. Circus before entering the business on his own. His circus advertised such oddities as a horned horse and "uncouth" sea cow.

72

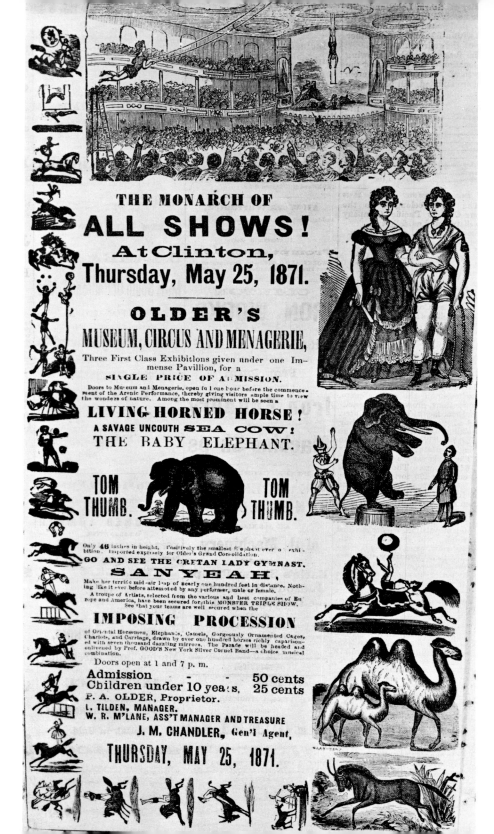

the same time. Howes personally bowed out of the business about that time, but his title, Howes Great London Circus, would survive another fifty years.

One other circus complex completed the picture of major shows prior to the Civil War. This was Spalding & Rogers — the innovator, the inventor, the experimenter. If other shows were satisfied with the equipment and procedures developed at the outset of trouping, Spalding & Rogers was not. This show would perfect new systems for larger tents, for seating, lighting and transportation.

It began when Gilbert R. Spalding determined that he must take over management of the Nichols Circus because it was in arrears on both a substantial bill for paint Spalding had sold it and for money he had loaned to it. For about five years he operated Spalding's American Circus. One of his performers was a rising young clown named Dan Rice, and in 1848 Rice was set up with a show of his own, with Van Orden, a brother-in-law of Spalding, as an executive. This show traveled by steamboat on the Mississippi, opening at St. Louis, playing Galena and Nauvoo among other Illinois

Eighteenth-century circuses usually played indoors, but by the end of the next century every major show had become a tented enterprise. A descendant of the earlier circus, however, was the indoor show which played exclusively during the winter. Shipp's Circus, established in 1884, was one of the first of these winter shows.

73

Adam Forepaugh began his own circus in 1866 and operated it until his death in 1890. The street parade above is billed as Great Adam Forepaugh Show, but was under the new management of James Cooper.

landings. It switched to the Ohio to play Cincinnati and Pittsburgh territory, then returned to the Mississippi and finally went south to New Orleans.

Rice continued an erratic career, sometimes on his own and sometimes with circuses financed by Spalding. Rice became a national figure, comparable to a Will Rogers or a Bob Hope, as a commentator on current events. But he became too much entwined in those events. A personal vendetta against Spalding influenced his business dealings as well as his public statements. Rice became unreliable because of his drinking habits, and often the clown who appeared under his name really was J. L. Thayer, while the true trainer of his animals was Charles W. Noyes. Thayer left Rice earlier, and Noyes joined him in 1863 to launch the Thayer & Noyes Circus.

Meanwhile, Gilbert Spalding had paired up with Charles Rogers to troupe the Spalding & Rogers Circus. It was this outfit which perfected portable bleachers and an intermediate circle of poles to give circus tents greater size and capacity. In 1852 work was completed on an arena or theater barge called the Floating Palace. It claimed to seat 2,500 people, making it one of the largest theaters in the country. Their own Spalding & Rogers Circus was aboard for the first two seasons and then they leased the Van Amburgh-Raymond show for the third.

In 1853 Van Orden, undoubtedly with Spalding's cooperation, experimented with moving circus wagons by rail. Two years later Spalding & Rogers was entitled The Railroad Circus, toured what was then the West, and made most of its moves by rail. In the following year, further improvements were made in the railroading process, and again most of the tour was made aboard cars rented from a railroad. In that season their experimental railroad unit was in the East, while a wagon show played the Middle West and the Floating Palace made the river route. Spalding & Rogers stayed thereafter with the Floating Palace until it was closed down by Civil War action on the river. One story is that the show's identity was changed to the Dan Castello Circus as it carefully wended its way through territory contested by both Confederate and Union forces. For the next season, 1862, Spalding & Rogers played it safer. They sent a circus to South America under Rogers' manage-

Opposite: This bill was posted in 1871, the year Cole began his successful show.

74

COLE'S SOUTHERN CIRCUS AND MENAGERIE.

ment and thus escaped war risks. They resumed operation in this country for 1864 and 1865.

Spalding then dropped out of most circus activity, returning only to join with the Flatfoots to place an American circus at the World Exposition in Paris for 1867. His partners were Flatfoots Avery Smith, Girard Quick and John A. Nathans. Despite an elaborate portable building of their design, the show did not do the volume of business expected. After three years in storage the Paris Pavilion Show was sold by Spalding to Dan Rice. Dan found soon that it was never intended for one-day stands, and he had to abandon it.

While playing the growing towns of the Mississippi Valley, Mabie Bros. attracted the attention of Pardon A. Older. He held an interest in their show for a time around 1849, but soon joined Hiram Orton in the Orton & Older Circus, another Wisconsin outfit. Miles Orton, son of the founder, continued with Orton Bros. Circus. Briefly he was married to Mary Ann Cole. She was a member of the Cooke family of British circus owners and a son by earlier marriage was W.W. Cole. After the breakup of her marriage to Orton, the mother and son formed the Cole & Orton Circus in 1871. Miles Orton joined as a rider. Only a year or two later it was the W. W. Cole Circus, and he was destined to become one of the most financially successful circus men in American history.

Meanwhile, the Mabie brothers decided to retire and sold off their show. The menagerie half went to John O'Brien and Adam Forepaugh. They operated it for a year as the Dan Rice Circus and then split up to go their separate ways. Forepaugh began use of his own title in 1866. O'Brien branched out on a twenty-five-year career during which he used a wide range of circus titles, sometimes operating several shows in a single season. He became the most notorious circus man of his time because of his unscrupulous business methods and shameless treatment of the public.

Dan Castello, who operated a circus through much of the 1860's, teamed up with Egbert Howes and others in 1868 and 1869 to take a circus to the West Coast, using the brand new railroad for some of the show's moves.

The name of Robinson figured strongly in circus business at this time. One reason was the Yankee Robinson Circus, founded in the middle 1850's and grown to major proportions by 1866. It played mostly in the Mississippi Valley, headquartered at Indianapolis and included such big show features as a forty-horse hitch in its parade. Forty-horse teams were originated by Spalding & Rogers and were seen in a few other shows of this period.

The name also was prominent because of John Robinson, who began as a bareback rider for the Flatfoots and in the 1840's began a show of his own. The John Robinson Circus was a household name through eight decades. Once it was the partnership of Robinson & Eldred. Another time it was Robinson & Lake, but for the most part, first one generation, then another, and finally a third operated it as the John Robinson Circus.

Just before the Civil War, Robinson's agent was Fred Bailey, a man who claimed relationship with Hackaliah Bailey of early elephant fame. Bailey took on a runaway boy as an apprentice bill-poster. This lad changed his name to that of his boss and teacher and thus James A. Bailey came to circus business. He progressed to the post of general agent for Hemmings & Cooper Circus, and then in 1873 became a partner in Cooper & Bailey. At this point, the stage was set and a cast selected for the golden age of American circuses.

3-The Golden Age

William Cameron Coup had been in all the right places to see the potential for a new circus form. Now retired from his position as manager of the Yankee Robinson Circus, he was "at liberty," in the ideal position to partake of that age-old privilege of showmen — sitting back and planning the sure-fire idea for a new show. He contacted Dan Castello and together they approached Phineas Taylor Barnum with a plan whereby they would rent that museum man's famous name and use it on their new circus.

Barnum's name meant much at the time; he was a national celebrity. Long before these circus years, the young Barnum had exhibited an aged Negress whom he claimed had been George Washington's nurse, a tale the public found difficult to swallow. Upon discovering the smallest midget he had ever seen, Barnum dubbed him Tom Thumb and exhibited him before European royalty and then to crowds at theaters, museums and concert halls. He also managed the American tour of Jenny Lind, the "Swedish Nightingale," a singer of high cultural standing. Throughout his career, he had developed Barnum's Museum in New York City. There he displayed every sort of invention, discovery, rarity, oddity, animal and performer that he could obtain. Among them were a Cardiff giant and several other features that brought charges of "humbug." Barnum's way was to wink off such assertions in a fashion that made the public want to see even his counterfeits. His contact with circuses had been limited but he had had several business dealings with the Flatfoots and other circus men. When Coup and Castello made their offer, Barnum agreed to become their partner.

For 1871 they launched a giant wagon circus called P. T. Barnum's Museum, Menagerie & Circus. They had Admiral Dot, the Eldorado Elf; Col. Goshen, the Palestine Giant; some Fiji cannibals and a giraffe. Under Barnum's name and with Coup's skills it thrived. It was a major show from the first, claiming six hundred horses were required to move it. The long established shows of the time were surprised by its success and startling size. But for Coup it was only the first step.

For the very next season, he took the giant step and arranged to move P. T. Barnum's Great Traveling Exposition and World's Fair aboard sixty-five railroad cars. This was the first full-blown railroad show. Coup, recalling the lessons of earlier part-time railroad outfits and adding his own genius, developed the plan for placing ramps at the end of the cars, then pulling wagons up the ramps and along the length of the flats. His ideas for crossover plates, runs, snubbing posts, pullup and pullover teams and other elements of railroad circusing remained in constant use throughout the age of shows that moved by rail.

The parade included the "Revolving Temple of Juno with a 20-camel hitch." There were "telescopic golden chariots made in

Opposite: A publicity battle over a white elephant raged between Forepaugh-Sells and Barnum-London in the late nineteenth century. Ringling's sacred elephant of 1927, however, was truly white. {1927}

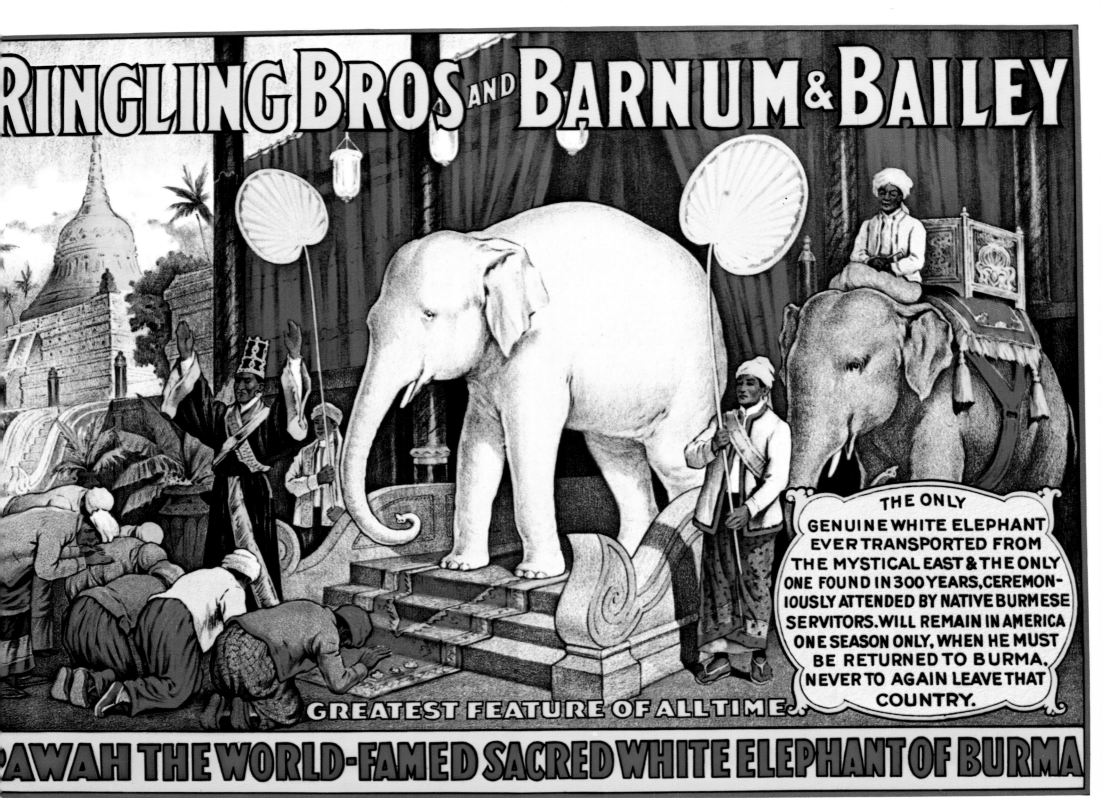

London," automatons called "The Dying Zouave" and "The Sleeping Beauty," stuffed birds, portraits of celebrities, a whale's jawbone and much more. The show closed at Detroit in November and was expected to winter in New York. Barnum, however, leased his name and animals to Pardon A. Older for a winter tour of the South. Old Phineas had been in the habit of renting his name out to first one and then another showman for such minor activities, and did not realize that now things were different. Coup was infuriated at the thought of someone else sharing in benefits of the title he presumed to control. But Barnum did not let up. For 1874 and 1875 he leased similar title rights to John O'Brien, whom Coup knew to be a scoundrel.

At the end of 1875 Barnum found himself alone. O'Brien shuttered his Barnum show; Coup ended his Barnum association largely because of displeasure over the museum man's insistence upon renting out his name. Even boastful P. T. Barnum knew that he was not the man to operate a new giant railroad circus single handedly. He turned to the old veterans of circus business, the Flatfoots. That group, now headed by George F. Bailey, operated the Barnum Circus from 1876 through 1880.

During the same winter that Barnum was turning his show over to the Flatfoots, James A. Bailey was converting his to railroad operation. He had progressed from billposter to owner. For the 1876 season he took his show first to California, then in November sailed for Australia. Cooper & Bailey played a full route "down under," staying until April of 1878. Then the show sailed from Auckland, New Zealand, to Lima, Peru, and during the fall of that year played a half-dozen principal cities in South America. This was an ambitious undertaking, but it was not a profitable tour. Cooper & Bailey limped home. There Bailey found that other shows were even less well off than his. The venerable Howes Great London Shows had run onto bad times. Under the management of James E. Kelley, it had gone deeply into debt. A rigged sale put it under control of James Reilly, a poster printer. Eagerly, he sold the Howes show to Cooper & Bailey, and this combination toured in 1879 and 1880.

Now the Flatfoots wanted out of their Barnum obligations and Bailey was ready for further expansion. So Bailey and Barnum joined together with James L. Hutchinson, a concessionaire, and they came out as P. T. Barnum's Greatest Show on Earth & Howes Great London Circus & Sanger's Royal British Menagerie. In typical modesty, Bailey let his name slip out of the title.

To the dismay of his partners, P. T. Barnum had a propensity for renting out his famous name, even to the most disreputable of showmen.

Above: Barnum's first major venture in circusing, announced in this double-
page spread in 1871, was a traveling show which included
curiosities from the Barnum Museum and a small menagerie.

Left: This ad illustrates the features in the Barnum show's first circus parade. 1871
was its first and last year as a mud show. The next season, his circus,
under Coup's direction, went on rails — the first to do so.

While associates and employees referred to Phineas T. Barnum informally, such was not to be the case with James A. Bailey. Rare was the time any trouper called him Jim to his face. It was Mister Bailey. Here was a man of great ability and modest manner, preferring to stay in the background while Barnum took the literal and figurative bows before the public. Though Barnum is hailed in history as a great showman, it was the efficient, unassuming Bailey who was indeed the master circus man. He came to the Barnum show when it was near collapse and he built it into a powerful show machine. Then he would do it all a second time. But then and now the little man with the borrowed name was little known outside of circus circles.

The Barnum-Bailey-Hutchinson partnership continued through the 1885 season and covered the period when the Barnum-London show presented Jumbo, the elephant, and when it conducted a deadly publicity battle with the Forepaugh Circus. Each claimed a white elephant. Barnum – London owned a true white elephant, but its color was not white enough to be convincing. Forepaugh had a creamy white pachyderm, thanks to artificial coloration. The vituperative battle that took place damaged forever the credibility of circus advertising.

Adam Forepaugh's policies toward the public were the same for the circus as Barnum's had been with the museum: A little flimflam and humbug will help the people enjoy it all the more. He came into show business by selling horses to the Tom King Circus and having to join it to collect his money. Forepaugh stayed in the field to build the biggest circus in the world. Because of his first name, he found it first convenient and then profitable to use Biblical references in his advertising. He played upon the idea that, just as the world had begun with one Adam, so the circus world owed its being to this Adam. But his circus was operated on something less than religious precepts. Blustery and crude as a person, Forepaugh's circus was the same. His advertising was deceptive, his treatment of employees was cruel, his handling of the public was cavalier.

In this period Bailey and Barnum were partners in conflict. The flamboyant Barnum irritated the conservative Bailey and refused to take any directions, and consequently Bailey sold his interest. The buyers were W. W. Cole and James E. Cooper. The latter, of course, had been Bailey's recent partner, while Cole had operated a highly successful railroad circus until selling out in order to take the Barnum - London position. He, too, had toured Australia; then he had rebuilt his circus from the ground up, designing cars and wagons as a unit for maximum efficiency. Cole and Cooper, however, amounted to a caretaker administration.

It seems likely that Bailey was letting Barnum suffer without him and held a plan to approach the old museum man again. And suffer he did. While Bailey was away, Barnum lost the lucrative contract for Madison Square Garden. The winner was their chief rival, the Adam Forepaugh Circus. The best that could be salvaged by the Barnum people was a joint appearance. So the two shows, Barnum & Forepaugh, combined for the Garden date in 1886. Moreover, the Barnum show agreed to a four-year route pact which divided territory between Barnum and Forepaugh. By now Bailey had made his point. In October of 1887 Barnum agreed to give Bailey full command of the show and add his name to the title. From that date onward it was the Barnum & Bailey Greatest Show on Earth.

Bailey no sooner came into full charge than a major fire swept through the winter quarters, and it was necessary to rebuild the show before spring. Bailey not only accomplished that feat, but in the next winter took Barnum & Bailey to London. They played a successful date despite opposition from English showmen and returned in time to start the 1890 season in New York as usual.

While Bailey and Barnum were finding their common ground and moving on to new successes, the rest of circus business also was doing well.

The Sells brothers were Columbus, Ohio, auctioneers who took auction wagons on the road and often followed circuses in order to benefit from the resulting crowds. Those crowds convinced them they should have a circus of their own. Three brothers started it in

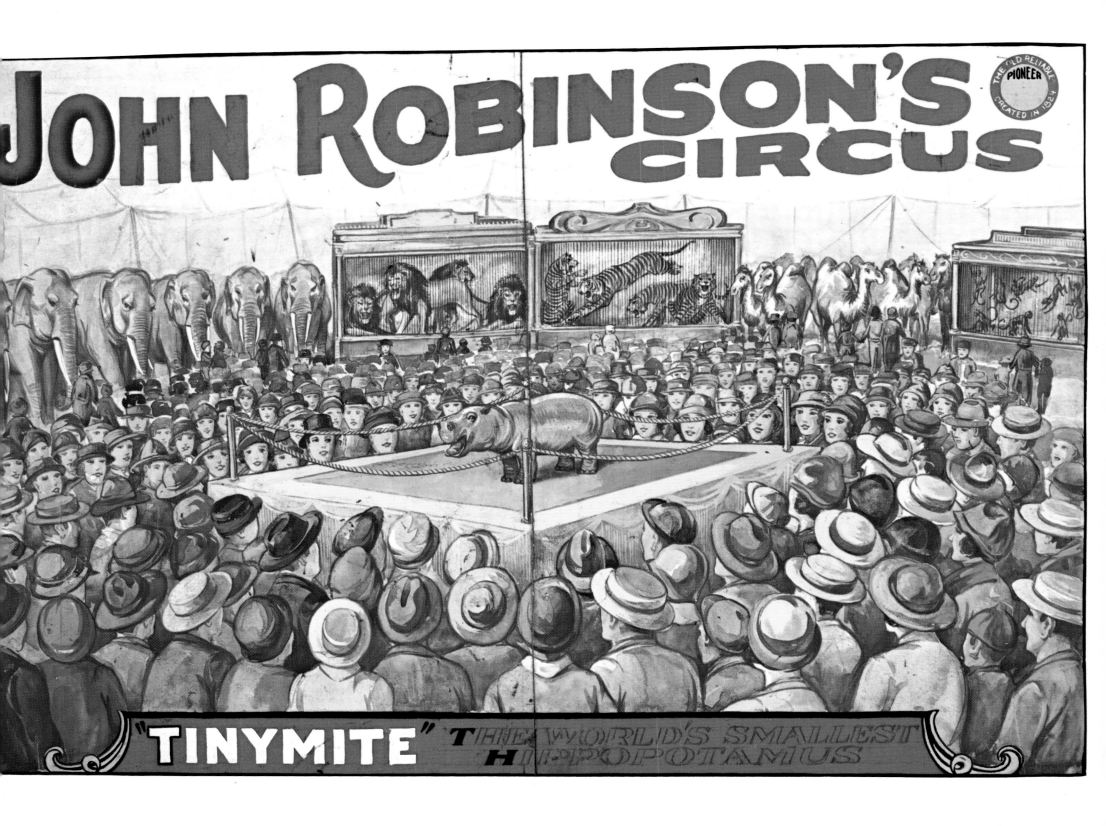

1872 but they did not do well until a fourth joined as treasurer. Thereafter, their luck — or their accounting — improved and they began to make money. The Sells show provided stiff competition to the other major shows of the time. Subsequent history would see their name bought, sold, stolen and borrowed by a steady progression of showmen, extending to the present and attesting to its value as a circus title.

Meanwhile, the Adam Forepaugh Circus, sometimes larger than the Barnum operation, was rolling along not only with its own show but, also, in renting surplus equipment to other showmen. It outfitted the Montgomery Queen Circus which operated in the middle 1870's, and there were others which utilized Forepaugh rental property. When the Queen show failed, Sells Bros. bought much of its equipment and came out in 1878 as Sells Bros. Great European Seven Elephant Railroad Show. This freed the old Sells wagon equipment, so it was used by their brother-in-law for the S.H. Barrett Circus. Sells Bros. experienced much opposition from Howes Great London, but that show was already in its financial difficulties and would not long survive.

By the 1880's a substantial number of significant new shows were coming on the scene. Old Dan Castello found a new angel and they came out as the W. H. Harris Nickel Plate Shows. The Hilliard & Main Circus was succeeded by the second generation Walter L. Main Shows. Frank A. Robbins came out on equipment rented from Forepaugh. As several livery stable owners before him, Ben Wallace found he had to foreclose on a circus, and thereby became a showman. This started the Great Wallace Circus in 1884. The sale of W. W. Cole had resulted in establishment of the Lemen Bros. Circus. Of special interest was the establishment in 1883 of Buffalo Bill's Wild West. Still underway was the ancient John Robinson Circus. And like a last touchstone with the old days of the Flatfoots, the Van Amburgh Circus closed in 1883. Even so, the title would find later usage.

A group of young showmen from Baraboo, Wisconsin, had been inspired by visits to the John B. Doris Circus and the Dan Rice boat circus, among others. Now they determined to enter the business themselves and made a deal with old Yankee Robinson for use of his name. They were the brothers Ringling (an Americanized version of the German name, Rungeling), and they were to become the most famous circus owners in the world.

The title of the new show became Yankee Robinson & Ringling Bros. Great Double Shows, Circus and Caravan. For 1884, they had nine wagons and rented farm teams to make the moves. One of the Ringlings had been with the Yankee Robinson Circus, and now the five brothers learned much from the old showman before he died later the same season. The Ringlings made great progress but looked back over their shoulders one more time when they leased the Van Amburgh title in 1889 to use along with their own name. That winter they became one of Forepaugh's customers, buying eleven railroad cars and several wagons. Beginning in 1890 it would be Ringling Bros. Railroad Shows. Adam Forepaugh died in January of 1890, and James A. Bailey moved at once to buy the show. His partner again was James E. Cooper, who fronted the enterprise. Bailey's interest in the Forepaugh show was kept secret.

Extending the 1891 season, Sells Bros. followed the route of Bailey and Cole to Australia. But Australian interests convinced authorities that Sells' horses were diseased. The stock could not be unloaded, but rather than give up the trip, the Sells show bought all new horses in Australia and set about to train them as they played the route. This and other difficulties made the trip a losing venture. Back at San Francisco in June of 1892 the Sells show resumed normal operation.

The financial panic of 1893 damaged several circuses. John Robinson was in a weakened condition. Sells Bros. already was staggered by Australian losses. The Forepaugh show, under Cooper-Bailey ownership, closed at the end of the 1894 season. About the only outfit making big money in 1893 was Buffalo Bill's Wild West, which by a coup had obtained a lot across the street from a main entrance to the Chicago World's Fair. It played there for most of the season.

Opposite: Dressage acts were designed mainly to please the eye. {1903}

The Young Buffalo Wild West Show typifies the set-up preferred by such shows. Tents were not used since the quarter poles and rigging interfered with riding demonstrations. Instead, a canopy was raised over the spectators' seats, leaving the center area open for the Wild West presentation.

Buffalo Bill Cody had started with a show that played ball parks and similar grandstands for extended engagements. Annie Oakley, a young sharpshooter whose first show experience was with Sells Bros., joined Buffalo Bill in 1885. The next year, when Adam Forepaugh controlled Madison Square Garden, Adam booked the Cody show in from Thanksgiving until February. A month later Buffalo Bill's Wild West show sailed for England and a four-year tour of Europe.

The Wild West was patronized and hailed by royalty throughout its tour. Queen Victoria had two command performances, and continental royalty reacted the same way. This tour gave opportunity for recruiting cavalrymen of each nationality and Cody's show thereafter featured "Rough Riders of the World."

Back in America for the Chicago Fair and a subsequent season at Brooklyn, the Cody show needed help and turned to James A. Bailey. The Wild West could handle its performance, but getting the show from town to town was a different matter. Bailey received a fifty percent interest in the show and responsibility for providing rolling stock, financial support and winter quarters. Bailey sold half of his share to W. W. Cole. The Forepaugh show, owned by Bailey and Cooper, was closed, partly so that its railroad cars could be assigned by Bailey to move the Buffalo Bill outfit. Other Forepaugh equipment went to Columbus, Ohio, for a new combination with Sells Bros. The Forepaugh-Sells show then was owned by Bailey, Cole, Lewis Sells and Peter Sells. Bailey's three shows — Barnum & Bailey, Forepaugh-Sells and Buffalo Bill — conducted an opposition campaign against Ringling Bros. in 1896. In 1898, he took the Barnum & Bailey show on a five-year tour of Europe, leaving Forepaugh-Sells and Buffalo Bill to hold the territory against incursions by Ringling Bros.

For 1898 the Ringlings leased John Robinson, a circus they needed in the opposition battles and one which was available because of continued money troubles stemming from the 1893 depression. Also helping Ringling was the Gollmar Bros. Circus owned by their cousins. This outfit had started in 1890, using the wagon show equipment abandoned by Ringling when the latter went on rails. Gollmar soon outgrew wagons and it, too, became a

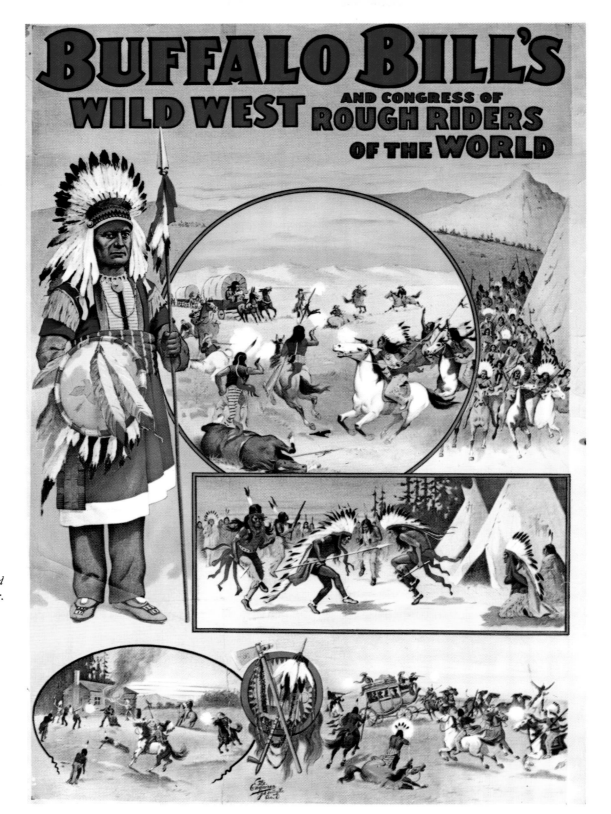

International roughriders were recruited during a successful European tour.

PHOTO BY
MERRYMAN STUDIO
PAWNEE OKLA.

Above right: In 1883, Buffalo Bill Cody and his partners initiated the Wild West show. The exciting show they produced lasted for thirty years and was widely imitated.

Above left: Major Gordon Lillie, known professionally as Pawnee Bill, also owned a Wild West show. He later became a partner of Cody, and their production was billed as Buffalo Bill's Wild West and Pawnee Bill's Great Far East Show.

Left: Pawnee Bill holds the lines of his team hitched to a Concord Coach. The stagecoach was a symbol of the West and no Wild West show was complete without one.

Ringling is the most famous circus name of all time. Standing left to right are Al, Alf T., August, Charles and Otto; seated left to right are John, Mrs. August Ringling, Sr., August Ringling, Sr., Ida and Henry. {c. 1895}

railroad circus, normally playing Minnesota and the Dakotas, where its chief competitor was Campbell Bros. Circus.

In 1898 the Barnum & Bailey show had gained phenomenal business in England. Consequently, in April 1899, Bailey organized Barnum & Bailey, Ltd., as a British stock company. Most buyers were British, but fifty-one percent of the stock was retained by Bailey and his close American associates.

Barnum & Bailey returned to the United States for the season of 1903, and for the occasion presented a gigantic street parade which included a number of new wagons built to commemorate the show's European tour and its return. It owned a winter quarters plant in England and a train designed for European railroads. So starting in 1903 Bailey routed the Buffalo Bill show on a four-year tour of Europe, using former Barnum & Bailey cars and quarters.

In order to settle the estate of Peter Sells, Bailey was forced to buy the entire Forepaugh-Sells show, but he turned around and sold half at once to Ringling Bros. This was an indication of things to come. In the past Bailey had stepped in at every juncture to buy major shows or save them from disaster, but that role now would fall to the Ringlings. James A. Bailey died in April 1906. In June the Ringlings bought Mrs. Bailey's share of Forepaugh-Sells and after the 1907 season, the Ringlings also owned Barnum & Bailey's Greatest Show on Earth. The Ringlings indicated no interest in the Cody show, and Cody, deeply in debt to the Bailey estate, had little control of things. Consequently, Mrs. Bailey sold out to Gordon Lillie, known professionally as Pawnee Bill. Lillie had been an associate of Cody's in early Wild West show days and then set up a rival show of his own. He had sold it off in the winter of 1908-1909 to such shows as Campbell Bros. and the Mighty Haag Circus. Pawnee Bill then bought two-thirds of the Cody show, and consequently it became known as Buffalo Bill's Wild West and Pawnee Bill's Great Far East.

Left: Gollmar Bros., cousins of the Ringlings, began a wagon show in 1890 on abandoned Ringling equipment. It, too, became a railroad circus and normally played Minnesota and the Dakotas in competition with Campbell Bros. Circus.

Opposite: Ownership of Al G. Barnes has changed hands many times. {1934}

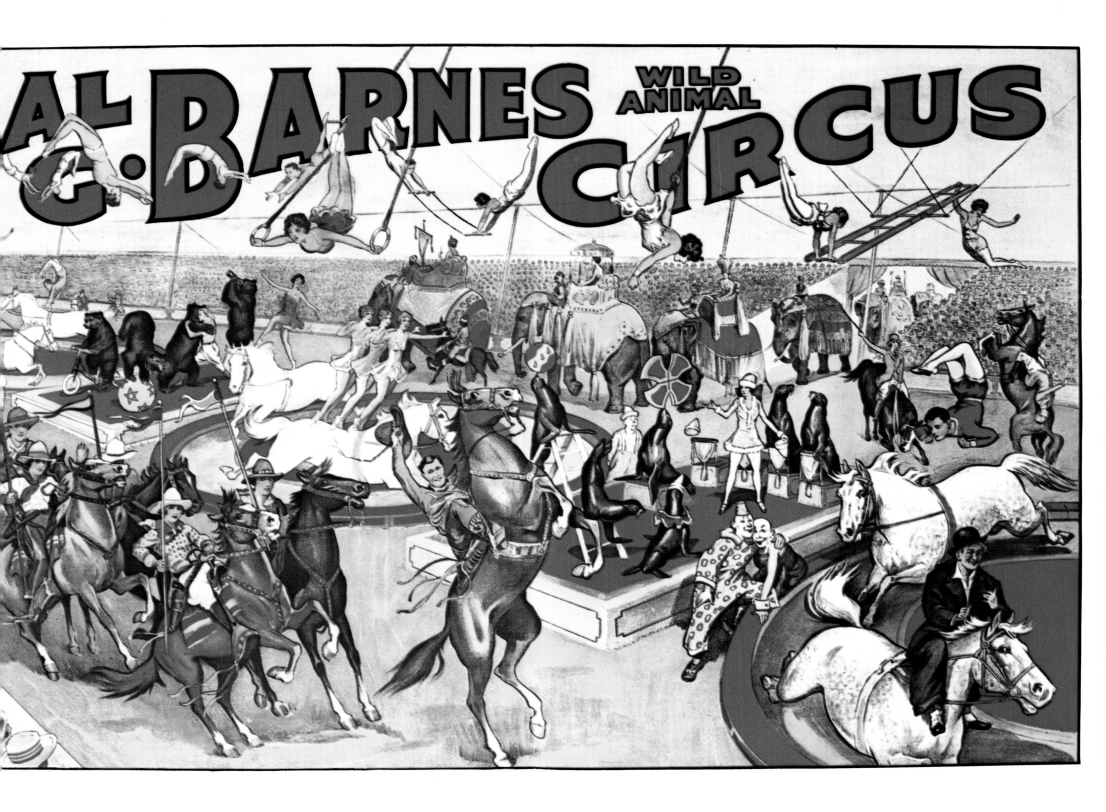

4 -The Early Twentieth Century

While the Sells Bros. Circus still was in operation, Willie Sells, an adopted son of one of the brothers, gave up bareback riding in favor of management. He promoted one angel and then another in the series of circus operations which included the William Sells Great London Show of 1891, then Sells & Renfrew, Sells & Gray, and Sells & Downs. The latter was a partnership of equally crafty characters, Willie and Martin Downs. Each tried to beat the other, and Willie lost. However, Downs continued with a circus which he named Cole Bros.

Willie looked around for something to do and found work as general agent for a show owned by the proprietors of the *Denver Post,* the Great Floto Show. It was named for their sports editor simply because the owners liked its sound, and now they hired Sells in order to wrap up that name. The show came out in 1908 as Sells-Floto Circus.

Almost at once the adventuresome editors-turned-circus-men began the use of posters which depicted not just Willie but also his famous father and uncles. Ringling Bros. took exception to this plan, and in Federal Court won a suit which barred Sells-Floto from using the pictures of the original Sells Bros.

This was part of a continuing battle between Sells-Floto and Ringling. The Sells-Floto owners, Harry Tammen and Fred Bonfils, scored more than once. With their great political power they obtained legislation in Colorado, Kansas City and Texas which would strike a show the size of Ringling with extra taxes and high license fees. The same laws left shows the size of Sells-Floto with nominal fees. In Texas, for example, a Sells-Floto-inspired law would charge Ringling a prohibitive license fee for each performance. As a partial answer to this, Ringling replaced its usual two-show schedule at Texas towns with a single continuous perform-

ance. In order to do this, performers took turns to keep a ring busy from the time the afternoon performance usually ended until the regular starting time for the night performance.

As part of the upheaval after the death of Bailey, the Ringlings decided to discontinue the Forepaugh-Sells Circus, so it was stored at their Baraboo, Wisconsin, winter quarters for the 1908 and 1909 seasons. When Sells-Floto began use of the contested pictures, Ringling found itself claiming ownership for a title it was not using. Therefore, in 1910 and 1911 it revived the Forepaugh-Sells show, but put it back on the shelf when the excitement died down.

The St. Louis World's Fair of 1904 inspired several entrepreneurs to move into outdoor show business. Fire Chief George Hale of Kansas City had won international competitions with his teams of fire fighters. Their show at the St. Louis Fair was such a hit that later it was loaded onto circus equipment and taken on the road. At the same time several other companies duplicated the plan with fire fighter shows. The Forepaugh-Sells show added a feature called "Fighting the Flames" as part of its regular circus performance.

Another feature of the fair was the Boer War Show. Horses for it were supplied by a Missouri dealer named William P. Hall. As a result of this combination of show business and horse trading, he became a dealer in circus horses, elephants and even complete shows. He bought Harris Nickel Plate and Walter L. Main Circus for openers. Thereafter he was buying and selling equipment, sometimes having several complete shows organized and opened out of his Missouri headquarters. As he accumulated elephants they were leased or sold to other circuses and eventually Hall owned

Opposite: The Sells-Floto union resulted in one of circusdom's most distinctive titles.

Animals have always been a prime feature of circuses. Goliath, a gigantic sea elephant {above left}, starred with the Ringling show from 1928-1931. This odd-looking creature fascinated the crowds. Elephants, of course, are indispensable. Liz {above right}, one of the old elephants on the Ringling herd, was a performer and was broken to harness for work. Performing horses {below left} were often owned by their riders and were stabled in the pad room.

one of the largest herds of elephants in show business.

St. Louis fair goers had seen the Mulhall Wild West performers and after the fair, not only the Mulhalls but also the Miller ranch family opened tented enterprises. The Millers combined with Edward Arlington, a Barnum & Bailey veteran, to put out the Miller & Arlington 101 Ranch Wild West Show, starting in 1908. Colonel Fred Cummings, who also had been active at the St. Louis Fair, subsequently started the Cummings Wild West Show.

Biggest of the fair's features was the Carl Hagenbeck Wild Animal Show. This famous German dealer had been persuaded by American showmen to organize a show for the fair, after which it would be put on the road. Thus in 1905 Carl Hagenbeck Trained Wild Animal Show joined the ranks of American circuses.

Hagenbeck had been a supplier of wild animals to American shows for many years, and as such, he was on a friendly basis with most showmen in this country. But when he opened a new circus he became a competitor, and suddenly all of his former customers seemed to turn on him. They scheduled their shows in opposition to his, seeing that one or another of them was giving the Carl Hagenbeck Wild Animal Show more competition than it could stand. Hagenbeck himself never left Germany, but his son and his American partners operated their outfit for two seasons. After a railroad wreck and unprofitable tours of the United States and Mexico in 1906, it was decided the show must be sold.

The American partners approached Ringling Bros. and a transaction seemed to be assured until the Ringlings discovered the Hagenbeck side had no money with which to carry out their joint plans. The deal collapsed and the Hagenbeck owners turned next to Ben Wallace. The absentee partner, Carl Hagenbeck, was pleased about the possibility of selling to Ringling but highly distressed at the mention of Wallace. He knew Wallace's show had many troubles and that it was infested with petty gamblers. Nevertheless, the partners on the scene went through with the sale, and Ben Wallace combined his show with the superior Carl Hagenbeck equipment to make up the new Hagenbeck-Wallace Circus of 1907. Carl Hagenbeck sued, asserting that while the equipment had been transferred, it implied no right for Wallace to use the Hagenbeck name. The suit was unsuccessful, however, and despite animosity between the two men, the names of Hagenbeck and Wallace became permanently linked in circus history.

One of Wallace's cohorts who helped establish his low reputation was Jerry Mugivan. Mugivan had climbed from the ranks of petty confidence men to become first a ruthless manager, then a successful circus man and finally an Indiana banker-showman of substance. In 1904, Mugivan and his partner, Bert Bowers, joined to buy a tattered and tiny show that had pirated the title of Howes Great London. Immediately they changed the name to the Great Van Amburgh Shows, thus despoiling two old titles with the flick of paint brushes. By their fourth season they had increased from ten- to fifteen-car size, and during the 1908 tour, they changed the title back to Howes Great London. For 1911 they fielded a second show as Sanger's Great European Circus, a title they retained until late 1913, when it became the Famous Robinson Circus.

Mugivan and Bowers had acquired the Robinson name by purchase from Danny Robinson, and they continued its use in this form until 1916. They had long wanted to own the John Robinson title and Danny's name was as close as they could come until 1916. Actually, the John Robinson Ten Big Shows had closed in 1911, but it took another five years before the family sold the title.

Jerry Mugivan had been in and out of the Hagenbeck-Wallace deal of 1907. That show had changed hands since then, and by 1918 it was owned by Ed Ballard. A disastrous railroad wreck at that time led to the show's financial failure, so Mugivan and Bowers stepped in. They joined with Ballard in reorganizing the show, starting with the 1919 season. At this time, Tammen and Bonfils had grown weary of circus business, and their Sells-Floto show was not doing well. So after the 1920 season, Mugivan, Bowers and Ballard purchased Sells-Floto.

In 1917, the partnership incorporated its Howes Great London Show into its John Robinson outfit, which had been called Famous Robinson until the previous year. Mugivan and Bowers, however, revived Howes Great London in 1920, and the following year it acquired equipment from a show using the aged title of Yankee Robinson, which had closed at the Hall farm in Missouri after the 1920 season. In 1922 the Howes show was called Gollmar Bros., and the next season it was absorbed again by the Mugivan-Bowers John Robinson Circus. Thus, by 1923 their Hagenbeck-Wallace, Sells-Floto and John Robinson circuses were all of substantial size. Mugivan, who was the prime mover of the three-way ownership, and his partners would make their circus power felt for the rest of the decade.

The Ringlings operated Barnum & Bailey and their original Ringling Bros. as separate circuses until after the 1918 season. Ringling Bros. Circus did not return to Baraboo that fall, but

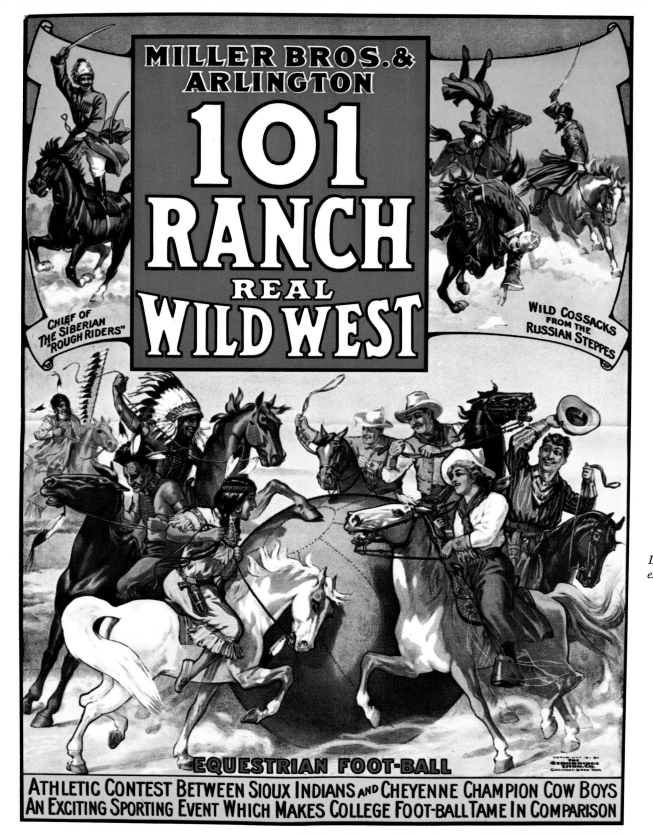

Left: The 1904 St. Louis World's Fair prompted this expansion of the real Wild West. {1911}

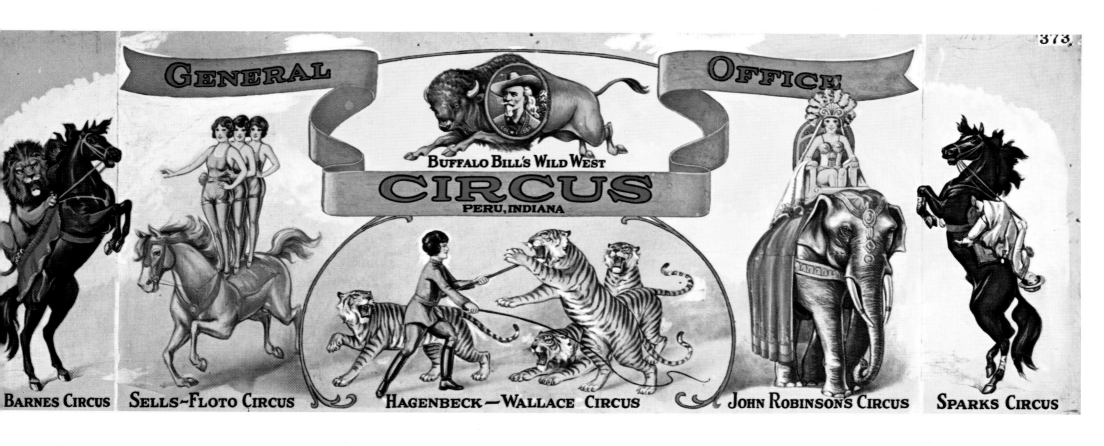

GENERAL OFFICE

BUFFALO BILL'S WILD WEST

CIRCUS

PERU, INDIANA

BARNES CIRCUS   SELLS-FLOTO CIRCUS   HAGENBECK—WALLACE CIRCUS   JOHN ROBINSONS CIRCUS   SPARKS CIRCUS

*This letterhead designed for the American
Circus Corp. underscores the power it once held.*

Twelve different species are represented in the canine pyramid above, a feature of Gentry Bros., which found a formula for success in the dog and pony format. The show passed from Gentry hands in 1916 and the title was last used in Depression years.

rather, went to Barnum & Bailey quarters at Bridgeport, Connecticut. The two were combined for the 1919 season and thereafter. This show increased to one hundred railroad cars, twice the size of its nearest competitor. Mugivan, Bowers and Ballard, however, could give the Ringling circus much trouble with their trio, which now comprised the American Circus Corp.

After the Buffalo Bill Wild West & Pawnee Bill Great Far East Show collapsed at Denver in 1913, Buffalo Bill appeared first with Sells-Floto and then in 1916 with 101 Ranch. The Miller Bros. had had a losing experience in sending a second unit to England just in time to be closed by World War I, so they were apprehensive about operating during war years and elected to sell their show. It was purchased by their former partner, Eddie Arlington, in conjunction with Buffalo Bill and heavyweight boxing champion Jess Willard. Unfortunately, Cody died just before the show opened and Arlington soon sold his interest to Willard. The show completed the season but then disappeared from the scene.

By 1925 Miller Bros. was ready to try it again. It bought a revival of the Walter L. Main Circus and added other equipment for the 1925 edition of Miller Bros. 101 Ranch Wild West Show.

The American Circus Corp. had expected to eliminate parades as the Ringling show had done earlier. But the independents still featured street marches. These included such shows as Christy Bros., Robbins Bros. and 101 Ranch. The latter in particular stressed its parade in opposition battles against the Corporation, even to the point that the powerful Mugivan, Bowers and Ballard shows were obligated to revive their parades.

Completing the scene in the middle 1920's were two shows owned by Floyd and Howard King. When the Walter L. Main show equipment was sold to Miller Bros., the Kings leased that title and created a circus to use with it in 1925. The next year they purchased the Gentry-Patterson Circus and reverted to the Gentry Bros. Circus title. The original Gentry Bros. Dog and Pony Show had been in its prime during the 1890's and early 1900's. At one time they operated four nearly identical units. These performances featured dogs, ponies, monkeys and other lesser animals as well as elephants. The dog and pony format was highly successful and the Gentrys were careful to offer quality performances in clean surroundings. Their reputation, if not their size, was the equivalent of Ringling Bros. However, the family lost control in 1916 and others operated the Gentry show until 1922. Then it was combined with the James Patterson show until King Bros. acquired it and opened

Christy Bros. was one of the few outfits independent of the Corporation in the 1920's.

Above: Madison Square Garden's biggest single money-maker in the early twentieth century was Ringling Bros. and Barnum & Bailey's Combined Shows.

Below: Sells-Floto came out in 1908 and, during its years of trouping, played rare indoor engagements like that at the Chicago Coliseum.

100

in 1926. This Gentry edition failed in 1929, the year the Kings called their other show Cole Bros.

By that time, the American Circus Corp. of Mugivan, Bowers and Ballard also had acquired the California-based Al G. Barnes Circus and the Sparks Circus which, like Gentry, held an enviable reputation comparable to that of the Ringlings. Expectations within circus business were that the expanding American Circus Corp. might even acquire the Greatest Show on Earth.

John Ringling, last of the surviving brothers, was a principal stockholder in Madison Square Garden, and the circus was the Garden's biggest single money-maker. But in 1929 the Garden management and Ringling's fellow directors wanted to close down the circus on Fridays during its extended run so that sports events could be presented. John Ringling, not interested in losing a lucrative weekend night, resisted this change. When word reached Jerry Mugivan, he announced to Garden management that he would be pleased to bring his Hagenbeck-Wallace and Sells-Floto circuses in combination and augmented by the appearance of Tom Mix. Furthermore, he would be delighted to close on Fridays. Garden management was about to accept that offer, so John Ringling had to move decisively. But he also acted impulsively. In the fall of 1929 he purchased the American Circus Corp. outright.

SPARKS CIRCUS

A SENSATIONAL EXHIBITION BY
FIGHTING, FOREST-BRED MALE LIONS

Sparks held a reputation comparable to that of Ringling Bros. and Gentry. {1925}

5-The Depression and War Years

John Ringling set himself up as circus king of the world. But his reign would be short-lived. One day he bought the American Circus Corp. and held title to nearly every major circus worth the effort. Just a few days later the stock market crash had plunged his circus world into the abyss of depression.

He had made his point. When he bought his major competition, Madison Square Garden had to allow the Ringling-Barnum show to play there on Fridays in 1930. But this was small consolation because the crowds were small every day of the week. Not only was Ringling-Barnum losing money, but now he also had Sells-Floto, Hagenbeck-Wallace, John Robinson, Al G. Barnes and Sparks circuses eating money every day as well. The circus business was about to experience its greatest cutback.

Fine old titles would disappear from the road and a new set of circus names would take their places. The circus business had never faced such a crisis as the Depression of the 1930's and it would never be the same again.

John Ringling had to swing the ax first — or more accurately, he had whole circuses to spare and could close some. Other circus owners could only cut down the size of their more limited outfits. The 1930 season saw the last of the John Robinson Circus as a separate entity, though the title would be appended to others a couple of times. Nearly ninety years of circusing under that name came to an end. Sparks Circus lasted through 1931. Sells-Floto was shelved after the 1932 season, then it borrowed the John Robinson name to help its own in the South.

At the end of the 1932 season, the king's own role was taken over by a regent. John Ringling fell behind in his payments and the bank stepped in. It named Samuel Gumpertz to manage the Ringling Bros. and Barnum & Bailey Circus and its remaining subsidiaries. Gumpertz was a Coney Island midway man and amusement park operator who knew show business.

Meanwhile, the independently operated circuses were succumbing to the same financial ills. In 1929 Howard King closed Gentry Bros. Circus. George Christy took out a smaller show than usual in 1930, but his Christy Bros. Circus closed in July. Floyd King's Cole Bros. Circus lasted until August that year. The Miller Bros. 101 Ranch Wild West Show collapsed dramatically at Washington, D. C., in August of 1931. The unpaid employees protested and damaged some equipment before it was finally loaded and shipped back to Oklahoma. Robbins Bros. Circus held out until September 1931. En route to Lancaster, Missouri, where it would be parked among the ruins of many other circuses at the Hall farm, Robbins Bros. had some employees thrown off the train while it was underway. This was the old circus practice of "red lighting," so that troublemakers or unpaid employees could conveniently be left behind. In this instance one of the victims died and the Robbins owner went into hiding.

When the Ringling-Barnum show observed the fiftieth anniver-

Opposite: While the Depression ruined many smaller circuses, the Hagenbeck-Wallace show continued to present outstanding performances.

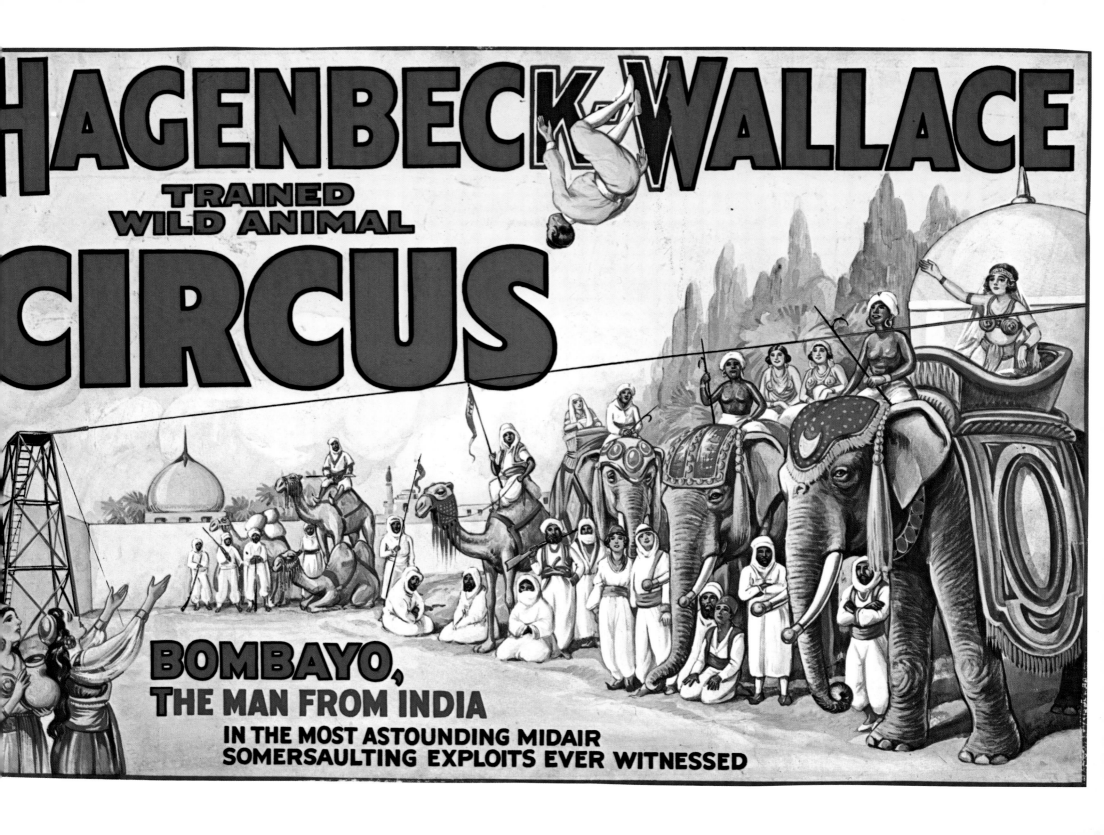

Above: Clyde Beatty left Hagenbeck-Wallace to form Cole Bros. & Clyde Beatty Circus in 1935. Its success promised a new future to the blighted shows of the Depression years.

Left: The 1937 season was better financially than 1936. Ringling-Barnum played Patterson, New Jersey in 1937.

sary of Ringling Bros. Circus in 1933, not many other shows remained to look on. The principal ones were Al G. Barnes and Hagenbeck-Wallace, both of which Ringling owned anyway. No one yet really noticed the little truck shows to which some of the unemployed circus people were turning. Hagenbeck-Wallace in 1934 presented an outstanding performance that included many of the all-time circus greats — Clyde Beatty, Alfredo Codona and the Cristiani family. Moreover, it revived the street parade. Business was good and showmen saw hope for the future. One was Jess Adkins, manager of Hagenbeck-Wallace, who now left that show and joined with Zack Terrell, another veteran manager of units for the American Circus Corp. They lured Clyde Beatty away from Hagenbeck-Wallace and proceeded to assemble an all new show, Cole Bros. & Clyde Beatty Circus. After so many failures and foldings, the opening of a new circus of major proportions was a shot in the arm for the entire business, and this new show, starting in 1935, was successful.

The Ringling-Barnum Circus continued without interruption but its management made changes in its subsidiaries. For 1935 the Hagenbeck show title was expanded to read Hagenbeck-Wallace-Forepaugh-Sells Combined Circus, thus reviving one of the long idle circus titles, but only for a brief moment. The entire operation was shelved for the next season, and then in 1937 the Hagenbeck-Wallace title was leased by Ringling to other operators, primarily an old Corporation employee, Howard Y. Bary. In that season, too, the Barnes title was expanded to read Al G. Barnes & Sells-Floto Combined Circus, while in some cases the posters were even more elaborate, reading Al G. Barnes, Sells-Floto and John Robinson Combined Circuses.

That 1937 season was pretty good for the shows, good enough that several expansion plans were put into effect. For the next year, Adkins and Terrell would double their operation, fielding not only their new Cole Bros., but also a second new outfit, this one wearing the old Robbins Bros. name. Tim McCoy, the movie star, had even more elaborate plans. He would leave his starring role with Ringling-Barnum and put together his own show, building it from the ground up as Col. Tim McCoy's Real Wild West Show.

By this time the Depression years had determined which of the new motorized circuses would rise to the top, and several of them had grown to positions of relative prominence, although many veterans of the railroad circuses would have nothing to do with

This mired quarterpole wagon could be interpreted as a symbol of the forlorn condition of most circuses during the Depression of the 1930's.

these mud shows. Hard times had taken the same toll among these smaller struggling circuses as with the big shows. Dozens of motorized circuses had appeared briefly and then faded from view. A few of the real veterans, dating back to wagon show days, survived now on motor trucks. Among these were the Mighty Haag Circus, Atterbury Bros., Orton Bros. and a brief Depression-born revival of the Gentry show.

Of more significance was the rank of some of the newcomers, shows that survived and grew in Depression seasons and now were big enough and brave enough to move in on the routes of larger cities once played by the now defunct railroad shows. In this category were Barnett Bros., which originated in Canada; Russell Bros. Circus; Downie Bros., a pioneer among motor shows and now operated by Charles Sparks; Seils-Sterling; and the Tom Mix Circus. The latter grew out of the remnants of the Gentry truck show with the help of Sam B. Dill, a former manager of John Robinson. Now the Mix show played a route that took it from coast

105

to coast and into some of the nation's largest cities, considered quite an accomplishment for a truck circus in 1937.

These were the new names of the 1930's, the new breed of shows that traveled by truck to fill the void left when many rail shows disappeared. Names like Mix, Barnett, Russell and Downie took the place of Robinson, Floto, Sparks and Gentry. Now, after 1937's encouraging results, showmen were expecting great things of 1938. The Depression apparently was over.

But shows were not very far into the new season when it was apparent that all was not right. The beautiful new Tim McCoy Wild West Show folded in a matter of weeks. Charlie Sparks closed Downie Bros. Circus, although he reopened it briefly in the fall. The Tom Mix Circus folded permanently. Owners of Seils-Sterling decided it was time to sell out and retire. Adkins and Terrell shuttered their larger Cole Bros. Circus early and continued with the smaller Robbins Bros. The leased Hagenbeck-Wallace Circus collapsed in California. Even an old perennial like the Mighty Haag fell by the wayside.

Ringling Bros. and Barnum & Bailey, which sometimes seemed immortal, now met serious difficulties. Union organizers had chosen this already disastrous year as the time to press their demands against circuses. While the show was at Madison Square Garden workingmen refused to perform their duties and performers stepped in to keep the show going. But this only served to build the union pressure to a higher peak. Eventually, at Scranton, Pennsylvania, a strong union community, the Ringling show was hobbled by a full-blown strike. For several days it was not even possible to load the equipment, but finally the defeated circus rolled toward winter quarters in mid-summer. There a new train of Ringling equipment was made up and shipped to the show's lone subsidiary, Barnes-Sells-Floto. It continued the season with the most elaborate title in circus history. In its full form it read, Al G. Barnes, Sells-Floto & John Robinson Combined Circuses Present Ringling Bros. and Barnum & Bailey's Stupendous New Features.

If circus men thought the early Depression years were bad, now they knew that things could be even worse. The 1938 season was the most disastrous since the 1860's. Of the railroad shows only Barnes-Sells-Floto and Robbins Bros. completed the season. Neither of them went out again, although their parent organizations resumed touring, along with several of the new truck shows.

The decade of depression and this final recession had revolutionized the circus business. Hereafter there would be few baggage horses and more tractors, few parades, few railroad circuses. Most of the old names were gone and even some of the most promising new titles were shot down in their infancy.

That toughest season happened to be the time that a young Ringling picked up the banner of his family's show and set out to be the showman his uncles were. John Ringling had died in 1936, and a year later two nephews, John Ringling North and his brother, Henry Ringling North, were able to pay off enough debts and raise enough capital to regain control of the circus. Sam Gumpertz retired and a new day began for Ringling-Barnum. The North brothers began by presenting a super feature, that sneering, evil-looking gorilla, Gargantua the Great. They produced a spectacle featuring Frank "Bring-em Back Alive" Buck, of wild animal fame, and in general they revitalized the show.

But they barely had their feet under the desk when they were hit by the first of an almost unbelievable series of catastrophes. First was the strike and its resulting financial losses at a time the new management could least afford it. Loss of income from the Hagenbeck-Wallace rental was a minor irritant but complications of their initial season convinced the Norths that there was no time in their schedule for any subsidiary. So Barnes-Sells-Floto was retired from the road. Now the absence of the great titles of the past was nearly complete with the exception of the Ringling-Barnum show.

The next disaster struck, however, not at Ringling but at its new rival, Cole Bros. This show had survived the difficult times with an abbreviated edition in 1939. Back in winter quarters it prepared for the next season. Then, in February 1940, a disastrous fire swept its winter quarters, burning valuable wagons, animals and equipment. Only by monumental effort in the few available weeks was a show put back in working order. Help came from its rival, Ringling-Barnum, which offered the loan of some substitute equipment from its idle Hagenbeck-Wallace lineup. With this aid and its own efforts, Cole Bros. managed to make the 1940 tour, but one of the partners, Jess Adkins, was stricken with a fatal heart attack. Zack Terrell continued alone.

Ringling-Barnum played out a normal season for 1939, a year notable for North's experimentation with air conditioning the big top. Eight air conditioning wagons were utilized along with canvas air ducts to feed cool air into the tent, but the cooling effect was minimal. This also was the first year that the circus carried no baggage horses. Since the drivers were blamed for some of the violence during the previous year's strike, John Ringling North

The clown's admiration reflects the feelings of the crowd. {1898}

*Above: In 1937, a year after John Ringling's death, his nephews
Henry {left} and John Ringling North regained control of the circus;
Samuel Gumpertz retired and the brothers began to revitalize the show.*

*Below: Mrs. Charles Ringling, the Norths' aunt and mother of Robert,
owned one-third of the shares in the Ringling circus.*

sold off all the baggage horses and substituted trucks and tractors.
Cole Bros. followed suit shortly thereafter.

Now the economic climate changed entirely. War in Europe and
rearmament in the United States generated industrial activity which
ended the Depression. Now circuses attracted abnormally good
business and would continue to do so for several years. Their
troubles came by a different route. Ringling, for example, had good
crowds in 1940. It grossed over a million dollars in New York and
Boston alone and enjoyed tremendous business everywhere.
North's innovations for the performance in this season and
thereafter won acclaim from critics and the public. Old circus hands
and many circus fans found fault with the new format, but it was
successful at the box office and resulted in bigger and more colorful
production numbers for the circus.

The strike and its repercussions comprised the first bad luck for
North and his Ringling Circus. Then late in the 1941 season the
show reached Atlanta, Georgia, and the elephant men noticed that
some of their charges were acting strangely. As the day wore on one
and then another elephant became violently ill. Frantically, the men
tried to determine the cause, but they were unsure and too late.
Eleven of the forty-seven elephants with the show were stricken. Six
died before the day was out. Five more would be lost in the ensuing
few days. Circus people were helpless to aid the elephants and
looked on the tragic scene as other pairs of elephants towed the
casualties away. In time it was decided that the animals had eaten
grass and weeds which had been sprayed with arsenic weed killer at
an earlier stand.

The next tour began with conflict between the circus and the
musician's union. In the end the circus band went on strike,
presumably against its will, and the show proceeded for the rest of
the season with the playing of recorded music.

Then at Cleveland, on August 5, still another disaster struck.
This time fire swept the menagerie tent, killing forty animals
including two giraffes and three elephants and causing $200,000 in
damage. But the show went on. In fact, that very night it gave a
performance again, including the "Happy Holidays" spectacle.
Outside of the big top, however, men were struggling to save the
lives of animals by using newly developed drugs made available by
the military.

The elephant department, hard hit in two seasons, would sustain
one more loss. Walter McClain, the popular elephant superinten-

dent and a human dynamo, had come to Ringling when the Barnes show closed and had brought with him the policy of using elephants to unload the train and pull wagons. The United States was in the war by this season and manpower was short. So McClain volunteered to help the train crew. In addition to his elephant duties he substituted at the dangerous job of poler. While unloading the train at Jacksonville, Florida, in November, a wagon broke loose and crushed him to death.

Just as John Ringling North had been in and out of favor with his Uncle John, so he would be in and out of favor with the circus profession and his own fellow stockholders. This son of the Ringling brothers' little sister had taken summer jobs on the circus and attended Yale, then worked on Wall Street. His Uncle John had once chased him off of the circus, later named him executor of his estate, next took him out of the will — but forgot to replace him as executor.

North's playboy ways bothered some circus men, who resented having to wait until mid-afternoon for North to arise and start his day's business. The other stockholders thought him high-handed. Traditionalists objected to his "turning the circus into a musical" full of Broadway show girls — the "North Starlets" he called them. But others applauded his decisiveness in replacing baggage stock, his resistance to strong-arm methods of union organizers, his creation of big spectacles the circus could boast about.

The North brothers voted one of the three blocks of Ringling stock. Another was owned by Mrs. Aubrey Ringling Haley, widow of the Norths' cousin, and the third was owned by Mrs. Charles Ringling, aunt of the Norths. While John Ringling North owned only seven percent of the stock outright, as executor of his uncle's estate, he also voted the thirty percent then owned by the State of Florida. He had been elected president each year through 1942, but in 1943 Robert Ringling, son of Mrs. Charles Ringling, was elected president. One of the issues that brought the change was North's recommendation that the circus suspend operations until after the war. The other stockholders feared that if it ever stopped, the circus never could be started up again. They also believed the circus should continue its contribution toward maintaining wartime morale, and, indeed, the Federal government encouraged it along these lines.

The experiences of Cole Bros. Circus during wartime years were typical of all circuses. It was difficult not only to buy equipment but

The North Brothers introduced Gargantua the Great to the public in 1938. He was one of the most highly billed circus attractions of all time.

Right: Patriotism was the order of the day after the United States entered World War II. Ringling-Barnum's 1942 finale at Madison Square Garden featured performers in wartime costume and huge pictures of General MacArthur and President Roosevelt.

Below: 1940 saw the end of the Depression and one of Ringling's best seasons. The Old King Cole spectacle at Madison Square Garden was an elaborate display with beautifully robed elephants and a host of elegantly attired drummer girls.

to hire men. The show sent agents into employment offices of big cities and into the Dakotas at wheat harvest time in an effort to recruit workmen. It published want ads in newspapers of each town it played, a practice typical of all circuses then. Since new canvas was not available, Cole Bros. used its 1941 tents for an extra season. Despite the demands of wartime traffic, the railroads were moving the show on time. Business for Cole Bros. and the others was quite strong, and their performances reflected the availability of money. Patriotism was the order of the day. The Cole Bros. finale in 1941 and 1942 brought all of the performers into the rings and a giant tableau, with the cast dressed as soldiers, sailors, nurses and war workers and Uncle Sam, held the honor spot at the center ring. At the last minute a huge flag was unfurled, fireworks went off and huge pictures of General Douglas MacArthur and President Franklin D. Roosevelt were displayed.

By 1943 the Cole show, among others, was cooperating in the effort to sell war bonds. It donated a block of seats at each performance for war bond buyers. In this same year, Ringling carried an extra ticket wagon and parked it downtown each day as a sales point for war bonds. By 1943 the manpower situation was becoming more critical. Workmen were fewer and the show moved slower. In addition, many performers had been drafted and now those of an older generation were called back to work.

The war years brought a new combination of titles to the leading positions in circus business. Ringling and Cole were the big railroad shows. The Barnett truck show now was retitled and combined with Beatty to become the Clyde Beatty-Wallace Bros. Circus. Another Depression-proven show, Russell Bros., took over the Western route once the private property of the Al G. Barnes Circus. New and growing were Mills Bros. Circus and King Bros. Circus, while the tiny Davenport Society Circus suddenly blossomed forth in 1944 as the new Dailey Bros. Railroad Circus and it increased steadily in size over the next several years. The Dailey show was the last of the rowdy racket outfits. It thrived on trouble and was permeated with petty gamblers and thieves.

Under its new leadership, the Ringling show came out in 1943 with one spectacle called "Let Freedom Ring" and another entitled "Drums of Victory," while a third featured the new Liberty bandwagon. The menagerie lost the previous year could not be replaced entirely. Ringling carried only about ten cages and exhibited its animals in the open air for lack of a menagerie tent.

One crowning disaster was in store for Ringling-Barnum. It opened the 1944 season at New York and starred Emmett Kelly in the spectacle. Wartime business continued good as it moved through the East. So a large crowd was at the matinee at Hartford, Connecticut, on July 6. Fire broke out on the big top while the Great Wallendas were on their high wire. Merle Evans' band switched to its disaster march to alert everyone on the show to the trouble. The fire spread like a flash across the canvas, causing poles to fall. The audience panicked in an effort to escape. Many did not realize they could duck under the tent at nearly any spot. Instead, they fought to reach the door by which they had entered. Blocking the hippodrome track was the animal chute for transferring cats to the arena for Alfred Court's wild animal act. It was over in an instant, but the tragedy and repercussions would be felt for a generation. One hundred sixty-eight persons had lost their lives in what was one of the worst disasters on record, one of the most devastating fires in history and the worst catastrophe in the history of circus business.

For the second time in a half-dozen years the circus would pick up its tattered remnants at mid-season and limp back to its Sarasota, Florida, home. At the outset it accepted liability for the fire and promised payment of claims against it. An office was opened at Hartford to handle this dreary business. Just short of a month later, the circus reopened at Akron, Ohio, now playing stadiums and ball parks for lack of a tent and allied equipment. Meanwhile, the State of Connecticut filed manslaughter charges against several of the Ringling executives and department bosses. The men pleaded *nolo contendere,* anticipating fines or suspended sentences. They were astonished and shocked when, instead, they were sentenced to serve a year in prison. Among other repercussions were new ordinances and state laws throughout the country to require fireproofing of all such tents. For several weeks nearly every circus, wherever it was playing in the country, found that city fire fighting apparatus was assigned to the lot for the day.

Wartime business continued at such a high rate that several new shows came out and others were enlarged. The operators of Ringling and Cole knew that it was difficult just keeping their existing organizations staffed and moving. The prospect of big profits, however, encouraged other showmen to seek out idle equipment and open new shows. The Dailey Bros. Circus added more cars to its train each year and in 1945 operated Austin Bros.

The tiny Davenport Society Circus was reborn as Dailey Bros. Railroad Circus in 1944. The show thrived for the next several years.

Circus as a second unit. In the same year the new Arthur Bros. Motorized Circus was converted to railroad operation, utilizing Hagenbeck-Wallace equipment that had been stored in California. Russell Bros. Circus bought Beckman & Gerety carnival equipment and moved up to the railroad category in 1945.

Ringling resumed tented operation in 1945 and utilized all-metal seats. As the labor shortage continued, it devised a plan for sending a layout crew and stake driver a day ahead of the show to pound the stakes that would be needed when the circus arrived. Chances were that arrival would be late and every minute counted.

For the 1946 season Robert Ringling was succeeded by James Haley as president of the corporation. Already the show could state that twenty-five percent of the gigantic fire claims were paid. All funds in excess of those needed to prepare for the next season were paid to the survivors of Hartford victims. This was fortunate for the show and the claimants, for otherwise there was the specter of

bankruptcy. However, as these strong business years went by, Ringling was unable to accumulate any sizable reserves that it might otherwise have anticipated.

James Haley continued at the helm for 1947 and increased the size of the train to a phenomenal 109 cars, largest ever in the history of any circus and twenty-three cars larger than during the previous season. Now the war had been over long enough so that new performers could be imported and there were newcomers throughout the Ringling performance. The circus was traveling with twenty-six new sleepers that had been army hospital cars and came to the circus as a war surplus purchase.

By 1947 Mills Bros. Circus had grown to twenty-five-truck size and featured the Western movie star, Jack Hoxie. Floyd King had been working for other circuses since his show closed in the Depression, and then in 1946 he joined the post-war trend and, in partnership with H. J. Rumbaugh, he opened King Bros. Circus. King and Mills both made use of equipment from the Clyde Beatty Circus, and that same year Beatty went west to join Art Concello in what had been Russell Bros. Pan Pacific Circus and for 1946 became the Clyde Beatty Circus. This was the first such outfit to enter western Canada since the war. It found a veritable gold mine in every town along the way. Extra performances were required to accommodate the crowds in town after town. Even in rainstorms the circus gave three performances a day for turnaway crowds. The phenomenon of the Beatty show's tour of Canada remains one of the high points in recent circus history.

That year a newcomer had built a new motorized show with the expectation of trouping a tented ice show. When ice-making gear proved to be unsatisfactory, he converted it at the last minute to circus operation and leased the Sparks title from Ringling. A year later this Sparks show was outfitted with all new wagons and moved by rail. It toured Canada but fell far short of the business enjoyed by Clyde Beatty. The show managed to cross the border and then closed down for good. Two years later the Beatty Circus would buy this Sparks equipment and replace its old wagons with the new Sparks units.

Opposite: Alfred Court was a master of his trade. {1941}

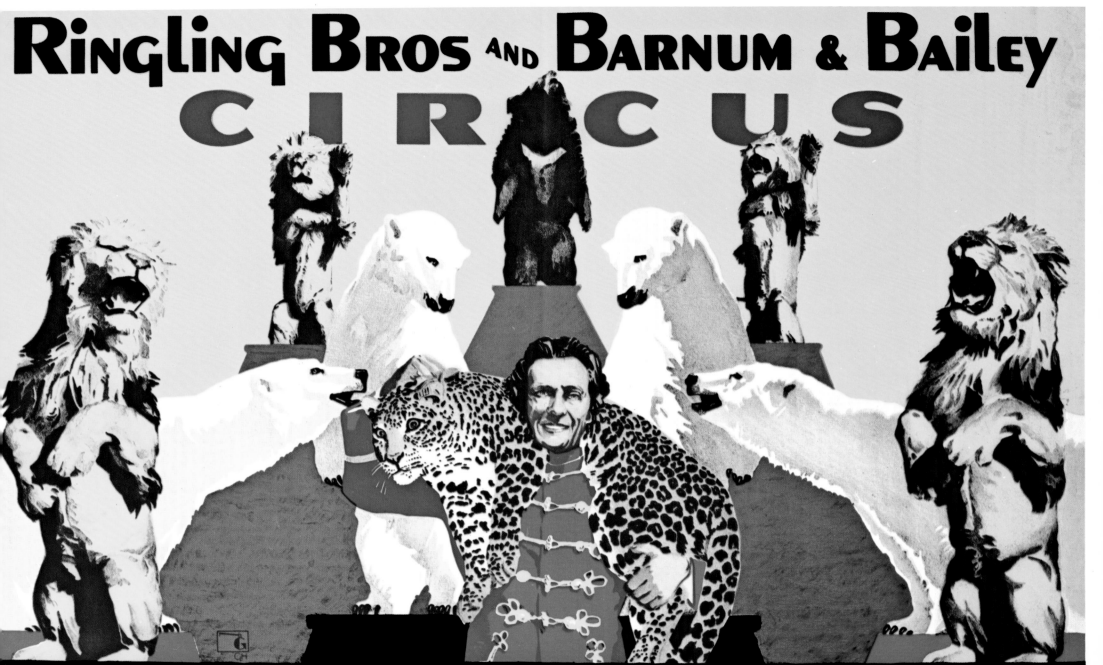

6-The Post-War Years

One notable factor about the 1947 circus season was that both John Ringling North and Arthur M. Concello were off the road, a situation they soon would correct. In November, North headed up a combine which bought the Ringling stock heretofore held by the State of Florida. A week later the Haleys sold their stock so as to give North a total of fifty-one percent and to give Mrs. Charles Ringling forty-nine percent. North was elected president and he named Concello as general manager. They took over in the final days of the season and feverishly began preparations for the new show and new season. In 1948 Ringling came out on ninety cars with new retractable seat wagons invented by Concello, with new cages and revitalized leadership.

Art Concello, who was partial to big cigars and big bank accounts, came to management by way of the trapeze. As a youngster in Bloomington, Illinois, he joined the Flying Wards, later formed the Flying Concellos and mastered the rare triple somersault, as did his wife, Antoinette. Soon he owned several flying acts and booked them on Ringling-owned shows. By 1947 he had amassed that sizable bank account and loaned it to John Ringling North. It won North the stock and won Concello the general manager's job. There he proved to be a tough taskmaster. He instituted efficiencies to save time and money. In a business and a show sometimes hidebound by tradition and habit, Concello did not hesitate to force change. He had held the job before and would lose it again but in the meantime he held a tight rein and made the circus hum.

Out west the Clyde Beatty Circus toured aboard fifteen cars and its performance featured Beatty's twenty-two lions and tigers. In the Middle West, Cole Bros. Circus had come out of the war years in good financial position but Zack Terrell was weary. At the end of the season he would sell his outfit to Jack Tavlin, a former associate of Concello on both the Russell and Ringling shows. Tavlin had a personal vendetta against Ringling, and with Cole

Bros. he expected to put the bigger show out of business. Before that attempt got underway, however, Cole Bros. took its steam calliope to Washington for the Truman inauguration and in the parade it played "Meet Me in St. Louie, Louie" and "The Missouri Waltz." Among the truck circuses Floyd King was not faring so well. He had taken over full ownership of King Bros. Circus for 1948 but business was poor. When the season closed it was broke.

The next season, 1949, served to develop some predictable results and to set the stage for a new phase of circus history. First, as might have been expected, Tavlin caused the Ringling show no difficulty, but his own operation of Cole Bros. Circus was not successful, and at the end of the season, he sold it to Arthur M. Wirtz and associates, owners of the Chicago Stadium. They brought on Hopalong Cassidy, who was at his peak of television popularity, and retained Tavlin as general manager. From April until July the show played at stadiums and ball parks and made little use of its tents. The show went under canvas July 5 but closed July 22, thus ending the sixteen-season career of Cole Bros. Circus. Mills Bros. Circus sought to buy parts of the Cole show, including cage animals and lead stock but was unsuccessful.

Equally predictable was Floyd King finding a way out of his difficulties. Among those to whom he owed back salary at the end of the 1948 season was one of the branches of the Cristiani family. In lieu of that salary he transferred a fifty percent interest in the show to Lucio Cristiani, who represented the principal branch of the famous bareback riding family. This partnership would produce one of the most successful circuses of the next several years.

Ringling's activities for 1949 were a harbinger of things to come. It played several indoor engagements as an experiment. As always it played New York and Boston in permanent arenas. This time it

Opposite: The mixed animal act required great daring on the part of the trainer. {1923}

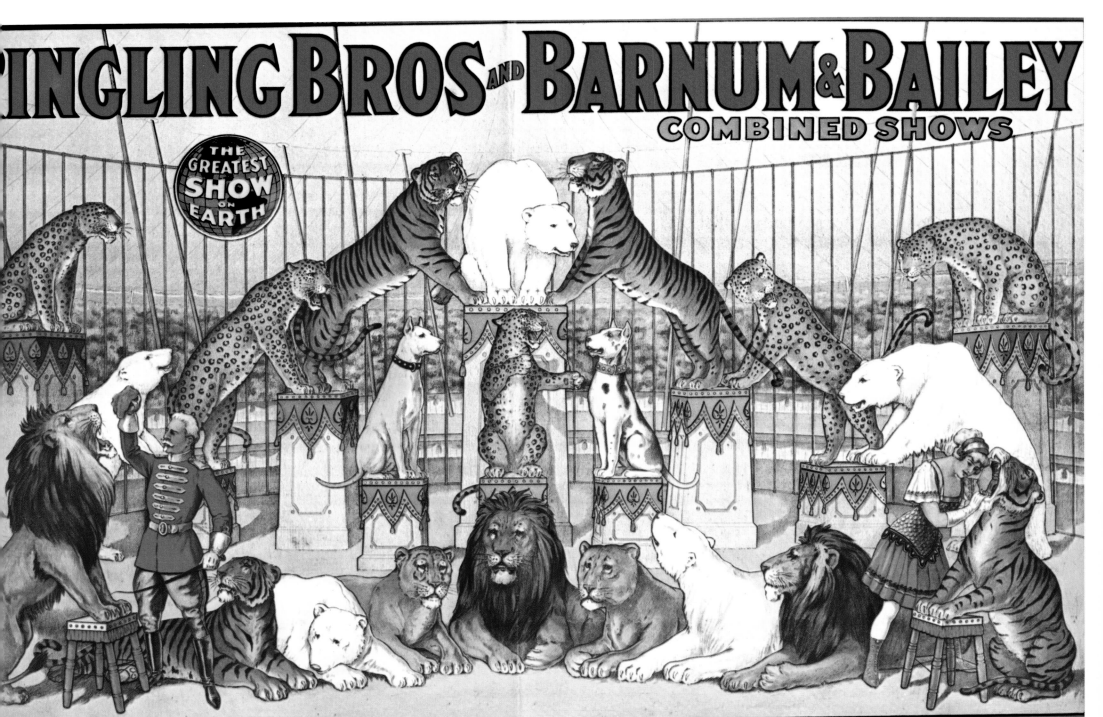

also tried indoor stands at St. Louis, San Francisco and San Antonio. While some of these experimental stands were not financially successful, the maneuver revealed the direction of Concello's and North's thinking. In a half-dozen years that would be the direction the circus would move. After the regular season, Ringling sent nine carloads of equipment and animals to Havana, Cuba, for the first of several annual Christmas shows there.

The array of tented circuses had still another new complexion. None of the ancient titles survived, not even any of the Depression-nurtured truck shows remained on the roster. Those in addition to Ringling were Clyde Beatty, Mills Bros., the King Bros. combination with the Cristianis and the new, growing Al G. Kelly & Miller Bros. Circus.

Kelly-Miller was owned and peopled by troupers who grew up with Seils-Sterling and a host of smaller circuses where Obert Miller had been a pony trainer. When his sons, Dory Miller and Kelly Miller, returned from the service, they were ready to make their mark in the circus business. The 1944 show of twelve trucks and three elephants grew to nineteen trucks and six elephants by 1946 and two years later to thirty trucks and eleven elephants.

As the decade of the fifties got underway, Kelly-Miller boasted of thirty-two trucks, fourteen elephants, sixty horses and an elaborate menagerie that included a giraffe, hippopotamus, and rhinoceros. In contrast to Mills and King, this was a Western show, after the pattern of the old Campbell Bros. and Yankee Robinson. Its performers wore cowboy boots and ten-gallon hats. The show made long jumps with ease and its performance raised as much dust as a rodeo. They carried a lot of horses and they felt Indians were a necessary part of every circus performance. The show came out with one of the most energetic promotional plans ever seen even in circus business, using an extra large number of posters for every town and mailing a courier to every box holder for miles around. It equipped an airplane with a loudspeaker and flew to all the surrounding towns to announce the presence in the county of Al G. Kelly & Miller Bros. Circus. As the show continued to make good profits and to grow, it was cited by many troupers as

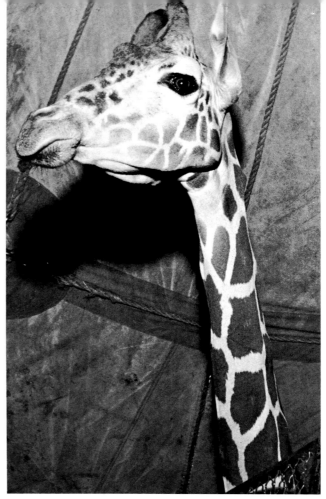

As the decade of the fifties got underway, the dust-raising, Western-oriented Kelly-Miller show boasted of an elaborate menagerie that included a giraffe and a hippopotamus.

116

proof that a tented circus still could operate on the strength of its own advertising alone.

In contrast, however, a larger group of showmen was turning to telephone promotion, or to some other variety of local sponsorship. They decided the time had come when the circus could not generate adequate business simply by erecting its posters and arriving in town. Instead, they said, it is essential that a show develop an advance sale and that it benefit from association with a local organization.

In the simplest form of sponsorship the circus agreed to pay a percentage of its gross to a local organization, which in turn would supply the show grounds, local license, water supply and local use of its name in selling tickets.

More complex was the telephone promotion system under which there were two simultaneous ticket sales. In one, members of the local Rotary Club, police department or Shrine lodge sold tickets to their friends and neighbors for the circus that would be coming. Simultaneously, promoters hired by the circus installed a battery of telephones and called all of the businesses and many of the individuals in town, asking them to buy tickets to the circus for underprivileged children. When a merchant agreed, the phone man would dispatch an agent to deliver the tickets and pick up the money. As the system was further refined, the buyer sometimes never saw his tickets, which instead were delivered directly to a school or youth organization. Mills Bros. was a particularly strong advocate of telephone promotion, while King and the others would turn to it increasingly each year.

Such promotion started in the Depression years with merchants' free tickets, a plan by which the circus supplied a block of tickets at reduced cost to a merchant who would distribute them at a low price or free to youngsters in the town. Details of telephone promotion were perfected by Polack Bros. Circus, leader among the new species of indoor circuses.

Indoor circuses had existed since the beginning, but in a modern sense they began when Robert Morton rented some equipment from Gentry Bros. Circus and presented a show for a local organization in the 1920's. At about the same time, Orrin Davenport, a famous rider with Ringling, Hagenbeck and other circuses, was contracting winter dates. Circus performers always had tried to earn extra money by playing winter dates. Many played vaudeville and some left circuses early in the season in order to play fair dates. Davenport arranged to use acts owned by the Ringling Circus together with others he contracted directly. Then he took

Above: American Indians have trouped with many circuses down through the years. Ninety-two-year-old Nabor Felix {shown here} has worked in many shows and in 1969 was part of the Clyde Beatty-Cole Bros. Circus.

117

As the fifties progressed, more and more shows played indoor engagements in permanent arenas. The cream of all indoor stands was New York City's Madison Square Garden, which until 1958, Ringling Bros. and Barnum & Bailey usually played as its first stop of the season's tour.

this package to Grand Rapids, Detroit, and other cities as their annual Shrine Circus. Morton, following the same pattern, formed a partnership with George Hamid that resulted in the Hamid-Morton Circus. The Polacks switched from operation of carnivals to sponsorship of bazaars which featured circus performers. Soon they were presenting winter shows under auspices of the American Legion, chambers of commerce, service clubs or lodges.

Indoor shows covered the same type of preliminaries as had the motorized circuses. A few early examples were operated by suitcase promoters, some of whom disappeared or failed to produce any performance. Little by little, however, these circuses gained stability and respect. By the late 1940's such shows as Polack, Hamid-Morton, Orrin Davenport and the Tom Packs Circus were leaders in the field. The Polack show played so many towns that it was necessary to open a second unit. In hiring acts it guaranteed the people more than forty weeks of work each year, an unheard-of situation in circus business.

In many towns sponsors and shows worked together to build highly successful engagements. Indoor circuses presented strong performances utilizing the best performers. In many cities the Shrine Circus changed the thinking of the population so that the circus was no longer a seasonal thing. It was just as logical to

118

attend an indoor Shrine Circus at the local auditorium in February as it was in May. While there were numerous organizations producing and promoting such shows, almost invariably they were publicized under the name of the local sponsor. Thus the title of Shrine Circus came into prominence and even though it designated no single or specific organization, it had the same effect on the public and the name gained the same sort of value that had been held by such titles as Sparks or Cole or Hagenbeck-Wallace.

During the 1950's these indoor circuses grew to the stature of second echelon shows. They took the place vacated by the railroad circuses that were second in size only to Ringling. The indoor, sponsored shows played major cities and booked many of the principal acts. Often the indoor shows outshown the tent circus as represented by Mills, Kelly-Miller and Beatty. The big top circuses, however, were thriving and active, with the King show setting the pace.

Floyd King was a man of two distinctly separate but simultaneous circus careers. In one he was among the foremost general agents, the expert in deciding where shows should play and adept in not only contracting the difficult towns, but garnering strong publicity for his show. He had been agent for Cole Bros. Circus and its Robbins subsidiary. In his other career he was a circus owner and manager. But here his fortunes varied. Either his show was scraping bottom, operating with no customers and no money, or it was coining profits at a merry rate. King thrived in either condition.

As an owner and in partnership with Lucio Cristiani, King was on an upswing in 1950. Their outfit joined the select group of shows that exhibited a giraffe and it toured western Canada. The next year it registered large profits in New England and the South. As King Bros. & Cristiani Combined Circus in 1952, it carried twelve elephants, the Zacchini cannon act and it successfully revived the street parade. The show operated on a very heavy advertising budget. In addition, it utilized local organizations as sponsors. It made a creditable showing in competition with Ringling when routes of the two shows coincided.

The next season brought even bigger business. The show traveled on fifty-four trucks and gave not only a street parade but advertised a free balloon ascension as a method of drawing crowds to the show grounds. In only a handful of stands did the balloon actually get into the air and soon it was abandoned. But crowds kept coming to see King-Cristiani. The only problem was the partners no longer could get along with each other. Although the show was making its greatest profits ever, King was determined to end the partnership. Reluctantly Lucio Cristiani agreed to a split.

Opposite: This art style, popular during the post-war years, continues today. {1966}

Ringling Bros

THE GREATEST SHOW ON EARTH

WAY in

ADMISSION 2 NUTS

LAWSON WOOD.

Barnum & Bailey

Above: The human cannonball act was popularized by the Zacchinis, Fearless Gregg and the Great Wilno, the latter shown here blasting from his cannon.

Left: In 1951 the famous Hanneford Troupe, led then by George Sr., came over to the Clyde Beatty Circus from the old Cole show.

The Cristiani family then joined the little Bailey Bros. Circus to play the route of ball parks and fairgrounds. In 1954 the Bailey-Cristiani show made a historic and spectacular trek to Alaska. It became the first show to play that territory where elephants and snakes had never been seen, and their show did great business.

Meanwhile, Floyd King formed a partnership with his long-time associate Arnold Maley and in 1954 they put out King Bros. Circus with fifty-four trucks and sixteen elephants, including ten bought from the defunct Cole Bros. Circus. It was a big circus and the new partners decided to expand. As King Bros. & Cole Bros. Circus, they opened on nearly seventy trucks in 1955, making it the biggest truck show ever. But there was no business to match. Despite strong advertising, telephone promotion and every kind of effort, the people just did not come out. The show had substantial overhead, including payments on obligations to Cole Bros., to Lucio Cristiani and for wintering expenses. This burden, together with the daily costs of operating such a large show, soon had this circus in trouble.

The pattern was not dissimilar on the Clyde Beatty Circus. In 1951 it took the long hard trek through western Canada but it found the public in some towns still angry with circuses because of the way Dailey Bros. had behaved, and King Bros. had played the other towns too recently. Business was far short of expectations.

Beginning with that season the Clyde Beatty Circus was the only railroad circus other than Ringling. It could take its choice of experienced executives. Among those putting in seasons were Ira Watts, Denny Helms, Buster Cronin, George Smith, Leonard Aylesworth, George Davis, Dan Dix and many others from shows of earlier years. Frank Orman, during his stay as general manager, induced many department heads from the old Cole show to join Beatty. Also coming over was the George Hanneford family, an outstanding bareback troupe. The combination of Beatty's animals and the Hannefords' riding provided a superb nucleus for a performance of superior quality. They added a street parade in 1954.

Now Concello was out of the management picture at Ringling and turned back to the Beatty show, buying control of it at Christmas time in 1954. A fixture on that circus was Bill Moore, serving then as general agent and always exerting an abnormal influence over the affairs of Clyde Beatty. Concello fired Moore, but Beatty sided with the agent. The outcome of the violent arguments

Opposite: Circus men capitalized on people's interest in the unusual. {1898}

The Barnum & Bailey Greatest Show on Earth

BLUE-BEARD'S CHAMBER

CHASTE, CHARMING, WEIRD & WONDERFUL SUPERNATURAL ILLUSIONS, ASTONISHING MAGICAL ACHIEVEMENTS VIVIDLY PRODUCED. LIVING & BREATHING HEADLESS BODIES, TALKING HUMAN HEADS, REVOLVING SPRITES, BEAUTIFUL MERMAIDS, GRUESOME GNOMES & CURIOUS FLYING PEOPLE. CREATED BY ROLTAIR, THE MAGICIAN.

PRINTED IN AMERICA

THE WORLD'S LARGEST, GRANDEST, BEST AMUSEMENT INSTITUTION

that ensued was Concello's withdrawal from that outfit.

Concello had managed the Ringling show in the early fifties. He experimented with local sponsors but avoided telephone promotion. By elongating the big top, he created room for the menagerie animals and thus eliminated need for a separate tent. This and other economies were invoked to tighten up the operation. However, John North disagreed with some of Concello's operating policies, and after the financially unspectacular tour of 1953 Concello was replaced by Frank McCloskey. Advertising policies were reversed through the heavy use of posters and billboards. Thirty billposters were utilized, the most since 1947, and the 1954 season was better financially.

However, all was not well. Conflicts and unrest on the Ringling Circus were unbelievable. There were new union difficulties and endless clashes of personalities. At Minneapolis-St. Paul in 1955 McCloskey and several of his key staff men resigned. Lloyd Morgan became general manager, but few other experienced department heads remained. Consequently the show found it increasingly difficult to move on time, and through much of the 1955 season it missed matinees because of late arrivals. There was business to be had, but Ringling was not ready to accommodate the customers.

Thus, at the dawn of the 1956 season, the principal tented circuses were in turmoil. Ringling could not keep to the pace of one-night stands. Beatty had just experienced the torment of internal dissension and repeated change of command. King Bros. was overextended, deeply in debt and winning little business. Mills Bros., at a peak of thirty-nine trucks and seven elephants, found a highly successful formula for dealing with local sponsors and had enjoyed repeated profitable seasons. But in 1956 it sensed trouble and experienced difficulties in getting over the road, so it cut back to fewer trucks and half as many elephants. Kelly-Miller, off the pace from its peak of fourteen elephants, thirty-two trucks and as many as sixty horses, nevertheless was rolling in good shape. It was one of the few shows still relying on its own promotion rather than on some local sponsor plan. But this was coincidence and not the reason for success here or troubles elsewhere.

Even the new King Bros. partners came to a parting of the ways. Now they divided their big circus into two. King took one and Maley took the other for 1956. The dissension and division marked the show for trouble at the outset, but lack of business sounded the finale. The two units struggled from town to town,

abandoning trucks for lack of drivers or inability to repair them, moving only on credit and courage. They struggled through the spring but then could move no more. Meanwhile in the Los Angeles area, Clyde Beatty Circus, with the Cisco Kid as an extra feature, opened its season but found no business and quickly fell behind on wages. At Burbank on May 9 the American Guild of Variety Artists ordered its members not to work unless paid. That closed the show and it was taken to Demming, New Mexico, where an attorney said the Beatty show would file for bankruptcy.

Superstitious circus people believe that trouble comes in threes, but the Ringling show had been having its troubles in larger quantities than that. John Ringling North rejoined the show in Ohio after an extended absence and was dismayed by the disorganization that he found. On the Heidelberg race track outside of Pittsburgh in July, John Ringling North ordered the circus closed. In a public statement, he said this circus no longer could exist under canvas and that after a period or reorganization it would return to play arenas as an indoor operation. It was a time of supreme crisis, not only for the Ringling Circus but for all of those who follow the tent show business.

Three major shows, King, Beatty and Ringling, now had closed in 1956. Three times in less than twenty years the mighty Ringling circus had ground to a halt in mid-season — once after the strike, once after the fire and now, for what many people feared would be the last of a great institution. For the third time in two decades the defeated Ringling Circus rolled into Sarasota at mid-season.

Surviving shows reacted immediately. The frisky Kelly-Miller circus took the expedient way. It came out with huge posters reading: "Last of the tented circuses, see it now or miss it forever." Its business perked up as townspeople took children and grandchildren for one last look at this great American institution. A more significant move took place in New Mexico. Frank McCloskey and Walter Kernan, who earlier had resigned from Ringling managerial posts, had taken over the concession department on the Beatty show. Now, through purchase and manipulation of mortgages, they acquired that circus and re-opened it on August 29. It was staffed by a broad cross section of circus management. There were several Ringling department heads, including the boss canvasman. Floyd King was general agent and there were others held over from the original Beatty staff. This railroad circus played to strong business through November 20 when it closed at Sarasota, Florida. On that day the era of the original, traditional railroad circus came to an end. Both Ringling and Beatty announced they would resume business on trucks.

Opposite: Each season the horse acts seemed more thrilling than ever before. {1930}

123

7-The Circus of Today and Tomorrow

Picking itself up from another of its periodic seasons of catastrophe, circus business moved into 1957 with trepidation. The public thought there were no more circuses and troupers themselves were not really sure. The titles to consider were Ringling-Barnum, Clyde Beatty, Kelly-Miller, Mills Bros. and the new Cristiani Bros. Circus. Beatty was an all new operation — motorized and sponsored, but good signs were quick in coming and in the end the show netted $320,000, making it the best Beatty season since the phenomenal post-war tour of Canada. For the next two seasons it opened at Palisades Park, opposite New York City and then it played engagements on Long Island, both locations comprising a challenge to Ringling's New York appearance.

Ringling-Barnum itself ventured out of Sarasota in April 1957, and was on familiar ground at Madison Square Garden and Boston Garden. Thereafter its indoor operation would be new and strange to people who had spent their entire lives under canvas. The first several stands were less than encouraging and many mistakes were made. Then in June 1957, Ringling played the Charlotte, North Carolina, coliseum, the eighth stand of its tour. At Charlotte there were big crowds and a successful engagement. Those three days convinced Ringling management that the new plan could work.

A major departure in the system provided that Ringling would work with local promoters in each community. Much of the trouble in transition resulted from efforts to find the proper promoters and weed out those who were not up to the project. It developed that in many cities no capable promoter existed, so more and more the circus turned to promoters it knew elsewhere and asked them to take on additional towns. One was Harry Lashinsky of Charleston, West Virginia. Another was Irvin Feld of Washington, D. C.

The show also found it must re-think its calendar. Playing indoors, it no longer was so dependent upon good weather and could operate nearly all year. The first season ended in February and the second opened in March, not at New York but at Charlotte. Experiments in playing outdoors during the hottest weather were not successful. These fairground and ball park dates soon were abandoned in favor of finding air conditioned arenas. The 1958 season was stretched out by adding a month in Mexico. By 1959 the show's new routing pattern was established. It would open in January at Miami Beach and play its way northward to spring in New York. Then it would appear in arenas all around the country before closing in November. Over the Christmas season it would be in winter quarters to rehearse its new edition.

There appeared to be only one executive forceful enough to push the Ringling show back into the old business in a new way. That was Art Concello. In their on-again-off-again relationship, North asked Concello to take on the chore, and North himself agreed to participate from a distance. He remained in Europe. For three seasons, the Ringling circus experimented with motorized movement. They shipped some elephants by railroad baggage car but moved most of their equipment by truck and trailer. The overall change to indoor format reduced the Ringling payroll from about

Opposite: Every performer has a role in the colorful opening spectacle. {1928}

1,000 people to aproximately 225. No longer was it feeding and housing everyone. No longer did it carry its own seats, its own electric generator. Now it carried only a circus performance and used facilities of the modern arenas being opened in city after city.

Concello solved the transport problem by designing an all new variety of circus train. Starting with the coaches Ringling already owned, he converted some to stable cars and some to tunnel cars. Into the tunnels were drawn a new form of circus wagon, designed to fit inside these cars as well as inside arenas. The train was put into use early in 1960 and proved to be an instant success. Subsequently, more cars were added to it.

About as soon as the principal problems were solved and the pressure was off, Concello and North found that once again they could not work together. Succeeded on Ringling by Rudy Bundy, Concello then followed a familiar trail. He participated in an abortive attempt to join the Clyde Beatty organization. In 1966 he purchased the share of the late Walter Kernan, but the other two partners came to early disagreement with him, and after several weeks he sold his interest to them.

Elsewhere in the business both tented and indoor circuses were finding the going rougher. Mills Bros. for several years threatened to make further cutbacks, and then in 1967 it did not go out at all. Its principal advance agent had quit and the show simply had no route to follow. Cristiani Bros. Circus enjoyed spectacular success in 1957, netting $100,000, and for the next season put out a circus of classic proportions and quality. It reached its peak by playing the former Ringling stand on the lakefront in Chicago. The show, however, experienced contracting and routing problems. In 1959 it played Chicago suburbs with disappointing results and nearly folded before reaching Los Angeles. There it played a successful and profitable engagement, but it was not enough to save the show. It collapsed at the end of that season.

Over on the Kelly-Miller Circus the family was jolted by the unexpected death of a principal cog, Kelly Miller. His father, Obert Miller, soon retired and D. R. Miller continued alone. He expanded the circus for its twenty-fifth anniversary and moved it on a

The 1969 edition of the Clyde Beatty-Cole Bros. Circus, after turning in consistent profits the season before, opened again to large crowds.

Wild animal acts were placed early in the program since the heavy and cumbersome steel arena had to be set up before the show. {1927}

combination of semitrailers and piggy-back wagons that approximated rail show design. However, more troubles set in. Miller bought a steamboat to take his show on a tour of the Maritime Provinces of Canada. The old boat developed many troubles and had to be pumped out. Finally at Halifax it simply sank, taking with it much of Miller's circus property. Personally, he survived a train wreck and the crash of a private airplane and the government made demands for back taxes.

The Kelly-Miller circus was forced to sell its rhino, hippopotamus and many elephants. The giraffe died and key department heads retired. Before long Kelly-Miller Circus was down to the standard format of small shows using an 80 by 200-foot big top and traveling on about twelve trucks. Miller had turned to telephone promotion and finally he leased the circus to Joe McMahon. This proved unsuccessful, and McMahon closed the show in August 1968.

Even the established indoor circuses were experiencing troubles. Davenport died and his dates were divided among several rivals and former employees. Morton died and Hamid found it difficult to keep the established route of sponsors. The once invincible Polack Circus also lost dates to such newcomers as the Hubert Castle Circus and to the long established but growing Clyde Bros. Circus. The sponsored indoor circus field was divided up so many ways that few of those circuses could claim a lengthy route. Performers worked for one and then another of the indoor producers.

By 1968 the circus business was at another of its periodic low points and was poised for still another recovery and revitalization. And then it began. Just before the season opened, John Ringling North sold his circus. He believed there were no likely successors in the Ringling family to take on its operation. The principal buyer was Irvin Feld, who by now had come to promote a large proportion of Ringling's arena engagements. Feld was associated with Judge Roy Hofheinz, impresario of the Astrodome at Houston. This new management gained public attention by opening a school to train new clowns and by offering stock in Ringling Bros. and Barnum & Bailey Combined Shows, Inc., for purchase by the general public.

But their most important achievement was to organize and open an all new circus. A single Ringling-Barnum Circus could not play all of the desirable arenas in cities across the country, so a new circus was added. For 1969 Ringling-Barnum's red unit played the established route, while Ringling-Barnum's blue unit played a new series of towns, including an extended stand at the Astrodome.

Once again the irrepressible Ringling-Barnum was on the rise. Once again the indomitable circus business was moving to the high side of its endless cycle. While Ringling was doubling its operation and looking for more new fields to conquer, Clyde Beatty-Cole Bros. Circus was turning in consistent profits and it was operating subsidiaries named King Bros. and Sells & Gray. A former wire walker with his Hubert Castle Circus loomed as the new major power among sponsored indoor shows. Mills Bros. sold its equipment to a growing grandstand show named James Bros., which promptly began tented operation. Remnants of Kelly-Miller were used in the enlargement of Carson & Barnes Circus, an operation launched with help from the Millers and now managed by D. R. Miller.

The titles might change rapidly — Davenport to Castle, Mills to James, Miller to Carson & Barnes. Some of the oldest names would continue to recur — Cole, Sells, Barnes, and, of course, Ringling, Barnum and Bailey. Every circus man was striving as always for that new idea for a sure-fire success. Every circus trouper as always was living in the faith that tomorrow's town would bring sunny skies and big business and that tomorrow's circuses would be bigger and better than ever before.

Opposite: Whatever the future holds, every circus trouper lives in the faith that tomorrow's circuses will be bigger and better than ever before.

Part III
THE WONDROUS ONE-DAY STAND

1-The Mobility of the American Circus

Rivaling the feats of performers in the ring was the daily miracle of moving the circus from town to town. Efficiency combined with self-sufficiency so that the vast majority of circuses moved every day, playing six different cities, towns or villages each week. Even the gigantic Ringling Bros. and Barnum & Bailey Circus played mostly one-day stands. The season of 1937 was typical, when it played 136 different cities, 116 of them for a single day each. In that period such cities as Memphis, San Antonio, Kansas City, Indianapolis, Buffalo, Columbus and Louisville were one-day stands for the Ringling show.

Movement never has been novel to the circus. Pioneer troupes of colonial times moved in and out of Albany, Boston, Schenectady, Philadelphia, New York, Charleston, Savannah. In later times the circuses of Europe moved from city to city. But these moves were infrequent. The shows played each city for a week or more. They usually nailed their seating together, a sign of immobility that brought ridicule from the ranks of American circus bosses. While circuses always have moved, it was only in America that the one-day stand came into full development. The amazing accomplishment constituted an attraction on its own, one that often rivaled the performance in the rings. Even after a tradition of more than a century's duration, one-day stands remained a mystery to much of the American population. In the few cities where the biggest shows appeared for a week or a month residents rarely realized the same extensive performance would be loaded up and reassembled in a different city each day for most of the season. Townspeople who gave it any thought at all usually supposed that the circus must alternate, moving on one day and performing on another. Yet the fact is the American circus developed and thrived upon the one-day stand. Each day between noon and midnight it presented two performances. Each day between midnight and noon it dismantled itself and moved across the horizon to set up for business in yet another town.

Key to this ability and breakneck pace was the matter of self-sufficiency. A circus could move onto a vacant pasture, create its own self-contained city and then move on, with only a handful of reasons to contact local people. It bought feed and food in each town and needed a local source for water. Even for these staples it carried an emergency supply of its own, and for every other sort of need the circus was self-sufficient.

It reached this goal by evolution. When early circuses discovered they could save time and money by feeding themselves they established the circus cookhouse and dining tent to eliminate dependency upon small town hotel dining rooms. Wagon show performers usually slept at hotels, but development of the railroad show meant sleeping cars replaced the need for local accommodations. Eventually nearly every circus filled all of its own needs, from blacksmithing to barbering. Circus horses and elephants provided power enough to pull the show out of the deepest mire without the need to hire local teams or tractors. Shows carried their own generators for electric power even before most cities were fully electrified. European circuses and American carnivals usually tied into local power sources, while the American circus carried its own.

Starting with the advance agents, the American circus was

Opposite: The circus tent made possible the demanding pace of the one-day stand. {1896}

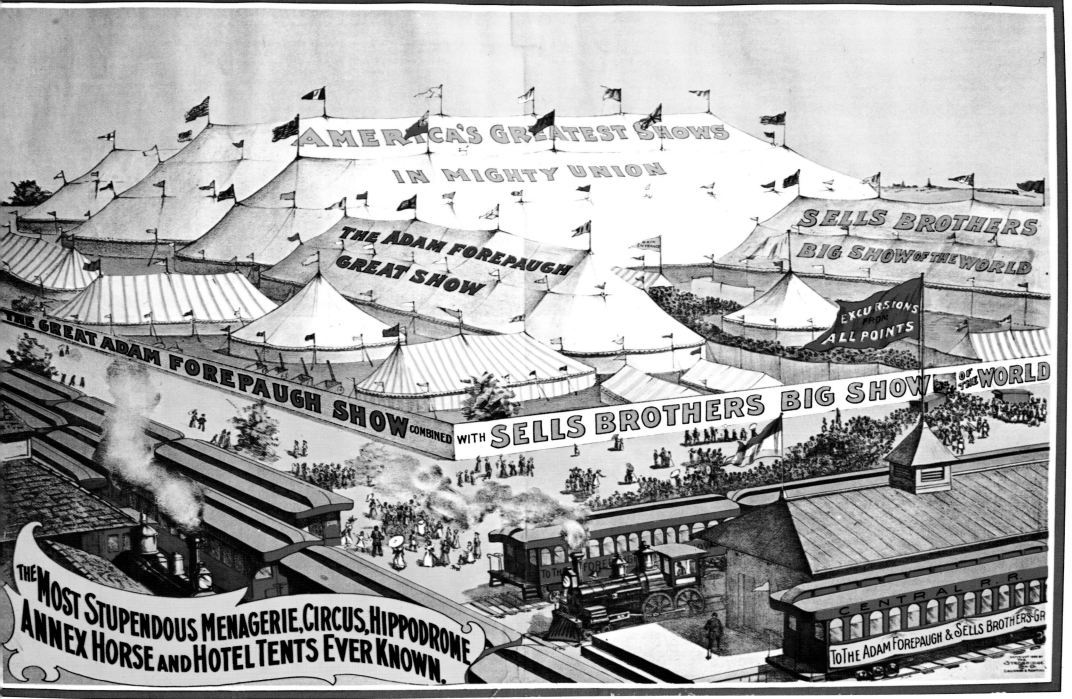

Setting up the big top is a smoothly run operation which never ceases to amaze onlookers. With the center poles in position, the huge bales of canvas are ready to be unrolled {opposite, right}. Sixteen-pound sledges slam down on the stake to drive it into the ground {opposite, above left}, then the men spread the canvas sections {opposite, below left}, lace them together and lash the canvas to bale rings at the center poles {left}. The tent slowly takes shape {below} and is ready at last for seats and rigging {bottom}.

COLE BROS. CIRCUS

RETURN HOME AFTER A TRIUMPHAL CONQUEST OF THE OLD WORLD

The cookhouse, which was capable of feeding every man on the show, helped the circus to become a self-contained city.

Every self-sufficient circus also carried its own light plant. The generator wagons above were with Ringling-Barnum in the 1930's.

designed to get up and go. In earliest times the single advance agent for a show could complete his tasks in a single day and then move on. Thus, he could keep the same schedule as the circus which followed him. As the chores of routing, promoting and contracting became more complex the single agent was replaced by an advance crew numbering as many as a hundred men. A single contracting agent came first and on his day in town he rented the lot, arranged for the license, contracted for the hay and grain, ordered the food for that future circus day, and then caught the local passenger train for the next town.

After him came the billposters, traveling two weeks ahead of the circus aboard a decorated railroad car and keeping to that important one-day schedule. Arising from bunks aboard the car, billposters ate breakfast cooked by the same steam which boiled a huge kettle of paste for posters. Then they fanned out through the town each with a hod of paper — that assortment of circus date sheets and lithographs which he would post on walls and windows throughout an assigned neighborhood. His fellow billers drove into the countryside and decorated country stores, grain elevators, giant barns and little feeder towns with the colorful posters which announced the coming of the circus. By sundown they had posted literally thousands of sheets, transforming the color scheme of that city or village and starting up the cycle of excitement that would cause thousands to buy tickets on circus day. Back at the advance

Opposite: Adequate transportation was essential to the mobility of the circus.

car the billers met a fellow agent who had arranged with local newspapers for advertising and publicity.

The accomplishments of billers and agents for each day were nearly as spectacular as those of their fellow troupers back on the show. But the success of one-day stands started with the fact that advance people spent no longer in the town than would the show. Otherwise they would lose their lead and soon be overtaken by the circus. In such a situation the show "caught up with its paper" and no greater crisis existed in circus management.

Last of the advance men was dubbed the "twenty-four-hour man." And here again the concept of the one-day stand was sharply pointed up. He was always in tomorrow's town checking on the others, seeing that the farmer had not plowed the pasture since the circus rented it, making sure that the feed and ice and milk and meat all would be delivered the next morning. He checked the roads and the railroads and in every fashion made sure the way was clear for arrival of the circus. His final responsibility was to meet the first elements of the show itself upon their arrival in the town. Then the twenty-four-hour men had nothing to do — except hasten to the next town and start the cycle once again. His title and his chores demonstrated the demanding pace of one-day stands.

The circus tent itself was another manifestation of self-sufficiency and the ability to make one-day stands. In fact the tent was developed as an answer to the situation which made one-day stands essential.

The earliest American circuses appeared at riding academies and livery stable yards with little or no property beyond the few

135

This group of dedicated Forepaugh-Sells Bros. billers stand beside their advance car in 1904 {above}. No walls were beyond the reach of the banner men. Each would fill his mouth with tacks to be picked from his lips with a magnetized hammer and then driven into the wall {below}.

costumes and props that were used in demonstrations of trick riding. As the circus grew in size and popularity, entrepreneurs in cities built structures especially for ring performances. Typical were those in Savannah, Albany, New York City and New Orleans. In several towns there were multi-purpose buildings designed to serve as theaters one time and as circus structures another. The Walnut Theater in Philadelphia and a theater operated by Dan Rice in New Orleans were examples. These multi-purpose buildings were fore-runners of today's modernistic multi-purpose arenas which accommodate hockey, trade shows, basketball, theatricals and circuses, all in quick succession. Those little halls of the 1850's could be converted quickly from proscenium to hippodrome, from stage to ring. This made for wider appeal to the public and greater usage of the buildings then as now. But there were critical limitations. Once in such a building the circus could accommodate only relatively small audiences. Even so, there was a limit to how long it could play profitably in a given town, and thus it found it must move on.

Not every village and town included a building suitable for circuses, and showmen soon saw that if sufficient audiences could not be attracted continuously in certain circus buildings, the circus would have to reach the audiences some other way. Shows would have to go where the audiences were rather than where the buildings were. Thus came the circus tent, and with it came the one-day stands.

Essential to the combination was adequate transport. Shows have moved by wagon and canal boat, by railroad and steamship, by motor truck and airplane. In sequence the showmen have made use of the best available mode of transportation and adapted each to the needs of one-day stands. The first of these was wagons.

For the villagers and the farmers who inhabited America during the century ending with 1930, the content of circus wagons — that is, the performance — always held great appeal. But a parallel attraction was the wagon itself and the caravan of which it was a part. In many of those years, anyone from over the hill or around the bend or just from the next town was a novelty. So the circus coming from even farther constituted a major occasion. The wandering circus held fascination for the ingenious Yankee who revered efficiency, whose great-grandfather had come from Europe and whose great-grandson might go to the moon. Much of America was inhabited by church-going homebodies who traveled little and felt tied to the farm by demands of livestock and crops. Circus wagons brought wonders from Araby and Asia. Time enough to relish those at the afternoon performance. But first it was amazing enough that these circus men had brought their wagons overland thirty miles since sunup.

Opposite: Blue ribbon winners were a feature of many circuses. {1904}

2-Wagon Shows

For the seven decades ending in 1870 all American circuses traveled by wagon. Some such overland shows continued until the era of World War I and a few remnants of the wagon show age lingered on until 1929. The pioneer troupes of Pool, Lailson and Caytano moved by wagon. But these transfers were incidental since the shows played longer stands and moved only occasionally. It may be that they did not own many wagons themselves.

The Robertson Circus of 1802 appears to have been one of the first to travel about the country to any great degree. Not until the introduction of the circus tent in 1826 by Nathan Howes did the circus embark upon the traveling routine by which we know it now. With a tent the show could move rapidly and perform in any community that gave promise of audience. In short order little circuses and separate menageries were criss-crossing the Eastern seaboard.

It was a circus owned by Howes and the two Crane brothers which crossed the Alleghenies in 1831 and went on to Mobile. Circuses had reached Chicago before 1836 and thereafter continued to press westward against retreating frontiers. June, Titus and Angevine of 1834 boasted of twenty-nine wagons, sixty-four horses, two elephants, fifty men and sixty animals. Its tent measured 170 by 85 feet. It spoke proudly of "an omnibus for the sole purpose of carrying the band and pulled by four beautiful bay horses." This outfit exhibited a horned Asian rhinoceros, the first of its species in the United States, and it featured Van Amburgh, trainer of lions and tigers. Just one year later the Zoological

Institute claimed forty-nine wagons and 120 horses. Since this undoubtedly was the June, Titus and Angevine show under a revised name, these statistics may have been influenced by circus-style inflation; it seems unlikely that the show nearly doubled its roster of wagons and horses in a single season. In any case, the panic of 1835 cut it back to a more reasonable rate of growth.

Buckley, Hopkins, Tuft & Co. of 1839 had twenty performers and forty horses. An 1840 circus under the aegis of June, Titus and Angevine was comprised of eleven wagons, one music carriage, three buggies, forty-three horses and two ponies. Still they grew. Sands, Nathan & Co. in 1859 had 110 people and 120 horses along with a new-fangled thing called a calliope. Van Amburgh & Co.'s Circus and Menagerie in the same season had 150 horses and 130 people.

By 1870 the George F. Bailey Famous Menagerie was advertising that "we do not travel by railroad as many small concerns are obliged to do, but with a working force of 240 men and horses." This was a big show claiming a seating capacity of five thousand for its tent. The circus opened by the Sells Bros. in 1872 counted 130 horses to pull its thirty-three wagons and cages. The Van Amburgh show of 1880 was powered by 170 horses. Yankee Robinson's Circus of 1869 claimed 220 horses, and the P. T. Barnum Circus in its first season, 1871, claimed to have 600 horses.

Opposite: Barnum & Bailey's Continent wagons were built to commemorate the show's triumphal return from its tour of Europe. {1903}

The Barnum & Bailey Greatest Show on Earth

SECTION 3-OF THE NEW HALF MILLION DOLLAR GRAND STREET PAGEANT.
THE MOST GORGEOUS OPEN AIR SPECTACLE OF MONUMENTAL MAGNIFICENCE EVER BEHELD.

THE WORLD'S LARGEST, GRANDEST, BEST, AMUSEMENT INSTITUTION.

Above: For the seven decades ending in 1870 all American circuses traveled by wagon. Some wagon shows continued in operation until World War I and a few remnants lingered on until 1929.

Left: Six grays help six chestnuts move Ringling Wagon No. 57 through the mud at Chicago's lake front show grounds.

When the young Ringlings opened for business in 1884 they had nine wagons and a handful of horses which had to be augmented by rented teams. For their second year they had twelve wagons and sixty horses. By 1888 there were eighty horses, and their final season as a wagon circus was 1889 when 110 horses moved the huge show.

Neither mountains nor rivers nor endless prairie stopped the circus. Shows ranged all over the country performing by day, traveling by nightly caravans that amassed annual mileage totals of nearly three thousand miles. Construction of the National Road out to Wheeling and on to Illinois country helped ease the way, but usually wagon circuses were in a continual battle with mud. Construction of bridges helped eliminate fording. But heavy circus wagons occasionally splintered the flooring and collapsed the timber bridges. Early circus documents reveal that the going was so tough in the muddy roads of springtime that circus horses became exhausted and wagon shows occasionally had to schedule rest periods of several days before resuming the arduous schedule of one-day stands.

Circuses developed a wide variety of specialized wagons for their overland moves. Weight was such a problem that seat wagons gave special trouble. Heavily laden with lumber, they became mired or demanded too many horses, so sturdy skeletons of wheels and gears comprised the typical seat wagon itself while seat planks were piled on top without benefit of wagon bed. Similarly, specially designed pole wagons were elongated to accommodate the center poles for constantly larger circus tents. Unnecessary weight was eliminated until, again, only the wagon skeleton remained to receive the weighty load.

Cages were designed in especially numerous varieties. The usual model had iron bars at the sides to contain the lions, hyenas and bears. Littler wire cages carried monkeys, mountain lions and other smaller species. Glass-sided cages contained snakes, and cumbersome dens with water tanks transported hippopotamuses as early as the 1850's. Giraffes, too, were carried by wagon circuses from the 1830's onward, though attrition among these fragile animals seems to have been high. Another modification typical of wagon circuses was the museum wagon. Glass-fronted cases made up the sides of such wagons which exhibited stuffed fish or birds or perhaps other curiosities of a museum nature. Between these side cases was cargo space.

When the heavy wagons became mired in the mud, additional horses called "hook rope teams" were used to pull them out. Here, twenty-two horses struggle to free a Ringling wagon in 1916.

141

Above: In this Walter L. Main Circus street parade of 1899, the calliope, smoking and blasting away, is bringing up the rear.

Below: The first bandwagon in the parade always had the most horses. This ten-horse team of Percherons illustrates a typical circus team.

Wagon circuses soon developed the special requirements for ticket wagons which also served as offices on wheels. These had doors and windows rather than brackets and tailgates. The wicket through which circus tickets were sold was placed at the back of the wagon and usually it was necessary to dig two trenches for the rear wheels so the window would be low enough for ticket buyers to reach with money. Bandwagons began as ordinary omnibuses designed to carry a dozen or fourteen people. But very soon showmen began to decorate these wagons with ornate carvings and oil paintings. Circus men went to the finest builders of their day — Stephenson, Fielding and Sebastian — for wagons that were at once rugged and ornate.

After Seth B. Howes imported elaborate tableau wagons from England to set the standards and style, circus men vied with each other to feature the largest and most ornate of all wagons. These were the subject of heavy advertising in advance as features of the street parade, although moving them from town to town on the poor roads and bridges of the day was a major undertaking. The calliope wagons and other tableau features of the street parades were similarly decorated. More prosaic were the special wagons built for such practical purposes as cookhouse operation. Soon each circus had an elongated wagon with hinged sides that opened to reveal a counter from which showmen could sell pink lemonade and candy.

The logistics of a wagon show move were dominated by the matter of sleep. However the matter was handled, there simply were not enough hours in a day, and teamsters who guided the circus wagons over the road were plagued by exhaustion and drowsiness.

Upon the completion of an evening show, performers and executives of the circus would go to their hotel for several hours' sleep, the time depending upon the distance that must be traversed the next day. Their lot was better than that of circus workingmen and bosses, however, because performers were not needed in the next town until midday and they could sleep later in the morning.

After a night performance the workingmen had quite a different schedule. Their immediate chore was to take down the seats and

Opposite: Cage wagons were constructed so that animals could easily be seen. {1901}

tents, load them in the wagons and prepare for the move. Baggage horses were undisturbed in their tented stables at this hour. Once the circus was loaded the canvas crew and other workingmen could grab their forty winks. Occasionally they, too, were quartered in a hotel. But more often they slept wherever they could find comfortable canvas or straw or, more rarely, in camp tents on the circus grounds. Their sleep was short because of the next day's schedule.

At six o'clock, or five, or four, or whatever time was dictated by the miles ahead, the boss hostler roused his sleepy crew. Already the camp fire was refueled and coffee was waiting. The men cared for their horses, loaded the last of the equipment, then hitched the teams and prepared to move.

They would follow the trail blazed by a circus man who had inquired about the roads or knew the way. His job was called "railing the road." Either late the previous day or even earlier on this morning he traveled along the roadway that would take the circus to its next town. Sometimes his wagon had a device at the side which would dribble flour from an inverted barrel whenever the release was tugged. This would spill a strip of white along the road and was used to indicate turns or other directions to the teamsters on the caravan that would follow. Often the way would be marked by the piling of stones or chopping of branches. Typically, rails from roadside fences were borrowed to be laid across a road as guides, which gave rise to calling the process "railing the road." Although night travelers were few, it was always possible that some other passerby would see the rail across the road and kick it aside. Or rain would wash away the flour strips.

Back at the circus lot the heaviest wagons started first. These comprised the baggage train and included seats, canvas, poles and trunks. In the darkness the circus caravan wended its way, watching for potholes, mires and rocks, and keeping an eye out for signals left behind by the road railer. Lanterns were hung from the wagon poles to light the way for horses. The convoy leader, perhaps on horseback, held high another lantern as he sought out landmarks and road signs. Behind him came the teams pulling heavy loads and guided by the weary circus crew.

Veterans of wagon show days recall these moves in varied ways. Some remember only the rainy nights when wagons became mired

hub deep in mud. Teams from several wagons had to be concentrated to free a single wagon. Another wagon, its teamsters blinded by rainy darkness, might skid off the road and upset. Then the baggage train stopped and shouting men sought to help their fellow teamster free the panicked horses and try to right the wagon. Often enough it meant probing the darkness for lost parts of the wagon's load. If it was a cage, perhaps a valuable animal was injured or had escaped.

Other veterans remember the pleasant evenings or pre-dawn hours as weary times when the wobbling lantern on the wagon ahead mesmerized a driver, but his team of horses continued to plug along after the ones ahead.

Other pleasant memories include hearing the sound of creaking leather, snaffling horses and crunching wheels augmented by voices as the circus men visited. They might chat about other times with other circuses or discuss events of the day. Since teamsters often came from stagecoach jobs and canvas workers sometimes had been sailors, they traded tales of schooners on the high seas and stages on the roads or open plains.

As dawn came and farms along the way came back to life, townsfolk gathered along the road to see the strangers pass. Teamsters were known to wrangle chickens, eggs and fruit from farmers. If the show had elephants these big beasts generally traveled with the baggage train. No wagon show attempted to carry elephants on wheels. Instead these animals walked from town under the care of a handler who might walk or ride horseback. The elephants walked slowly and thus started with the first group. Moreover, their strength was valuable if a heavy baggage wagon became stuck. There are many tales of rural onlookers who were awed by the elephants. Sometimes young boys preserved the big round footprints in the soft road as a reminder or proof of the fact that an elephant had passed that way.

The sun had been up for several hours by the time the circus baggage train reached its destination. It moved through the town

Opposite: As the circus parade grew, the wagons evolved into ornately carved and painted vehicles including the fairyland tableaux. {1893}

144

The Barnum & Bailey Greatest Show on Earth

SECTION 12. DELIGHTFUL ILLUSTRATIONS OF CHILDRENS FAIRY TALES WITH CARVED GOLDEN CHARIOTS DRAWN BY TINY SHETLAND PONIES AND REAL ZEBRAS, EXACTLY AS EXHIBITED IN THE LAST DIVISION OF THE NEW MILLION DOLLAR FREE STREET PARADE.

THE WORLD'S GRANDEST, LARGEST, BEST, AMUSEMENT INSTITUTION.

Pole wagons were specially designed to accommodate the long center poles for ever larger circus tents. Unnecessary weight was eliminated until only the wagon skeleton remained to receive the load.

and out onto the circus grounds where the wagons were spotted in their appropriate positions and, without hesitation, the workmen began the task of erecting tents and seats.

Back in the previous town the cage train was now underway. This was made up of the lighter wagons, including the animal cages, the omnibuses for carrying performers or bandsmen and the several buggies that carried star performers or managers. Performing horses, ponies and camels trotted along in this speedier line of vehicles. Because of its lightness and speed it could start later, so performers got more sleep and made more of the move by daylight. Like the baggage train, they faced the risks of mud and poor roads but those on the later train usually avoided one problem. The baggage train, following the railing but risking the chance for mistake, occasionally missed a turn and discovered its mistake only miles later. However, by the time the cage train moved along it was easy to follow the ruts of the heavy baggage wagons and avoid those frustrating times for turnabout and back tracking.

It was arrival of the wagon show's cage train which evolved into the street parade. Near the edge of the new day's town this line of wagons would stop, perhaps by a stream or shade trees. Teams were fitted with plumes, wagons with flags; mud from the night's move was washed away from ornate wheels, protective canvas was peeled back from bandwagons, sideboards came off cages, bandsmen donned their red coats, and performers put on fancy bonnets and top hats. Then the revitalized caravan — with the band breaking into tune — made its grand entrance into town.

This procession was designed to attract as much attention as possible and lure the townspeople to the circus grounds. On arrival the cage train broke up as animals were taken to the menagerie and performers and horses moved to the pad room. These tents and others now were up and ready. The cookhouse was ready to serve breakfast, and workmen were completing the erection of seats and rigging in the big top. One of the show's specialists was the ring maker, who with adz and spade shaped the circular curbing of sod that would be the scene of this day's performances.

Thus the wagon show completed its move. From the time of

146

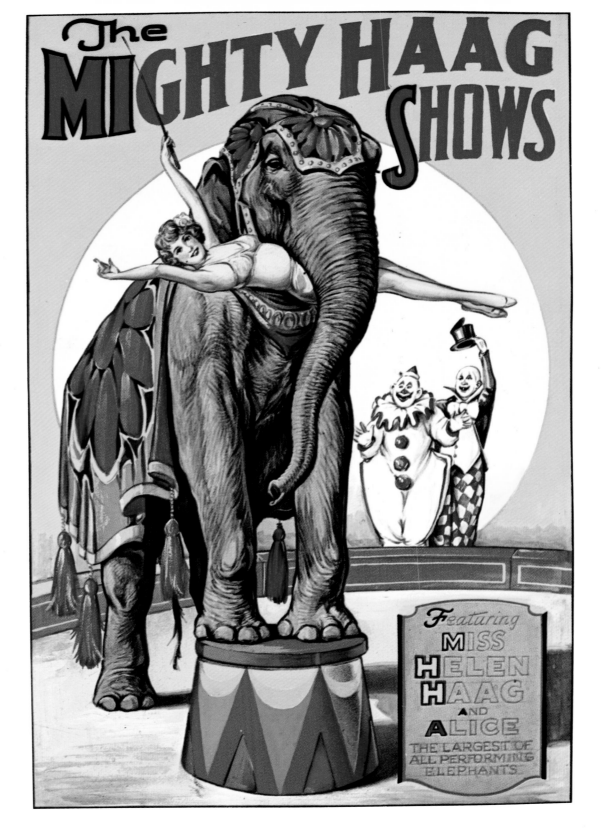

The passing elephants were an unbelievable sight to many rural boys.

Washington until the time of Coolidge, circus people somewhere were moving by this unchanging system. But midway in all those decades the sound of steam was heard and the lure of railroading made itself felt. When circuses first began to consider any other way of moving, many showmen shook their heads for the impending break with tradition. They declared these new-fangled ways would ruin circus trouping. Circusing had a special appeal to the wagon showman. There was a touch of similarity with the gypsy caravan of Europe or the wagon trains wending their way West. But most of all it was the way of life that had grown up with the concept of the American circus as it made its one-day stands under canvas.

The big shows forsook wagons in the 1870's, Barnum beginning the trend in 1871. Forepaugh followed reluctantly in 1877. The Van Amburgh Circus, in its dotage, lingered with wagons until 1883 and then passed from the scene. From that time onward, nearly every major circus switched to rails as soon as it became established. The new Ringling Bros. Circus was a good example.

Thus wagon shows became synonymous with small shows and since they lacked the firm advantage of high iron rails they became known as "mud shows." Mud shows played the high-grass towns — or small places. Their high wheels and light rigs, designed to navigate the muddy byways, were in contrast to the heavy wagons being utilized by railroad circuses.

While the most famous names and largest shows no longer were identified with wagon transportation, there remained a great tradition for overland trouping. The Orton Badger Circus in 1856 had been the first theatrical performance of any kind to appear in Kansas City, Missouri. Seventy-one seasons later Orton Bros. Circus played out the 1927 season as a wagon circus. William Newton had thirty-one wagons for his 1916 Honest Bill Shows. The next year, however, he had eight trucks and twelve wagons. Lamont Bros. in 1915 traveled on thirty-two wagons and Al F. Wheeler New Model Shows were of the same size. Sam Dock trouped the Great Keystone Show in 1921 with ten wagons, three

cages and one automobile. M. L. Clark Shows, a Southern tradition, had 175 horses to pull its sixty-five wagons and fifteen cages in 1911. These and others were among the outfits that continued as mud shows for generations, into the period immediately preceding World War I.

King of all the latter day wagon shows was the Mighty Haag Circus. In 1905 this outfit boasted of "100 horses and mules, mostly mules" as well as thirty wagons, two rings and two elephants. Its posters read "A Southern show for Southern people."

The Mighty Haag, like Orton Bros. and M. L. Clark, was bitten briefly by the railroad bug. Each tried its turn in that big-time category. Each prudently had stored its wagon show equipment, and each returned to it. The Mighty Haag was on rails from 1909 through 1914 but blossomed forth the next season with fifty-two wagons and 130 horses as well as three elephants, ten camels and nine cages. The Mighty Haag once again was back in its own element and once again began to thrive.

However, Haag bought its first truck in 1916 and owned seven trucks in 1919. The 1922 season involved seventy-six weeks of continuous trouping during which the show lost only three days. It moved on fifty vehicles including autos, trucks, wagons and cages. Still in 1928 this circus that had become a Southern tradition included ten cages and one baggage wagon along with its forty-one trucks. Finale for the mud show era came in 1929 when the Mighty Haag replaced its cage wagons with three trucks and bought another to substitute for the last overland baggage wagon.

It was the Mighty Haag which could set up its tents at a Kentucky crossroads, which only it could find, and be sure of capacity crowds. When the back roads gave out, the Mighty Haag used creek beds as avenues to probe further into the back hills of West Virginia, Kentucky, Tennessee, Alabama and Georgia. Wagon show troupers declared to a man that one had never really trouped with a circus until he had made a season with a mud show like the Mighty Haag.

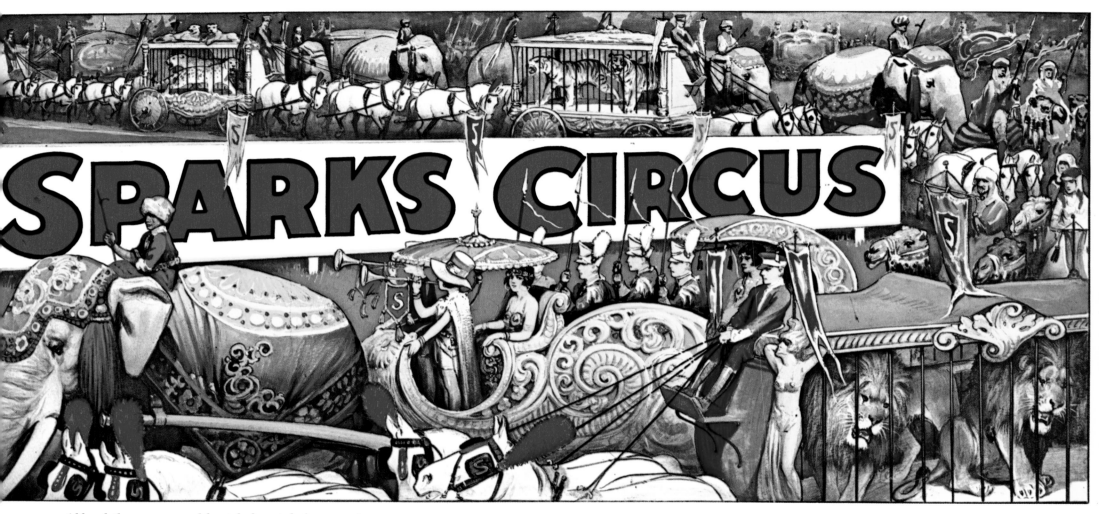

Although the wagons were elaborately decorated, they were also sturdily built to withstand the rigors of cross-country travel.

149

ALL AMERICA will celebrate THE GOLDEN JUBILEE of the
RINGLING BROS AND BARNUM & BAILEY COMBINED CIRCUS

3-Railroad Circuses

The age of steam brought the circus to its highest level. If wagon shows were colorful, quaint Americana, then the railroad circus was a big and powerful amusement machine. The very term "railroad circus" became synonymous for bigness. To many, a circus automatically was a big one simply by the fact that it traveled by rail. This was the mark of the big time.

Circuses flirted with railroads for nearly thirty years before making a binding commitment. Many were the wagon shows which hired cars and shipped home by rail at the weary end of a season. Mud showmen who found themselves in poor territory sometimes rented cars and loaded their wagons aboard in order to make a dramatic switch in territory. In the 1850's the Spalding & Rogers Circus, most famous for its operation of the Floating Palace, a plush riverboat theater that accommodated first one circus and then another, made extensive use of railroads, particularly in one tour which centered on Illinois and another which concentrated on New England and Canada. In all such cases the circus rented railroad cars and ultimately gave them up and returned to its wagon show ways.

Shortly after the transcontinental railroad was completed by the driving of a golden spike at Promontory Point, Utah, in 1869, a train of borrowed cars carrying Dan Castello's Circus completed its transcontinental route. Just two years later William Cameron Coup, with help from his partner, Dan Castello, and the man whose name they had rented, P. T. Barnum, put their year-old Barnum Circus on railroad cars of its own, thus launching the circus railway age. Now, circuses could be bigger and carry more paraphernalia, but, most of all, they gained enough mobility to permit them to choose which towns to play. Heretofore the limitations of horsepower dictated that a show must play within a limited range of its previous performance. When troupers developed the ability to rest aboard a

Opposite: On rails, the circus blossomed forth as never before. {1933}

train while railroaders rapidly carried their outfit between towns a hundred miles apart, then it no longer was necessary to stop over in the small towns or cities that might give only limited business.

All of America thrilled to the glamour of railroading. When this was joined with the universal appeal of circuses the result was exhilarating. Circuses quickly included the word "railroad" in their titles. While the shows did, indeed, travel by train the term "railroad circus" also carried a connotation of modernity. Railroading was exciting and advanced, and it remained in that category for decades, during which it brought the circus to an apex of development.

Railroad circuses developed extremely heavy wagons with wide iron wheels and a system for removing the pole or tongue so that each unit could be loaded close behind another on the flat cars. In contrast to the biggest wagons were the cross cages, smaller animal dens designed to fit crosswise on a flat car so as to take up less train space. Through the use of cross cages a circus could load many more animals in a given space. Another little wagon was the train light plant, a generator to furnish electricity both for the circus coaches and for the circus flat cars during times that no locomotive was present to supply other power for lights. Where wagon shows had been fearful of weight now railroad shows loaded not only the inside but also the exterior of their wagons with bulky circus plunder. Since railroads charged by the number of cars, money-conscious circus men learned to load maximum tonnage into a limited space. Then when they had devised every way of utilizing existing flat car footage — including brackets on the sides of wagons and storage bins on the bottom side of flat cars — they modified the rail equipment itself. Circus men developed the extra-long flat car which gave them bonus loading space for the same price. They designed elephant cars and horse cars of comparable length. Thus a circus moving on twenty extra-long cars might have required thirty or thirty-five cars of standard railroad dimension.

Specially designed seventy-foot elephant cars with solid sides could carry up to fourteen elephants. The animals were loaded sideways and packed tightly to help them keep their balance.

When most railroad cars were thirty-five and forty feet long, circuses switched to sixty footers, then to cars seventy and seventy-two feet long. This made circus freight cars as long as regulation passenger cars. It was a half-century later that railroads themselves took extensive steps towards lengthening their freight cars.

Circus trains soon took on a standard pattern. True, there were many variations and a single show might be loaded differently on consecutive nights. But the standard format began with stock cars immediately behind the railroad's locomotive. Next came the flat cars bearing wagons, cages and a few trucks or tractors. Finally there were the coaches. For a circus using baggage horses as opposed to the tractors of later seasons, a train was comprised of fifty percent flat cars, twenty-five percent stock cars and twenty-five percent coaches. A typical twenty-car show, for example, might have five stock cars, ten flat cars and four coaches. The fifth coach would be ahead of the show itself, serving as advertising car but counting in the total of twenty. To add a twenty-first car would be to pay for twenty-five, according to railroad tariff regulations. Therefore, shows, for the most part, counted their cars in multiples of five or ten.

Typically, the stock cars had slatted sides for horses and solid sides for elephants. In each case the animals were loaded sideways in the car and tightly enough together to assist each other in keeping balance. A seventy-foot circus car could carry thirteen or fourteen elephants or thirty-two baggage horses. Ring horses, camels, zebras and ponies required less space, so more were loaded in each car. Ponies could be double decked. No space was wasted. Extra poles for the big top were stored on the roofs of stock cars. If there was extra space inside it was used to carry reserve supplies of Cracker Jack, program booklets, tickets, soft drink flavorings, cones for ice cream, or even a spare big top. Often one end of an elephant car was fitted out as a bunk room and elephant hands lived with their charges.

The simple but systematic methods by which circus flat cars were loaded and unloaded held the secret for successful one-day stands with railroad shows. In the early stages of railroading some users loaded flat cars over the sides. Although in retrospect this may seem strange, it should be remembered that most box cars are loaded from the sides and hopper cars are loaded one by one. Therefore, why not flat cars?

It was early showmen — especially Coup on his pioneer Barnum show — who hit upon the efficient technique of placing ramps or runs at the end of a string of flat cars, then running wagons up the

Early circus men hit upon the efficient technique of placing runs at the end of a string of flat cars for loading and unloading wagons. This simple method contributed immeasurably to the ability of railroad shows to play successful one-day stands throughout a season.

153

runs across the first flats to their positions, beginning with the farthest car. Wagon followed wagon in prescribed sequence, bridging the spaces between cars with iron crossover plates. Teams of baggage horses brought the wagons to the railroad crossing then turned them over to train teams. A pullup team brought the wagon up the run where it was transferred to a pullover team that took it over the flats to its proper position behind the previous wagon. Horses, of course, walked alongside the flat cars. A rope connected the team to the forward corner of the wagon, and a member of the train crew guided the wagon down the string of flats. Upon approaching the previous wagon the new one was halted, its pole was dropped to the flat car deck and then the wagon was drawn into final position. Last duty of the train team was to jerk the wagon strongly against the chock blocks while train crewmen thrust another set behind the wheels, thus firmly anchoring the wagon for its night's trip. At the next day's town the runs were placed at the forward end of the flats and the wagons were towed off in the same sequence.

Wagons or trucks that were still called "wagons" were loaded in a strictly prescribed sequence according to which vehicles would be needed at what times the following day at the next stand.

Several elements of planning and design went into the organization of such a circus train. First the baggage wagons were built to fit their load. Thus, if stringers for the circus seating were sixteen feet long, the stringer wagon was built to accommodate a sixteen-foot load. Performers were told what kinds and sizes of trunks they could bring, and the trunk wagon was built to hold such trunks with no space to spare. Circus troupers counted camel-back trunks — those with curved tops — to be bad luck and one suspects that this superstition was inaugurated or encouraged by circus owners who figured that flat-topped trunks would load more efficiently in the wagons.

While wagons were of variable lengths the flat cars were of fixed sizes. So the next step was to group the wagons to make the most efficient possible use of flat car length. To do otherwise would be to require additional flat cars, and that would cost needless money for every move. The Hagenbeck-Wallace train of 1923 illustrated the degree of efficiency for using flat cars. The show was then using fourteen new seventy-foot cars. One combination of four wagons added up to only 63-1/2 feet, another to only 65. Three loads each totaled between 67 and 68 feet. Two more carried 69-1/2 feet each. Four loads added up to 70-1/2 feet or 71 feet each, calling for some overhang beyond the end sills of the cars. The other three

Left: Iron crossover plates bridged the spaces between the flat cars. The wagons had to be precisely grouped to make the most efficient use of available room since the flat cars were of fixed lengths.

Below: Various different teams of horses worked at the runs: one, the pullup team, brought the wagons up the runs, and another, the pullover team, took them over the flats to their proper position on the train.

155

Stock cars on a circus train were usually located immediately behind the locomotive. A typical train was composed of fifty percent flat cars, twenty-five percent stock cars and twenty-five percent coaches.

Opposite: The arrival of the circus trains was almost as exciting as the big show. {1938}

loads measured precisely 70 feet for seventy-foot cars.

In most cases there were four wagons to a flat, although the number frequently went up to five in the case of cages and down to two or three on the car which carried the extra-long pole wagon. No space was wasted because of those poles. A show's four center poles were loaded in pairs on the sides of the pole wagon while the bed of the wagon contained shorter quarter poles. Then a tractor or narrow wagon was loaded behind the pole wagon and between the extended lengths of its center poles.

After fitting the wagons to both the loads and the flats, the trainmaster's next task was to arrive at the sequence in which these wagons could be loaded and unloaded with the greatest relationship to the sequence and time at which they were used on the circus grounds. The loading order anticipated which wagons were needed first in the mornings and which were needed last at night.

Fortunately these needs often dovetailed. But in some cases there had to be an adjustment. For example, the seats could not be unloaded until after the tent was up in the morning, so canvas wagons should precede the seat wagons on the train. Yet at night the seat wagons were loaded before the tent was taken down and thus they were ready for the flat cars before the canvas wagons were. Perhaps the simplest answer came with those trainmasters who parked the seat wagons to one side until the others could be loaded. Another answer, however, for more complicated cases was to load the cars in one sequence, then utilize a switch engine during the night to re-position the flats so the wagons would roll off in a new sequence at the next town.

The basic loading order for typical circuses of the early twentieth century began with the cookhouse. The final meal of the circus day was served between the afternoon and night performances, so the dining department could be started to the train even before the night performance began. At the next town the cookhouse was needed first of all so that it could prepare breakfast. Thus, for both morning and night sequences, it could be first in line on the flat cars.

With it could be the steam calliope and any other equipment used only in the street parade. These things would not be needed until the parade early the next day.

In the next category were wagons for the menagerie tent, the stable tops and the cages themselves. At the old town the menagerie would come down as soon as the night show started. Since baggage horses already had been fed and cared for and now

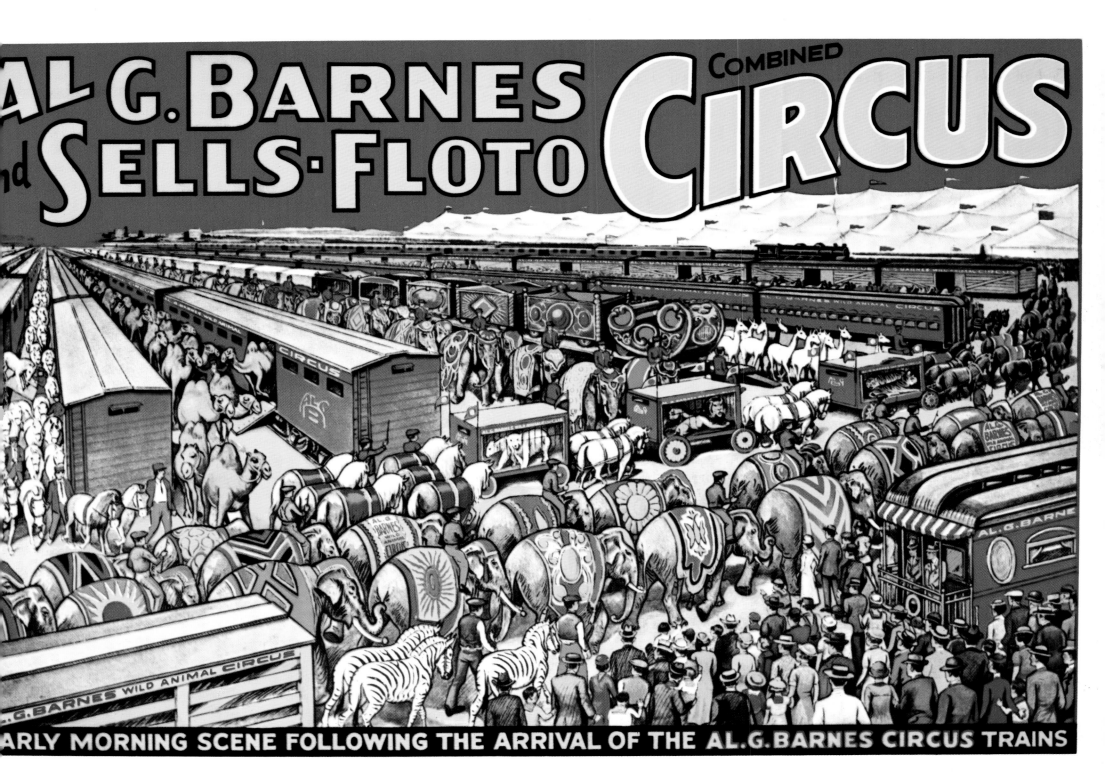

Behind the flat cars on a circus train came the several coaches.
Only rarely in circus history have individuals had a private
car to themselves, but often show owners had handsome staterooms.

would be working until midnight, there was no further need for the stable tops. Conversely the cages would be needed early in the new town so that they could be prepared for the parade. The menagerie and stable tops were among the first to go up.

Because the ticket wagon served as circus office, it might be needed on the old lot until the performance was over. Since the sideshow might win a few customers as the audience left the night performance of the main circus, its wagons were not available to the train until shortly after the night performance. But in the morning, that circus office wagon would be needed for conducting business at an early hour and the sideshow manager would want to get his department into operation as early as possible, certainly by noon, so as to catch the people who followed the parade back to the lot. Therefore the sideshow wagons and the big show ticket wagon usually followed the menagerie department's wagons onto the cars.

This early loading process steadily stripped the circus grounds of any equipment as soon as it had served its purpose in the evening. Circus goers always were surprised to come out of the big top and find that most of the rest of the circus already was gone. As soon as that audience cleared, the circus could load its seats, rigging and property wagons. Then the tent came down and was loaded into a

pair of hefty canvas wagons. Finally, the lofty center poles were eased to the ground and shouldered onto the brackets at the sides of the pole wagon. With the sequence of tomorrow's needs in mind, the trainmaster then sought a sequence starting with the pole wagon, continuing with canvas wagons, and following with those for seats, rigging and properties.

With the night show over, performers scurried to the pad room, that elongated tent with men's dressing space at one end, women's at the other, and performing horses in between. Costumes were loaded into trunks, saddles and plumes were placed again in the ring stock wagon. The wagons carrying trunks, pad room and trappings were loaded late on most show trains. They wouldn't be needed until afternoon on the next day and so their position late in the sequence was logical. Last in the typical loading order were the generator wagon and the circus light department; they were needed to illuminate the grounds until the last minute at one town and would not be needed until last of all in the next stand.

There were many variations of this idealistic form of the loading order. Many circuses placed their cages last in the lineup, with more thought for tomorrow's town than for tonight's, and especially if no parade was involved. Pole wagons often appeared later in a specific loading order because they were needed on the lot so late at night. During the unloading process, however, certain wagons ahead of them would necessarily be shunted aside until the all-important pole wagon came into place on the lot.

After baggage horses were replaced by trucks and tractors, railroad circuses had an increased need for shunting cars around after the train was loaded. This was so that the tractors used to load the train could be relocated in the lineup of cars to be available at the head of the flats for unloading early wagons in the morning.

Behind the flat cars on the circus train came the several coaches. Show trains were not normally noted for luxurious accommodations. The show owner or his principal stars might have staterooms or even as much as half a car. Only rarely in circus history have there been private cars reserved entirely to an individual owner or star. Outstanding examples included John Ringling, who traveled aboard his private Jomar, and Tom Mix, who had a private car while he was with Sells-Floto Circus. A few executives, bosses and performers had staterooms on some of the larger circuses.

But most employees were assigned to typical Pullman berths. Those with prestige and longevity won the lower berths. The first-of-May — or rookie — invariably was assigned to an upper berth. In

Opposite: Barnum & Bailey even built a train to fit European railroad clearances. {1902}

The Barnum & Bailey Greatest Show on Earth

VUE GÉNÉRALE DES 12 PAVILLONS, COUVERTS DE TOILE IMPERMÉABLE, TELS QU'ILS SERONT ÉRIGÉS ET SOUS LESQUELS SERONT DONNÉS CHAQUE JOUR DE LA SEMAINE DEUX GRANDES EXPOSITIONS.
CE SONT LES TENTES LES PLUS GRANDES ET LES PLUS BELLES QUI AIENT JAMAIS ÉTÉ ÉRIGÉES.

PRINTED IN AMERICA.

L'INSTITUT DE DIVERTISSEMENT LE PLUS GRAND ET LE PLUS MAGNIFIQUE DU MONDE.

the crowded conditions aboard show trains it was not uncommon to assign more than one man to a berth, particularly in the working-men's car. And in the lowliest of the circus train accommodations anything the Pullman company had originated was torn out and in its place were built sets of three-high bunks. Such a carload of humanity, unbearably hot and in frequent need of fumigation, was in sharp contrast to the plush luxury of private cars and tasteful fittings of the pleasant staterooms elsewhere on the train.

Space aboard the coaches was assigned according to one's job with the show. Thus, performers were segregated into one or more cars. If the show were large enough there would be a sleeper for the various family troupes and another for single girls. In another car would be the sideshow personnel plus perhaps the ticket sellers and bandsmen. Teamsters, canvasmen and cookhouse help would be relegated to the three-high bunks. No wonder they frequently chose to sleep, instead, beneath the wagons on the rocking flat cars.

A feature of most circus trains was the pie car or privilege car, that circus social center where employees could gather after the show and during the move to enjoy sandwiches and pie (thus the nickname for the car), as well as drinks, card games and general conviviality. Operation of the pie car was a choice concession and various specialists paid the circus for the privilege of operating it. On not a few shows the pie car included a card game, dice game or slot machine, and on such a show as Dailey Bros. Circus, it was policy of the management that the pie car with its games should retrieve for the owner much of the money he paid out in wages.

Often the show train would get underway just after midnight and arrive in the next town anywhere from five to nine hours later, depending largely upon the mileage, but certainly turning, too, upon the efficiency and hospitality of the railroaders on whose line the show was moving. If the arrival was early, the train was sidetracked and left alone until morning.

If arrival was late, it meant that no one aboard had breakfast unless he could squeeze into the pie car during the rush. Once on the lot, the show would concentrate on the big top performance rather than cookhouse and convenience of employees. In days of the street parade, the time of arrival of the train also influenced the timing, preparation and even existence of the day's street march.

The fantastic fact is that shows were able to arrive in town, unload the train, set up the myriad of equipment and gear, present a mile-long free street parade, reassemble on the lot and present afternoon and night performances, then reload the train and move on in the endless cycle of one-day stands. There was organization

and system to the circus way of doing. Without a maximum of efficiency no such tight schedule could have been maintained. But the system, like most, was successful in part because of its basic simplicity and good logic; no need to carry a twenty-foot wagon for an eighteen-foot load, no need to pay for twenty-five cars if twenty will carry it, no need to bring the light plant on the lot early when the cookhouse is needed first.

The distance a railroad circus might move often was forty to one hundred miles, but shows regularly made shorter and longer jumps. Shortest were those when shows moved from one location to another in the same city. Ringling Bros.-Barnum & Bailey, for example, used to play separate stands on each of two lots at opposite ends of Detroit. Similarly, it played two locations some seasons in Cincinnati. For many seasons it played Madison Square Garden in Manhattan and then moved to play a tented stand in Brooklyn. Similarly, there were smaller shows that often played a whole series of stands in principal cities. Chief among these was Gentry Bros. Dog and Pony Show, which annually "played the lots" in Chicago. It might play one or more days in each of a dozen different neighborhoods in such a city. Harris Nickel Plate Shows played the lots in New Orleans and elsewhere. In much later years showmen would take motorized shows on a similar series of dates in suburbs surrounding big cities, for by then suburbs had replaced the old neighborhoods of inner cities, just as trucks had substituted for trains in circusing.

In contrast to the short trips by circus trains were Sunday runs, those long jumps so named because most of them were made on Sundays. Circuses frequently scheduled no performances on Sunday and, therefore, could make especially long moves between Saturday and Monday towns. On such occasions they issued dukies — or box lunches — to personnel aboard the train since the pie car could not accommodate all of them. Similarly they scheduled feed and water stops so that animals could be cared for. The latter were especially typical of circus jumps to cover the great distances of the American West. Because of speed restrictions placed by regulating authorities and because of the frequently slow switching and transferring by railroads, moves on a circus train often were long and boring.

In addition to the jumps between stands were those long runs at the opening and closing of each circus season. The Ringling Circus, for example, moved each year from 1926 until 1957 from Florida to New York to start its annual tour. Sells-Floto once traveled from Denver to California, making no stops along the way, to avoid a

Though uncommon, circus train wrecks occurred from time to time, occasionally with disastrous results. A tragic accident on the Cole Bros. Circus {right} occurred on July 27, 1945, while the show was en route to Brainerd, Minnesota.

Feeding and watering stops for animals had to be scheduled on extra-long jumps, especially when the circus traveled in the vast West. Here, the Ringling show feeds its baggage horses at Dunsmire, California, en route to Fresno.

quarantine regulation on livestock. Similarly, the Al G. Barnes Circus jumped from its California winter quarters to Galesburg, Illinois, in order to leap across a quarantined area. These were extreme demonstrations of the mobility which railroading brought to circuses. In old wagon show days shows caught by the yellow fever, smallpox or any of the scourges of the time simply were put out of action and often with disastrous financial effects. Wagon circuses caught in coal mine country during a strike similarly had little choice but to play out their time and hope for better business later. But railroading meant that as soon as adjustments could be made in the advance advertising and contracting departments, a circus could move rapidly for great distances and pick up its tour again in more prosperous or promising country.

The biggest circus train ever was Ringling Bros. and Barnum & Bailey's 109 cars of 1947. More often that circus traveled on eighty or ninety cars and always was the biggest on the road. In 1929 the Ringling train was split into four sections as follows: The first section, or flying squadron, carrying the things needed first at the new town, numbered fifteen flats, four stock cars and four sleepers. The second section carried eleven flats, five stock cars and six sleepers. The third section moved fourteen flats, four stock cars, one storage car and four sleepers. Bringing up the rear was the final section with five stock cars, four elephant cars, a camel car, ten sleepers and one office car. These, in addition to the two advance advertising cars, were typical of the Ringling railroad equipment for many years.

Back in 1872 that first Barnum rail show utilized sixty-one cars. By 1889 the same show was using sixty-four cars of longer design,

and in 1898 it used sixty-seven cars for its tour of Europe. The Forepaugh-Sells Circus was Barnum's chief rival in the 1880's and its trains were nearly identical in size. The Great Wallace Show and the John Robinson Show both reached forty-five car size at their peaks. Hagenbeck-Wallace topped fifty, and Sells-Floto in 1922 claimed forty cars. Cole Bros. Circus had as many as thirty-five cars and as few as twenty as its fortunes fluctuated. Clyde Beatty Circus was on fifteen cars for its entire railroad experience. Dailey Bros. started at ten and grew to twenty-five cars. Christy Bros. grew to twenty cars. Floyd and Howard King juggled the Gentry Bros. and the Walter L. Main titles between their fifteen-car show and its companion ten-car unit. Over the years there were scores of railroad circuses, most of them in the twenty- to thirty-car class. Few reached forty or fifty, many started with ten or fifteen. The Great Depression dealt railroad circuses a near-fatal blow. The Christy, Gentry, Main, Cole, 101 Ranch, Robbins Bros., Sparks, John Robinson, Hagenbeck-Wallace, Sells-Floto, Tim McCoy and Al G. Barnes all passed out of existence during the decade between 1929 and 1939.

True, titles such as Clyde Beatty, Arthur Bros. and Dailey Bros. sprouted up as new railroad shows during the wartime period that followed. And in 1935 Cole Bros. had come out as a large and new railroad show which dwarfed any of the several predecessors operating under the same title. But the overall success of these late railroad shows was limited. Only Ringling Bros. and Barnum & Bailey and the Clyde Beatty Circus continued to move by rail. Then in 1956, the big Ringling show closed and declared it would not return to tents. The Clyde Beatty Circus closed down in mid-season but re-opened under new management and completed the year, only to announce then that it would divest its railroad status and start the next year as a truck show. The era of the flat car circus making one-day stands under canvas had ended.

For three shaky seasons the Ringling Circus traveled mostly by truck. Then it returned to railroading. This, however, was a new format. The show played arenas instead of tents and there were major differences in its railroad setup. By 1969 a second Ringling unit was opened; some forty-five railroad cars then carried the magic title of Ringling Bros. and Barnum & Bailey Combined Shows. Even so, the traditional flat car circus of one-day stands survives only in spirit at the Circus World Museum, where flat cars, runs, cross over plates, pullup teams and all the other accoutrements of a railroad circus continue in daily demonstrations.

Opposite: The modernity of the railroad circus appealed to the public. {1925}

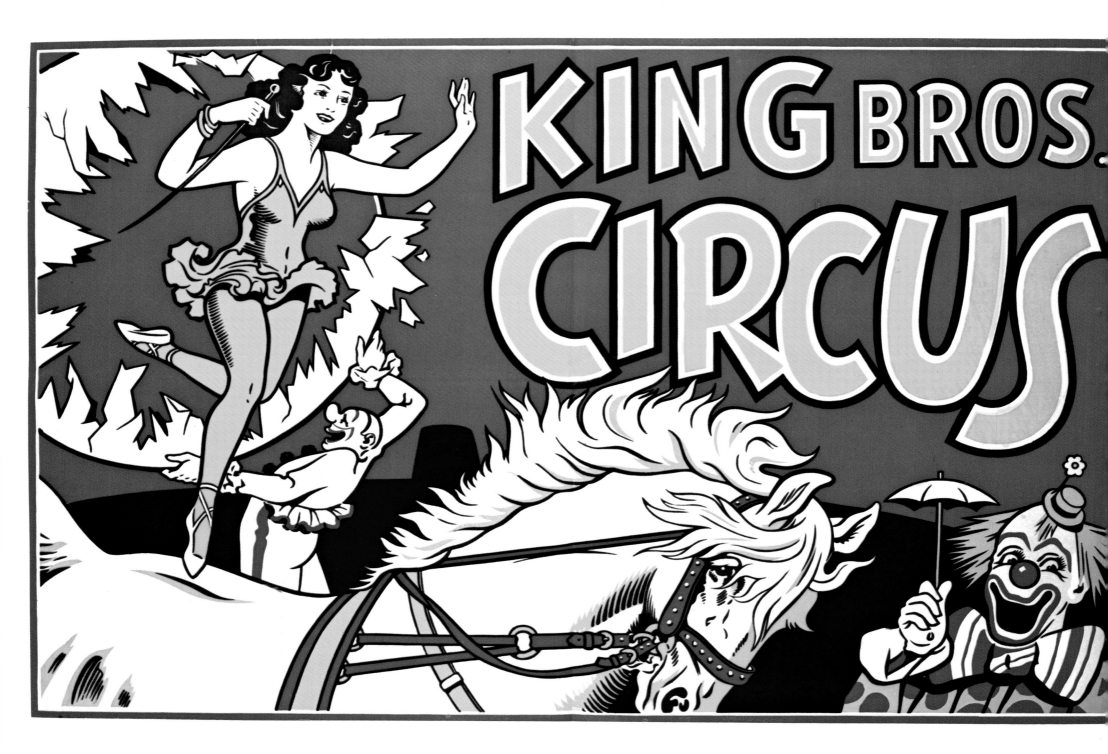

4-Motorized Circuses

The motorized circus picked up the banner for one-day stands and today the tented circus survives largely because of Ford and Chevrolet. Valuable new titles have been brought on the scene by gasoline, new traditions have been developed, great performances have been produced by truck circuses. But the going has been especially difficult.

When circusing switched from wagons to trains showmen boasted that the circus was being upgraded. But the changeover from railroads to trucks was a retrograde movement. In only a few cases did the old titles survive such a transfer or even attempt it. Instead, while the railroad shows were collapsing in tragedy, truck shows began to grow into the void. The old titles were cut off and new ones were built slowly.

Those long-term wagon showmen who had not converted to rails struggled into the 1920's and, reluctantly or not, found they must accept the motor age. Thus, long established shows such as Andrew Downie's, the Mighty Haag and Orton Bros. evolved into truck circuses. Meanwhile, a new breed of circus appeared, the truck show through and through. Among these were Russell Bros., Barnett Bros., Tom Mix Circus and Seils-Sterling.

Truck shows in the last of the wagon years for the most part could barely survive, while railroad circuses still succeeded. Just as there had been scores of wagon shows in years gone by and dozens of railroad circuses across the seasons, now there were many motorized circuses, and as with the others, most of the titles flashed but briefly on the public scene and then collapsed in failure. Those that began in second-class status during the railroad age and survived the Depression proved to be pretty sturdy operations.

They inherited advantages and disadvantages from both varieties of predecessors. No longer was the circus dependent upon the whims of railroads and train crews. No longer did the entire circus have to wait until the last and least was loaded before any could move. No longer did showmen growl in frustration as their train waited on a side track for switch engines that were long overdue.

Instead, the truck circus was free to go as it chose, finding not the mud of wagon seasons, but rather concrete highways all across the country. The maneuverability and the power to move great distances were not lost on the truck show. As equipment was improved, jumps of forty to one hundred miles, like those made by railroad shows, were not uncommon. But, in fact, the truck show was an overland operation as had been the wagon circuses, and it was from that element that the new truck shows derived many of their methods of operation. The new breed of overland showmen replaced wagons with semis and straight beds. Now highway routes were well marked and circus agents, instead of putting fence rails across the road, tacked arrows on the phone poles.

The first rumblings of ideas about motorizing circuses began about 1908. But it was 1918 when the Coop & Lent Motorized Circus hit the road and truck circuses became a reality. In those days equipment was far from dependable, but a dozen years made a great difference. Trucks became bigger and more powerful. Circus men learned how to build steering wheel shows and how to adapt the advantages of motor trucks to the peculiarities of circusing.

Opposite: King Bros., with seventy trucks, was probably the largest of the motor shows.

In 1932 Downie Bros. Circus moved on thirty-seven trucks. In the next season Seils-Sterling had thirty-eight, while Barnett Bros. had thirty-five. Russell Bros. had twenty-four trucks in 1941, and Lewis Bros. moved on twenty-five. Wallace Bros. Circus was a big one, with forty-six trucks in 1943. Mills Bros. had twenty-five trucks in 1947 and thirty-nine trucks in 1953, probably the peak of truck show operation.

The Tom Mix Circus, moving on sixty-five trucks, eased into the big time by playing Washington, Baltimore, Philadelphia and Toronto in 1937 and Chicago the season before. Wallace Bros., in 1942, turned a big corner by trouping seven elephants. King Bros., in 1955, opened with seventy trucks and may have been the largest motor show of them all. But it was the Al G. Kelly and Miller Bros. Circus of the early 1950's which set the pace for perfection and utilization of motorized circus equipment. There were thirty-two show-owned trucks, some sixty gasoline tanks in all, when one counted the power plants and private cars. It carried fourteen elephants, a giraffe, rhino, hippo, tapir and about sixty horses and ponies. There were a deep-freeze truck, restroom trailer, rolling wardrobe department and two giant spools upon which the canvas was reeled mechanically. Although motorized, the Kelly-Miller show carried six baggage horses and sent this hitch downtown with a wagon each day. It played small towns with heavy billing and presented a friendly attitude to the public. Kelly-Miller then made money while others lost, and had a long list of towns that gave it full houses.

While Kelly-Miller and the others carried a cookhouse, another refinement had come to trouping. There were no more wet nights in open buggies, no oppressively hot sleeping cars. Instead, truck showmen lived comfortably with their families in palatial house trailers. Many enjoyed meals family-style at home in trailers instead of at a cookhouse.

The new daily routine for one-day stands was a far cry from the demanding days of pioneer shows. Yet it still required the trouper's indomitable spirit. In some cases truck shows moved as soon as they were loaded after the night performance. In other instances

After several earlier, experimental truck shows had laid the groundwork, Andrew Downie in 1926 began his Downie Bros. Circus, a "second generation" truck show with new ideas. He mounted an air calliope in one of its trucks {above left} and its clown band on another. Note the special body the show constructed on the truck chassis.

On truck shows, large vans carry elephants, horses, camels and ponies. The wrinkled, unpainted front end of this Clyde Beatty-Cole Bros. Circus truck is undoubtedly due to the driver having missed an indicated turn and attempted to pass under a low bridge or trestle.

the show remained on the old lot until dawn of the new day and then made its jump. Eastern shows favored the night moves, and Western shows tended to move the next day. In the one case the dining department truck departed about seven p.m. and generally was set up on the new lot before its crew turned in. By the other operation the cookhouse stayed back with the show so as to serve coffee to drivers before making the move.

In either case breakfast was served on the new lot. Sometimes a truck called the flying squadron was dispatched to the new town early with a duplicate set of stakes so that the first work toward setting up the big top could be accomplished before the bulk of the show arrived in the new town.

In truck show operation, the twenty-four-hour man inherited the job of marking the road. On the afternoon before, he would make the drive to the new town, stopping periodically to place arrows on phone poles as guides to the drivers who would follow him. Initially such arrows were made of chalk, but later the poster printers supplied shows with printed arrows, and these were tacked up to guide the convoy. The twenty-four-hour man also checked the

Left: In 1936 the Tom Mix truck circus looked like this: compact, neat and attractive. The show itself, featuring Tom Mix and his horse, Tony, was appealing and very successful.

The majority of truck shows painted their vehicles in striking colors and designs to attract attention. This fine looking group of trucks {below and opposite} is winding up its parade, where it made a favorable impression on the towners who saw it.

possibility of detours, low bridges and other complications that could stall the move.

Only the earliest of truck shows tried to move in anything approximating a formal convoy. Generally, drivers started as they were ready and, in deference to traffic regulations and other motorists, they tried not to operate their trucks in a tight file. Some shows trouped a tank truck and bought gasoline wholesale, then delivered it to their own vehicles. Others filled their tanks from commercial trucks which came to the lot. For long jumps the twenty-four-hour man arranged for gas stops and each truck in turn stopped at the same station to refuel.

Bringing up the rear in any truck show move was the mechanic. Sometimes his operation consisted of a tool chest and truckload of spare tires. Best such operation was the Kelly-Miller mechanic's truck which was fitted with winches in case a show vehicle went off the road. Its mechanics were fully equipped to maintain the fleet of trucks, even to replacing burned out motors, an affliction that plagued many truck shows which had to entrust expensive rigs in demanding terrain to inexperienced drivers.

Rail show wagons such as stake drivers, ticket offices, power plants and cookhouses found their counterpart in the semitrailers of truck shows. Big vans also substituted for the larger stock cars, carrying elephants, horses, camels and ponies. Circuses had experimented during the 1920's with wagons which unfolded to become grandstands and others which mounted huge spools for loading canvas. But these ideas were not particularly successful until revived and modified by the truck showmen. Kelly-Miller Circus people devised the canvas spool truck and overcame the difficulties that had marked the rail show experiment in the same field. A principal difference was that the horse-drawn wagon spool drew the canvas across the ground and toward the wagon, whereas the motorized spool moved itself to or from the canvas, unreeling or reeling as it went. Kelly-Miller introduced the spool truck in 1946, and year by year more shows converted to this equipment until virtually every tented circus spooled its canvas.

During the second half of the 1950's nearly every motorized circus developed or acquired some form of retractable mechanical seat wagon. These and canvas spools were highly desirable as labor-saving devices. No longer was cheap labor available in quantity enough to assure building the circus seats in time each day. Hunt Bros., Mills Bros., Kelly-Miller, King Bros. and Clyde Beatty were among those who came up with various models of seat wagons.

Circus viewers for years had marveled at circus efficiency and ingenuity. They remarked about the inventiveness of circus men and cited the automatic stake driver as evidence of amazing mechanization. The fact is, however, that the mechanical stake driver dated back to 1903 and there was little difference between the rail show's operation then and in 1943, except that tractors had replaced horses.

But in the decade between 1946 and 1956 the motorized shows evidenced a great spurt of inventiveness and put into use highly original kinds of equipment which eased the demands on their time and manpower. Without them the one-day stands of tented circuses could not have been continued.

The switchover was difficult for truck shows. Their humble origins still showed while there were several rail shows to comprise the big time. Even the public thought twice about whether a truck show could be worth the price of admission and whether it wouldn't be wiser to wait on the chance a rail show might come their way.

In the time of Russell Bros., Tom Mix and Seils-Sterling, the truck show had to battle for every atom of prestige and recognition that it got. Then with fewer rail shows and with an upsurge among indoor circuses playing longer stands under local auspices at municipal arenas, the truck show business was no longer considered second rate.

Beatty, one of the all-time circus greats, rose from cage boy to circus owner.

The only difference between this 1969 cookhouse {right} and the much earlier one shown on page 135 is that the food is cooked in a truck rather than a tent. In a sense, the semitrailer {below} is no different from the railroad car on a circus: not an inch of space remains unused.

Above: As time went on, trucks became bigger and more powerful. Circus men learned how to build steering wheel shows and how to adapt the advantages of motor trucks to the peculiarities of circusing.

Almost imperceptibly the attitude of troupers and towners alike changed in regard to motor truck circuses. Now they were worthy places for big-name performers to appear. Now they were the practitioners and protectors of tent show tradition. Now they were the owners of some of the biggest elephant herds and the source of other animal acts that indoor shows might book in the winter. Train circus troupers once looked down their noses at the motorized outfits which inherited the earlier name of mud show. Now, if those people were to stay with their profession, they would have to join the truck shows. Hastening to work for motorized shows were many performers with rail show credits. Once there, they found this branch of circus business inhabited by many managers and bosses with rail show backgrounds, and among them also were the few remaining veterans of old wagon show days.

The motor show lot is that strange world where a big Mack tractor with a forty-foot Fruehauf trailer still is dubbed a wagon. It is here that a twenty-four-hour agent armed with a staple gun and pack of printed arrows says he's going to "rail the road," although rail fences have been gone for more than half a century. It is here that elephants are used to nudge vehicles out of the mud and where troupers will battle muddy lots all day and hilly roads all night in order to keep the show on the road.

For here is the last stand of the wondrous one-day stand.

Opposite: Contrary to this artist's conception, zebras were extremely difficult to train and rarely performed in the ring.

5-Wagons Roll

As the greater world turns, the circus world rolls. Everything is on wheels, and everything is ready to move. If it is any less, it is not circus. In no category of vehicles is there a greater variety of specialized contraptions than there is on the circus. Pantechnicons to Pullman cars, ice wagons to airplanes — no one has a greater or stranger roster of vehicles than the circus.

Motorized or horse-drawn, they all are called wagons by show people. Some are unique and some are not, but all are practical. Some are rare or notable because of their odd uses or strange cargos. Others come to mention because they take some ordinary procedure and turn it into a fully portable version.

Show wagons for special uses are in addition and in contrast to those ordinary box wagons or flatbeds utilized for moving more or less ordinary loads. Those squared off wagons to carry seat planks or show props or rolls of canvas can be considered just so many more ordinary wagons, albeit the blend of their loads comprises something unique.

Of particular interest are the specialized wagons. There are those odd vehicles from which stairways unfold, pictorial signs slide out, sides fold down to make walkways, undergear emerges to create a bally stand, and soon one has a pit show. This can contain snakes or chimpanzees or a wild man from Borneo. Customers pay the price and walk through the structure to see the oddity inside. Few realize how readily this outfit converts from show building to roadable truck.

Other circus wagons contain generator units for electrical power or offices for ticket sellers and circus managers. When under canvas the Ringling-Barnum circus included wagon No. 6, devoted entirely to a self-contained dishwasher unit. Two twenty-eight-foot wagons were the donnikers, or rolling restrooms. A few of the bigger railroad circuses included garage wagons. These usually were low with small wheels and bulky boxy bodies to contain John Ringling's Pierce-Arrow or the featured vehicle of Hagenbeck-Wallace's Chevrolet exhibit. Specialists in material handling and containerization will recognize that it was better for the circus to deal entirely with containers similar to one another. So the horse-drawn circus carried its automobiles in garage wagons.

Once loaded, there was no need to find an automobile driver; instead, the package could be loaded in the usual way developed for all the other wagons.

For more than sixty-five years circuses have used vehicles equipped with from one to three small pile drivers. These are used to drive tent stakes, and the three-way pile drivers clustered these stakes in exactly the right positions. Of course, circus efficiency dictated that the stakes themselves were carried on this wagon — no need to go elsewhere for a supply.

At the cookhouse again, Ringling-Barnum had two wagons given over to giant ranges where about 4,000 meals a day were prepared. These replaced an earlier circus version which merely loaded coal ranges into a box wagon. Many of the smaller circuses built rolling kitchens in semitrailer shape so they could begin their cooking immediately upon arrival at the new town. There was no wait for roustabouts to put up tents and tables and unload stoves.

No wagons were more specialized or utilitarian than circus canvas and seat wagons. There were many versions of seat wagons, differing in detail, but each unfolded, winched upward or expanded outward to create a large section of comfortable seats. Auditorium

Opposite: The Swan bandwagon served with five circuses as well as at Disneyland. {1907}

This wood panel adorned the side of an 1880 Sells Bros. cage wagon. Its graceful design shows the skill and care that were lavished on the décor of parade wagons.

chairs and ballpark bleachers generally stay in place, but circuses needed an efficient way to seat people quickly and then move on to the next town.

Equally special were the canvas spool wagons. Where else are there vehicles with giant reels upon which are rolled the acres of canvas? As with seat wagons, there were both motorized and horse-drawn versions. Either way they comprised some of the most unusual vehicles on wheels.

Accommodation of people drew much attention from circus builders. Before mobile homes were in use, wagon show people lived in the horse-drawn equivalent. Then motorized showmen built bunk cars — perhaps one for the clowns, another for the band, a third for workingmen. Such shows as Rogers Bros. and James Bros. trouped trucks which contained hospitality rooms for the accommodation and entertainment of officials from sponsoring organizations. Many motorized shows created their own equivalent of the railroad circus pie car, where employees could gather for

relaxation and sociability after the day's work was done.

While circus bunk trucks never were renowned for luxury, best of the lot probably is one built for Ringling and used mostly by the Clyde Beatty-Cole Bros. Circus as a dormitory van. Most extensive was the fleet of thirty-five-foot seat wagons carried by Ringling-Barnum to supply ten thousand seats. Extra-long pole wagons were one of the most utilitarian vehicles on any circus. Ringling's No. 43 pole wagon carried the sixty-foot center poles. The Tom Mix Circus pole wagon is recalled for its simplicity; a single pipe-like beam connected the towing tractor to the relatively distant bogey of trailer wheels.

Traveling ahead of shows were bill cars, the advertising department's rail or highway vehicles. These contained not only the

Opposite: The Lion and Mirror bandwagon began its career with Ringling Bros. in 1894.

176

Above: The sunburst wheels of this cage wagon, along with its mates, helped to create a kaleidoscopic effect as the big wagons rolled down the street.

Opposite: Columbia displays a setback design peculiar to a few Ringling bandwagons. {1897}

Above left: The America wagon, as it looked in 1937, was an ornate addition to Cole Bros. parades. A steam calliope was later built into the wagon.

Above right: Wood statues frequently decorated the wagons. This Adam Forepaugh wagon from the 1880's has six lovely ladies, one on each corner and one on each side.

Right: A wagon's motif was often taken from a foreign country. Typically, the top riders on the Russia tableau are dressed in the style of the country they represent.

180

storage bins for tons of posters but also work space for those who added date strips to the pictorials. There were sleeping quarters for the billposters and even a steam-heated vat for cooking their own paste. The railroad versions included a galley where billposters were fed, and their compact self-contained world might also have aboard a horse and buggy, a press agent's office, or a calliope instrument and stereopticon for advertising the circus.

Among the modern motorized shows none was better equipped than Al G. Kelly & Miller Bros. There were the usual vans for elephants and horses as well as a circus version of the tank truck to exhibit the hippo. One cage wagon combined the quarters of a polar bear with a display for refrigerators. The Kelly-Miller deep freeze truck didn't differ too greatly from the ordinary refrigerator van, but this circus unit made it possible to carry stocks of meat for both menagerie animals and people. Moreover, the refrigeration created distilled water, and this by-product was utilized by the concession department. Health officers said the circus water was more pure than that in many towns it visited.

The principal owner of the Kelly-Miller Circus lived in a three-room apartment, having all the comforts of home inside and the appearance of an ordinary semitrailer outside. The show's novel wardrobe truck had side panels which folded downward to create walkways alongside built-in closets. The center of the truck contained properties, including a clown car and other large items. One of the show's cage trucks had the ordinary bars on one side but van doors on the other. When it came time to move, half of the cage floor in each den folded upward, thus confining the small animal to half his daytime space. This created loading area all along the left side of the trailer and Kelly-Miller filled this with camels and other lead stock.

A tow truck is not adequate for the maintenance needs of a circus convoy, so Kelly-Miller had a fully equipped mechanic's shop built onto a semitrailer. If a truck broke down en route, this rig brought it in. On the show grounds, while others were concerned with performances, the mechanic was preparing for the next day's jump. His equipment was so complete he could virtually rebuild a truck or replace a motor. His unit was equipped with power winches designed to pull wayward circus trucks out of highway ditches and onto roads again. It got additional use in helping to free the circus from muddy lots.

A gilded Cinderella graciously accepts her slipper from the handsome Prince. Seven fairy tale floats were built for Barnum & Bailey in the 1880's; this charming float is one of the three survivors.

Above: The laughing mermaid on Five Graces bandwagon apparently has little diffi-culty in supporting the huge driver's seat. The wagon, built by Fielding for Adam Forepaugh in 1878, had the distinction of touring Europe with Barnum & Bailey.

One of the earliest multi-purpose wagons was on Cooper & Bailey Circus of 1879, when the steam boiler on a single wagon was used to power both the calliope and a pioneer electric dynamo. At one point the Buffalo Bill Show carried its own soda water wagon, carbonating its own water and making its own soda pop.

The finest things on circus wheels were the parade wagons.

These were the work of craftsmen in such shops as the Bode Wagon Works of Cincinnati; Sullivan & Eagles at Peru, Indiana; Moeller Bros. of Baraboo, Wisconsin; the Sebastian Wagon Works of New York; and the Beggs Wagon Co. of Kansas City. Connoisseurs can distinguish between the work of wagon builders as quickly as they can tell a Ford from a Chevrolet.

Bandwagons were the princes of parades and held the honored spot at the front. Masterpieces in this category include the Lion and Mirror bandwagon. It saw service first with the Forepaugh show where it was called St. George and the Dragon. The rising Ringlings bought it and their cousins, the Moeller Bros., converted it into the form by which it is best known. It was first used on Ringling Bros. in 1894 and now is at the Circus World Museum at Baraboo, Wisconsin.

The graceful Swan bandwagon was built by the Moellers and saw service with Ringling Bros., Forepaugh-Sells, Barnum & Bailey, Christy Bros., Ken Maynard and Disneyland. A favorite wagon among many connoisseurs is the Columbus-John Smith bandwagon, built by Sebastian for Pawnee Bill's Wild West Show in 1904. Later it was with the Mighty Haag Railroad Show and 101 Ranch Wild West. Making it especially unique is the fact that its wood carvings depict a different scene on each side — Pocahontas rescuing John Smith in one instance, Columbus landing in the New World in the other. Both the Swan and Columbus-John Smith wagons are also at the Circus World Museum.

The Five Graces bandwagon was built in 1878 by the Fielding Wagon Works for Adam Forepaugh. With even more artistic lines than most bandwagons, this one also had the distinction of touring Europe with Barnum & Bailey. Like many, it was with Forepaugh-Sells, Ringling and Ringling-Barnum. In 1934 it made an appearance with Hagenbeck-Wallace, and it now rests at the Museum of the American Circus at Sarasota, Florida. A few blocks away, at the privately owned Circus Hall of Fame, is the giant Two Hemispheres bandwagon. It was constructed by Sebastian for Barnum & Bailey in 1903 and later Ringling sold it to Robbins

Opposite: France is the sole survivor of a series of sixteen tableau wagons constructed for the short-lived United States Motorized Circus of 1919.

A fiery dragon completes the design on an 1880 Sells Bros. cage wagon. The gorgeous bas-relief carvings were usually gilded and placed on a brilliant background.

Both of these figures have evidently received a face lifting. These damaged carvings were crudely refashioned at winter quarters, but usually such work was done by skilled artisans.

Bros. Circus. It, too, is different on each side, since one shows wood carvings of the Eastern Hemisphere and one of the West. This is the biggest of all bandwagons, measuring 28 feet long, nearly 8 feet wide and 10-1/2 feet high.

Columbia bandwagon still shows a unique setback design peculiar to a few Ringling Bros. wagons. Its peregrinations took it from Ringling to Barnum & Bailey back to Ringling-Barnum, then to Christy and on to Cole Bros. Circus. It was the first wagon acquired by the Circus World Museum.

Among other principal bandwagons was the United States bandwagon built by Bode for Ringling Bros. in 1903, used until 1920 and then allowed to rot away at winter quarters. The John Robinson Circus featured its Golden Peacock bandwagon of unusual bird-shaped design. The Great Wallace Circus had an outstanding canopy bandwagon, lost in a 1917 wreck and replaced by a Bode product, the Carl Hagenbeck bandwagon, which was another of first-class design. The little Gentry Bros. Dog & Pony Show earned a permanent place in show wagon history by building twins. In order to equip two identical units of the Gentry operation, Sullivan & Eagles built a pair of identical bandwagons, a matching pair of ticket wagons and two carbon copy calliopes. These enjoyed the fine line of Sullivan & Eagles craftsmanship and delicate carvings. One of the ticket wagons survives at the San Antonio Public Library and one of the calliopes continues in modified form as a semitrailer truck operated by a movie chain.

Often parade wagons were built in a series and typical was the Cottage Cage series of the John Robinson Circus. Each of the wagons in this series had a different design of cottage-style roof, making them quite distinctive among all circus cages. The Barnum & Bailey show of 1883 and thereafter produced a series of twelve beautiful cages with statue corners. One survives in modified form and one survives in near original form, both at the Circus World Museum. Hagenbeck-Wallace Circus of the middle 1920's produced another distinctive series of cage wagons, some of which survive today.

Similarly, there were series of circus tableau wagons, those highly decorative vehicles which were features in the body of any principal circus parade. An outstanding series of tableaux was built by the Bode firm for the United States Motorized Circus of 1919. Sixteen bodies were built and mounted on trucks. Each of these represented a nation and included were the United States, Great Britain,

Beautiful scroll work embellishes a Wallace calliope {above} and the "B" for Barnum on Two Hemispheres wagon {right}. Both wagons are well over sixty years old.

Raucous, out of tune and belching black smoke, this lumbering calliope {pronounced kăl'-ee-ōp by circus people} was the grand finale of the Ringling parade.

Belgium, France, China, Panama, Africa, India, Persia and others.

The U. S. Motorized Circus did not last, but its parade tableaux did. After the failure of the circus, these tableau sides were removed from trucks and several of them found their way in 1925 to Robbins Bros. Circus. Some parade wagons were converted into truck bodies in their later years but only this series went in the other direction. The former truck parts were used as sides for new parade wagons with the Robbins show. These attractive units appeared next on Cole Bros. Circus, but most were lost in a fire and today the only survivor is France, at the Circus World Museum at Baraboo.

The greatest parade ever presented by a commercial circus was the Barnum & Bailey edition of 1903 to commemorate the show's return from five years in Europe. Heading the parade was the new Two Hemispheres bandwagon. In the lineup along with cages, mounted people and other features were twelve new parade wagons, certainly among the most specialized vehicles in the entire history of transportation. These were especially unique in that they served virtually no utilitarian purpose and could be used only as tableaux or floats in the street parade. The wagon boxes were only of half or two-thirds height and were topped by statues and other designs. Included were those called Funny Folks, Fairy Tales, Egypt, Phoenician Gallery, Siam and Balkis, plus Our Country with a depiction of hero Presidents. Eighth was the Golden Age of Chivalry, which featured a giant green dragon with two heads, now at Baraboo.

An additional feature in the 1903 parade were the so-called Continent wagons. During their European tour, Barnum & Bailey executives had become aware of the Prince Albert Memorial at London. This large statue complex included at each of its outer corners a symbolic stone sculpture representing one of the continents. Barnum & Bailey reproduced these continental groupings in wood carvings and put them onto otherwise half-height tableaux wagons that featured carved busts to represent the various tribes, peoples and nations of the continents. Some portion of each unit in this four-wagon series survives today. Some top carvings from Europe are at the Smithsonian Institution while the Ford Museum at Dearborn owns a portion of the Africa carvings. Both Asia and America were converted into full-height wagons, less the top statuary, and were used in that form by Christy Bros. and Cole Bros., and both are now at the Circus World Museum. America has taken on its third configuration, that of a steam calliope.

Circus parade wagons were decorated with gorgeous wood carved bas-relief, often gilded in gold leaf and rolling on sunburst wheels. Circus baggage wagons had to be sturdy enough to carry their weighty loads and still stand up under the brutal treatment they received when combinations of elephants and several eight-horse teams sought to yank them out of the bottomless mud of soft circus lots. Strange of design and cargo, circus wagons, by their custom design, extraordinary strength, and attractive appearance, contributed greatly to the success of traveling shows.

Opposite: Asia was originally a Continent wagon featured in Barnum & Bailey's 1903 parade.

6-The Street Parade

A major feature which all circuses had in common regardless of how they moved was the street parade. This midday mounting of all the show's performing features harked back to the earliest origins of show business. Medieval minstrels and Parisian buskers moved through the streets to attract an audience. Roving actors made themselves visible to the townsfolk even if they didn't formally promenade. Tented troupes of "Uncle Tom's Cabin" made street marches, with cages of bloodhounds and slave market floats. American minstrel shows marched through their town of the day in a parade they called "The 11:45." Toreadors and matadors parade before the bullfight and movies show coming attractions.

Like some of the other versions, the circus parade originated through the arrival of the troupe in town. They bowed and ballyhooed as they found their way into the community. Shows made these entries increasingly more elaborate and townspeople came to look for them, so that soon it was more than the mere entrance. Soon the circus company went direct to its lot and made more elaborate preparations for the street march.

In one early form a clown on a mule wended his way to the town square and reminded the folks gathered there that the circus performance awaited. Next, a showman sent a band to town on the same mission and soon that band traveled either aboard an elephant or in a wagon more ornate than any villager yet had seen.

The whole idea of the parade soon was for the circus to show its wares. Performers, horses, cages and elephants were in the lineup. The idea was for potential customers to follow the parade back to the show grounds, and in this they were successful. Once on the lot the townspeople were enchanted into buying tickets for the side-show and main performance. Street parades became a measure of a show's quality and a badge indicating its size. Small shows tried mightily to line up as many wagons and mounted people as possible. Big shows talked of mile-long processions reminiscent of the Mardi Gras and as glittering as a coronation. At one point this might have approached actuality. The biggest circuses — Barnum & Bailey, Ringling Bros., Forepaugh-Sells and others — competed fiercely in the parade department and spent freely to produce elaborate floats, tableau wagons, gorgeous bandwagons, unbelievable arrays of spangled costumes for a hundred mounted people, brilliant uniforms for a half-dozen bands and an array of mechanical music makers that boggled the mind.

Typically, the show owner or his high lieutenant led off the parade with a span of fine horses hitched to a shiny buggy. Behind him came mounted trumpeters in medieval costumes, and in each block along the route they wheeled their horses around and sounded their silver trumpets in a mighty fanfare. Sturdy Percheron horses came two by two around the corner until their total of ten or twelve or twenty-four or even forty had brought into view the Number One bandwagon. Able drivers in red coats and African sun helmets or military caps controlled every move of the matched team as it swung around the corner and into Main Street.

The bandwagon and every circus vehicle behind it turned on

Opposite: Two Hemispheres {right} is the largest of all bandwagons. {1909}

The circus brought the splendor of a larger world to the doorstep of every small town and village in America. Ringling Bros. paraded its magnificence before the townspeople of Black River Falls, Wisconsin, in 1892.

wheels which achieved a sunburst effect by painting a wooden webbing between the spokes with shades of yellow, orange and red. The wagon sides were encrusted with wood-carved gingerbread depicting monsters and goddesses from mythology or gold-leafed scrolls. Atop the wagon was the show's circus band and it blasted away with tunes such as "Barnum & Bailey's Favorite," "Ringling's Triumphant Entry," "Gentry Triumphant Entry" or any of a hundred other rousing circus marches.

Mounted people in sixes and eights were interspersed among the various parade wagons that followed. Some wore suits of armor, others dressed as Arabs or Royal Canadian Mounted Police. The body of the street parade included the show's collection of cage wagons, each drawn by four or more Percheron horses. These teams, which earlier in the day had moved the circus baggage wagons, now carried plumes and were bedecked in brass trimmings and monogrammed harness. Sometimes sideboards were in place on a cage and town boys on the curbstone could only guess about what monster it might contain. Other shows did not wait for imagination but instead primed the curiosity by proclaiming in red letters that this cage contained Royal Bengal tigers, racing ostriches or deadly reptiles. Somewhere back in the procession the biggest den of all was open to view and inside was the show's pride of lions. Sitting inside with the wild animals was the fearless circus trainer. As an alternate, advance newspaper advertising would have declared the parade would include "a living lion loose in the streets." This proved to be not so frightening a prospect as had been imagined. A sleepy lion was chained to the top of a tableau wagon and a circus girl kept it company. The fact remained that townspeople felt a chill upon realizing that nothing stood between them and the king of beasts.

Interspersed among the cages and other features of the parade were tableau wagons. These wood-carved floats depicted nations of the world, more mythology, or nursery rhymes and fairy tales. Atop one was the circus sideshow band featuring Negro musicians well-versed in grass roots jazz. Another tableau transported the clown band and riding on top were eight or ten clowns, many of whom could play instruments. Sometimes to fill out, a key instrument and its player were borrowed from the main circus band. Elsewhere in the march there might be tableaux with Scottish bagpipers or cowboy bands. Some shows gathered up the offspring of all their performers and fielded a children's band. The Gentry Bros.

*Cleopatra's Barge inspires awe in these New Englanders as it rolls by
in an 1890 preview of Forepaugh's Great Shows.*

The street march became a great advertisement of circus wares.

children's band was mounted on Shetland ponies. That show also introduced a ladies' band, and they rode in a finely carved bandwagon hitched to a team of black and white spotted ponies. In contrast was the big mounted military band of shows like Barnum, Ringling and Robinson. The man with a copper kettledrum mounted on each side of his horse raised his arms to spin the drumsticks masterfully between each battering of the drumheads.

The clowns brought comedy to each element of the parade. Often there was a clown police patrol wagon which stopped to "arrest" a lad or two in each block and give them a ride of fifty feet or so. Another clown rode the January cart, a stereotyped feature with a mule ready to demonstrate his forceful kicking. Other clowns walked along the parade route and amused the curbstone audience.

A children's section was featured in many bigger parades. Wood-carved floats depicted Bluebeard, Little Red Riding Hood, Cinderella, Mother Goose, the Old Woman in the Shoe, Sinbad and Santa Claus. More Shetland ponies pulled a cage of monkeys, and a couple of circuses featured revolving cages which usually contained exotic birds. Other cages brought the polar bears and hyenas and leopards.

Late in every street march came a long team and an extra-sturdy wagon with wood-carved letters proclaiming the blood-sweating hippopotamus from the River Nile. The hippo was there all right, but at high noon on most such summer days, he preferred the relative cool of his rolling water tank in the floor of the den and townspeople could not tell if his mouth really opened as wide as the posters indicated.

A Wild West contingent was a feature in every circus parade. There were mounted groups of cowboys and cowgirls as well as a retinue of Indians on calico ponies and dragging the double-poled travois. The Indians, resplendent in headdresses and war paint, delighted in startling their audience by cutting loose with a war whoop or so in every block. This section often included a cowboy band and invariably there was a stagecoach or Conestoga wagon pulled by lumbering oxen.

Tradition and stereotyping dictated that after the Wild West came the elephants. Circus men rode the heads of every second elephant,

Campbell Bros. Circus marches down an unpaved main street in 1908 {above};
Gollmar Bros. band, circa 1914, blares on atop the beautiful Mirror bandwagon
{right}; Barnum & Bailey's America tableau is followed by her sister wagon,
Europe, in 1904 {below}. Circuses competed fiercely in the parade department.
The size of the town was of little consequence as each show tried to outdo the other
in producing elaborate floats, brilliant uniforms and an array of spangled costumes.

193

The Walter L. Main band plays a rousing circus march as the troupers wend their way through Ogdensburg, New York, in 1922.

and their superintendent rode a speckled horse alongside the lead elephant. Sometimes one of the beasts carried a pretty passenger in a howdah, or miniature pavilion, on its back and usually there were bejeweled elephant blankets — though sometimes these were reserved for special occasions. On average days the elephants carried painted signs to advertise local merchants. The big round feet of these animals made a constant shuffling sound and this was punctuated by the jangle of their chains. Hoarse-voiced bull men shouted commands intended to sound strange and mystifying to the townspeople but which likely as not proved to be only directions to an elephant named Mary to "move up" or "come on." There was much swinging of bull hooks to punctuate the conversation, but the patient, dependable old elephants seemed to ignore the commands and merely continue to shuffle along.

Behind the littlest elephant, which brought up the rear of the herd, came the hay wagon. This was a circus baggage wagon decorated and disguised with bales of hay to hide the fact that it contained a trampoline. Clowns dressed in rube costumes bounced to great heights from the trampoline; to the people on the sidewalks it seemed that they were jumping in and out of a huge load of hay. This was a hilarious piece in the rural communities where haystacks were commonplace.

After that came the climax and the finale. This was the loudest monster of all. It shook the windows and deafened the ears. It bellowed black smoke that choked the throat and burned the eyes. This was no earthshaking dragon but, rather, the steam calliope. Inside the ornate wagon a calliope player was swathed in a cloud of steam as the thirty-two whistles of his steam-powered mechanical musical monster sounded off. He operated a keyboard which activated a series of tuned whistles, each as big and loud as the one on a firehouse or a steamboat.

Opposite: The parade became an attraction which rivaled the show it advertised. {1892}

The Barnum & Bailey Greatest Show on Earth

AN ENTIRELY NEW, GRAND, STREET PARADE, LED BY A TEAM OF 40 MATCHED HORSES
AND FOLLOWED BY THE GORGEOUS SPECTACLE OF THE RETURN OF COLUMBUS TO BARCELONA.

THE WORLD'S LARGEST, GRANDEST BEST, AMUSEMENT INSTITUTION.

Right: These excited lads are probably plotting how they will escape humdrum school days by running away and joining the circus.

Below right: John Agee leads Ringling-Barnum through downtown Paris, Texas. The parade was always headed by the circus owner or the equestrian director.

Below left: The grandest novelty of all was the mounted band. With their feet, these versatile musicians could manipulate an extra set of reins to direct their horses.

Above left: Circus animals are possibly the most well-traveled animals in the world. Although confined to small quarters, they are kept sleek and well-fed through the expert care of the menagerie crew.

Above right: Sells-Floto ponies pull a glass-sided den containing a varied collection of exotic snakes.

Left: A clown band delights Milwaukeeans with its inimitable music during a Hagenbeck-Wallace parade in the 1920's.

197

"Rain or Shine," the poster said and, like the mail, the parade almost always came through.

It played awful music. It was too loud for comfort and, despite the fact that its manipulator was as much plumber as musician, one never found a calliope with all whistles in tune at one time. The back end of a calliope wagon contained the upright boiler and an attendant kept it stoked with coal or wood so there was plenty of pressure whenever the player decided to render "Over the Waves" or "Go Tell Aunt Rhody." The raucous hoots and toots of the calliope served like the pipes of Pan. Inevitably, people fell in behind it and followed the show to the circus grounds.

The American circus was at its finest in presenting a good parade. One trouble was that they became too good. The parade comprised entertainment enough and some families decided against going to the performance itself. The tail was wagging the dog; the circus was putting time and investment into a feature which itself was an attraction that came to compete with the show it sought to advertise. Ultimately for this and other reasons, circus parades were discontinued. But then they had to be discontinued again and again, for abandoning the circus parade was like quitting cigarettes — one attempt seldom succeeded.

American circus parades began their period of major development when Seth B. Howes brought from England several ornate wagons that looked like gilded wooden wedding cakes. His American competitors soon tried to equal the style and size of the Howes wagons and thereafter circuses were continually building new parade equipment. Many of these remarkably sturdy wagons survive today and can be seen in demonstrations at the Circus World Museum.

The finest parade ever was the 1903 Barnum & Bailey production, and a fortune was spent to create it. Yet only a couple of seasons later the Barnum show tried to eliminate parades. The

Above: The crowds were intrigued by the imposing sight of massive elephants shuffling along single file down their street.

Below: A clown band rode on this beautifully painted wagon. Landscapes or Biblical scenes frequently appeared on the sides of the parade wagons.

The monster at the end of this 1933 Hagenbeck-Wallace parade is a calliope. Like the pipes of Pan, it lured the milling throngs to the circus grounds—only less musically.

march, however, survived for a few more years. Then, after Ringling and Barnum had been combined for a couple of seasons, that show eliminated its parades for good. There was no competition forceful enough to require their making the effort.

Lesser shows, like Sells-Floto, Hagenbeck-Wallace and John Robinson, continued parades into the 1920's when their parent corporation ordered abandonment of the street march. Independent circuses, including Robbins, Christy, 101 Ranch Wild West Show and Gentry Bros., continued to parade and caused the American Circus Corporation to reconsider. Then the Depression wiped out most of the railroad circuses as well as their parades.

The truck shows which followed maintained the tradition of circus parades. Some kept horse-drawn equipment in the transition years. Others painted or decorated their motor trucks and drove them in the parade. Even though interspersed among elephants and cowboys on horseback, trucks never quite transmitted the glamour that horse-drawn bandwagons held. But still they paraded and with success. The bands sat in ornate semitrailers and calliopes were mounted on truck chassis. In the parade of the Tom Mix Circus that Western star's famous horse, Tony, rode aboard a motor truck. And a few years later the Parker and Watts Circus devised a way to attach separate wheels to a semi and thus convert it into a wagon for its horse-drawn parades. Teams pulled its cages and other features. Few circuses between that 1939 edition and the 1950's made any major attempt to parade. Then came King Bros. & Cole Bros. Combined Circus of 1954. It presented a bandwagon and horse-drawn cages, a big hippopotamus truck and a motorized calliope, for what proved to be one of the latest and most successful attempts at revival.

The circus parade became a tradition on its own, a feature within a feature, a part of Americana and a part of show business that aroused recollections and lingered in memories all across the North American continent.

Opposite: The elephants invariably steal the show from their fellow performers. {1908}

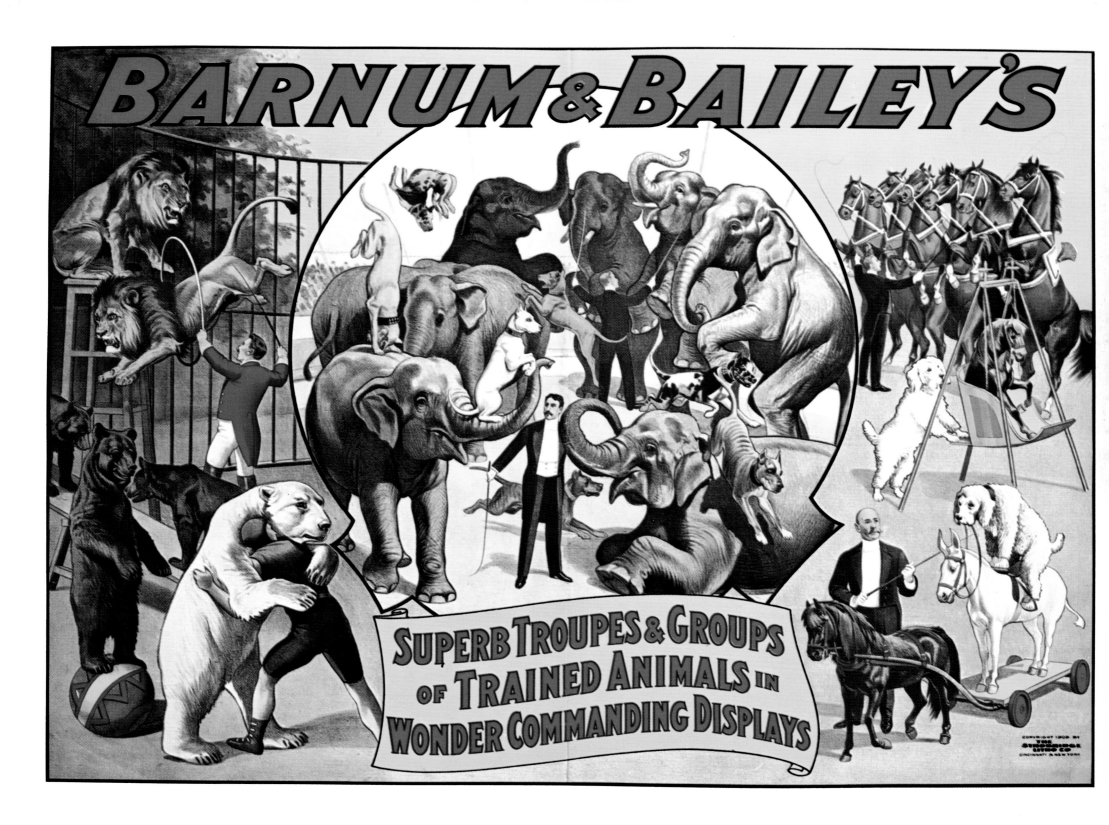

Part IV

THE BIG SHOW UNDER THE BIG TOP

1-"Step Right Up"

Excitement and an air of anticipation permeated the scene as people from the city were joined by those from the village and farms. Together they converged on the circus grounds to become that one-of-a-kind entity — the circus audience.

From a distance eager eyes sought to penetrate the skyline to see the circus. First in view were the tent peaks, with flags, banners and burgees flapping in the breeze. Soon after, one could hear not only the music, but also that intangible undercurrent of sound that marked every circus grounds.

The noise included specifics such as engines and generators and chain-driven trucks. It included oddities such as the roar of the lion and the squeal of an elephant. It included the whistles of circus bosses and the curses of circus hands. But usually all these and more sounds melded together in a compound of tension, excitement and noise comprised of indistinguishable elements.

As one street met another the traffic flowed together, until all were funneled into a single wayfare that brought them onto the circus grounds.

Whether they came by sidewalk, surrey, streetcar or sedan, circus audiences were all alike. Here was a true cross section of any population. Here were the especially young and especially old, the able and the ill, the rich and the poor. Somehow circuses seemed to attract more than their share of the handicapped, the pregnant, the crippled and the strange. Other events in town apparently were not worth the effort, but the once-a-year circus was intriguing enough to attract even those who must make a special effort.

As friends and neighbors met at a circus grounds, they first sounded a strange giggle that evinced not only the underlying sense of excitement, but also some strange sort of embarrassment. If they had met at the hardware store or football game, they would have spoken and moved on, but at the circus they giggled nervously and stated something about as original as, "Well, I see you came to the circus, too."

On every day, until now, this place had been just an ordinary pasture and had caused no interest. But today it was entirely different — no longer the familiar field but a place transformed into strangeness and excitement. Sometimes city show grounds were run over with cinders and rock and weeds. They were rough and dirty. More typical was a muddy lot. During the morning, all the circus wagons had turned off the road at a single entrance and entered the lot, which quickly became a mire. During the morning and again in time for the arrival of the afternoon audience, showmen had dumped bales of straw into that mud. It helped, but still the pedestrians hopped from dry spot to high spot and all too frequently skidded through the mud. But beyond was the circus and that made it all worthwhile.

Opposite: No circus is complete without the fat lady, the midget or bearded woman.

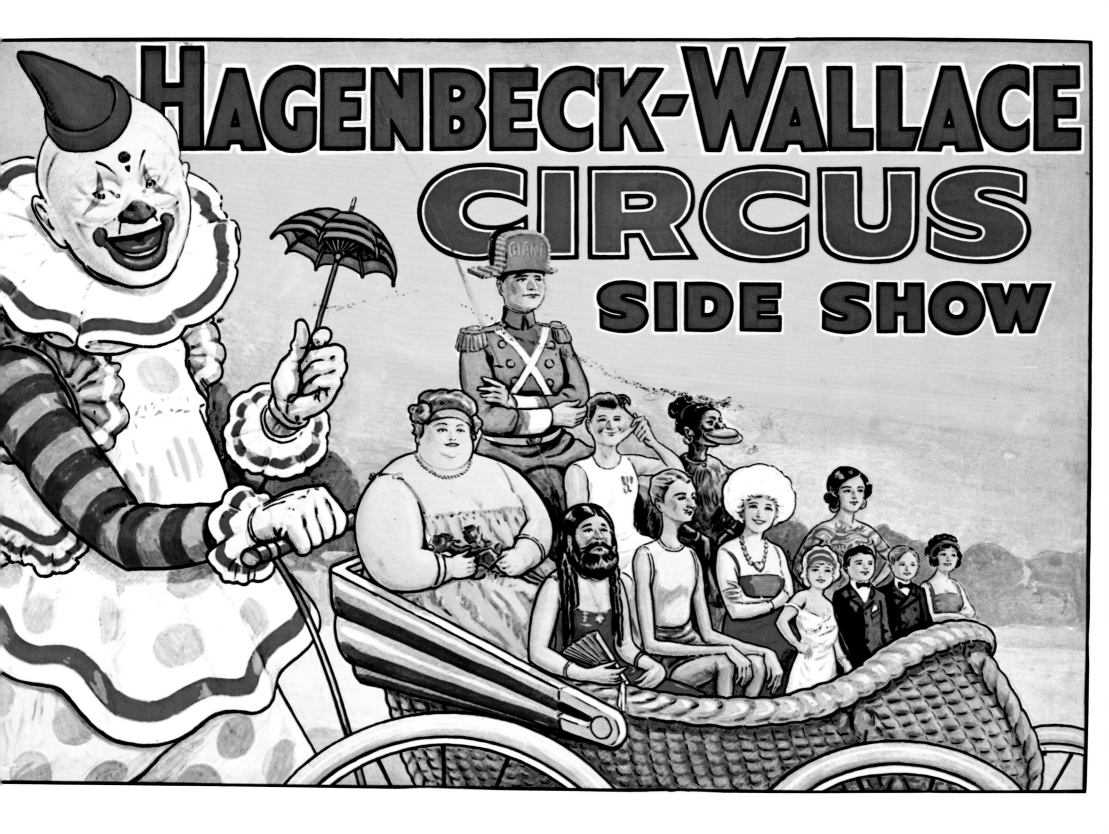

Ideally, the circus grounds were a grassy pasture where the pleasant smell of crushed grass blended with the stranger odors of the circus. There might be old ruts through the grounds, and the more knowledgeable circus buffs remembered those had been made last year by wagons of another circus. Sometimes in seasons long since gone, the midway was paved with wood chips or tanbark or sawdust, but as these materials became more difficult to find and more expensive, circus lot superintendents dispensed with such trimmings.

The layout of a midway was highly standardized. On one side was the sideshow. In front of its tent and bordering the midway was the banner line, that colorful collection of strange paintings depicting the weird exhibits to be found inside. There was a banner showing the Punch and Judy Show, another depicting the Southern Jubilee Minstrels. One might herald a magician and another a trainer of birds. There would be banners for the fat lady, magicians and sword swallowers. There might be Hawaiian dancers or Scottish bagpipers or someone who looked like Popeye or a human that could pass for a frog.

At the main entrance was a bally platform, where free attractions appeared while the sideshow talkers ballyhooed the wonders to be found inside. Usually there was a band made up of Negro musicians standing between the platform and the entrance; this was the justification for the minstrel's banner.

On the platform one of the attractions — perhaps the sword swallower — would perform his act as proof of the advertising and as an enticement to buy a ticket and see the rest. One sideshow talker might also be on that platform, but others were in the ticket boxes up and down the midway. This was the home of the phrase, "Step right up," as the talkers urged their audience to "come in a little closer." Their pitch or spiel was something unique in the annals of public oratory. They capitalized on an interest in the unusual, created a yen to see the weird, and convinced you that it was all there, that the price was right and that plenty of time remained for seeing the sideshow before the circus itself would start. This was accomplished in a highly specialized speech which built to a timely climax and, if successful, brought customers by the dozens to buy tickets.

Inside the sideshow tent there was an elevated platform for each of the attractions. The audience stood first in front of one platform and then at another. An orator directed their attention as he moved along the oval of attractions. He might introduce the fat lady so she could describe her size and then sell her photographs. The favorite sales item of circus sideshow giants was an outsized finger ring. He would show how it fit on his finger, then demonstrate that a half-dollar could be passed through the loop, and finally he would let you know that such a ring could be yours for just a quarter. A Negro dancer joined the band on a larger platform to present what passed for a minstrel show. The orator stepped up on another platform to present the Punch and Judy Show or to become a magician. A "pretty little lady" climbed into an enameled box and it seemed that he sliced her into sections. But then she stepped out unscathed. Chances are she was his wife and she would appear next as caretaker of the trained doves.

Outside on the midway again, the opposite edge was lined with concession stands and ticket wagons. First was a lemonade stand, where large glass tanks of pink or green lemonade were visible. There were castle-like towers made of Cracker Jack boxes and huge wicker baskets containing striped sacks of peanuts. Odors of onions and grease rose from the hot plate where a spatula-wielding attendant hawked his wares. Another stand might offer creamy frozen custard and still another sold cotton candy, that sugar concoction spun into a huge colored ball that melted away to nothing when eaten. If the peanuts were few or the ice cream drippy or the cotton candy sticky, it really did not seem to matter.

At the head of the midway was the novelty stand. This was a huge trunk opened to reveal its inventory of flags and canes and whips and birds on a string. Little kegs were set alongside the trunk to hold added supplies of circus novelties. Out of all this flashy color, surely something was bound to attract the eye of every little tyke that passed the stand. The novelty man was not above placing one of his products into the hand of a six-year-old, knowing full well the child would cry if his prize were taken away. Maybe, just maybe, the parent would conclude he would rather buy the toy whip than hear the tearful wail.

Further down the centerline was a platform where a salesman with an official looking cap accepted the free passes brought to the circus by those who had earned the show's favor. Some offered passes from the press agent. Some were railroad officials with free admissions. Some exhibited lithograph passes, indicating that their barn or shop windows had displayed circus advertising. This majordomo of the midway accepted the passes and awarded tickets in their stead. Honored guests received reserved seats at choice locations. Those with the lithograph passes sometimes found there

The persuasive voice of the sideshow talker draws young and old to his bally stand {left}, and their insatiable curiosity keeps the tents filled {below}.

Whatever their act or deformity, the sideshow attractions were proud of their profession {top}. Ringling's fat girl posed for this gag photo in 1937 {above left}. Jack Earle, also with Ringling that same year, was billed as the tallest man in the world {right}.

was a service charge to be paid and that their seats were in the less desirable bleachers. In the years during and just after each of the World Wars, there also was an admission tax to be paid.

But the great majority of circus goers bought tickets. In with the lineup of concession stands were the two ticket wagons. First, one came to the white wagon where reserved seats were on sale. Customers with little money to spend proceeded a little further down the midway to a red wagon where the general admission tickets were sold. As economic conditions varied from depression to inflation, the price of circus tickets varied, too. Good circuses in the 1920's and 1930's could be seen from general admission seats for fifty cents or seventy-five cents. When a show played remote territory or featured an especially powerful attraction or simply experimented in the wealthier communities, it might charge a dollar for adults and half as much for children. Inflation would increase these prices by two or three times, even seven times.

After waiting his way through the ticket line and paying his money, the customer finally held the priceless tickets in his hand. Now he turned to the crowded midway to find his family and together they moved toward the marquee. Humanity crowded and packed itself closely as it sought a choice spot in front of the main entrance. Now there was time to realize that the sideshow talkers still were at work, that the concessionaires still shouted and that the undercurrent of circus noises continued, paced by the rumble of the generator wagon just off the midway.

Finally the superintendent of the front door let down the chains and the audience could move through the piped entryway of the marquee, surrender its tickets and proceed toward the big show. First there was the menagerie to see, and it was free to ticket holders. One sidestepped the novelty stand in the canvas connectionway that linked the marquee with the menagerie tent. Inside was another big concession stand, but around the edges were the circus cages, each containing a display of animals. Crude attendants in coveralls barked at any townspeople who came too close. Sometimes the flies were unbearable and usually the heat was worse. But again, no one really seemed to notice or complain. The menagerie display varied strictly according to the size of the circus. There might be a single semi trailer divided into three or four dens, each containing a lion or bear or monkeys. Or, there might be a glittering circle of twenty or thirty or fifty brilliantly painted cage wagons. In the recent street parade, most of these same cages were probably closed. But now the side panels were lowered to make

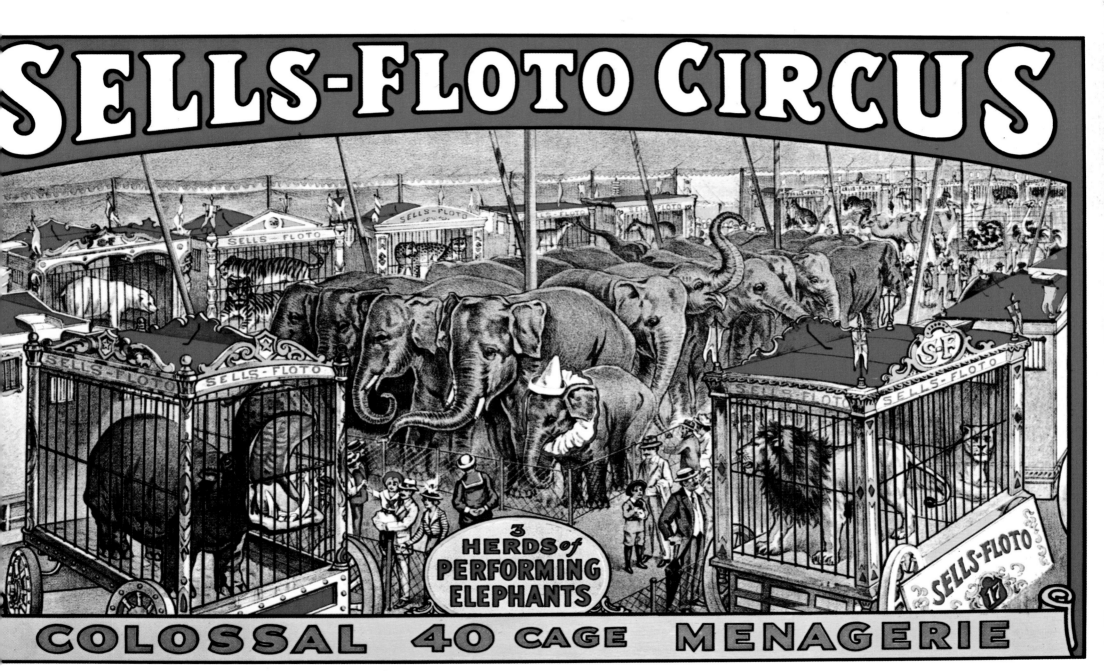

A menagerie of this scope featured a superb collection of wild animals comparable to that of a city zoo. {1920}

Above: The menagerie was as popular as the sideshow. Here circus goers could view and touch strange animals from distant lands.

Right: The playfulness of this sleepy lion belies his ferocity in the steel arena.

208

visible their cargos of tigers and leopards, ocelots and kangaroos, deadly reptiles and laughing hyenas.

Menageries of principal circuses actually were superb collections of wild animals, rivaling those of many zoos. While most cages were made with steel bars, some for birds or smaller animals utilized wire mesh and snake dens had glass sides. Such a super feature as Gargantua the Great, a Ringling gorilla, inhabited an air conditioned cage with plate glass sides. Typical of other special cages was the big one devoted to the hippopotamus. Half of its area was given over to a water tank, and likely as not the hippo was hidden therein. Giraffes were transported in high padded vans, but in the menagerie tall wire enclosures were assembled and the lanky animals were exhibited there.

In addition to the caged animals was the lead stock. This included zebras, camels, sacred oxen and, above all, elephants. Some of the major circuses carried six or eight zebras, occasionally using them as a harnessed team, and often including more than one species in their collection. During the first century of circus operation, camels were a popular feature, but menagerie customers did well to be wary, for camels can kick frontwards and spit with great accuracy. An eternal puzzle was why circuses bothered with sacred cattle or Asian oxen. Perhaps at one time these constituted an interesting attraction, but for the past half-century, few circus goers really cared about these docile beasts which looked too much like the cows in their own country. Perhaps it was because they were inexpensive and easy to feed. Perhaps too many showmen were not able to distinguish between the interesting and the ordinary among animals. In any case, these odd species of cattle were the most overlooked element of any menagerie.

It was a different story, however, with the elephants. They were the favorite of circus goers. In the menagerie the circus lined its elephants along the edge or down the middle. A peanut stand was close by so parents and children could feed the elephants, surely one of the great thrills of childhood, and an astounding opportunity for participation not only then, in the horse and buggy age, but now also, in a time when most chances for touching are filtered away through a television tube. Circus elephants, their hind legs chained to steel stakes, stretched forward to accept the peanuts. The swaying line of elephants might total a dozen or two, even three and, rarely, as many as four dozen in the herd of a single circus. Smaller shows, of course, exhibited only one or three or five elephants.

The delicate giraffe is rarely trained to perform, and is infrequently seen in the circus menagerie.

Latecomers who hastened through the menagerie tent noted that the elephants were draped with plush blankets, and attendants were slipping into red coats. For it was nearly time to start the main performance. Moving from the menagerie tent toward the big top, ticket holders met with more salesmen. One offered chameleons, tiny little lizards, safety-pinned to a green felt board. Purchasers could pin them to their lapel or take them home in a little box, there to terrorize sisters and mothers. Next came the program salesman. At the entrance to the big top itself, he declared that everyone needed a copy of his magazine of circus stories and details of the circus performance.

Now, again, the circus goer faced up to the question of seats. Upon entering the big top he was awed by its immensity. Overhead was the clutter of aerial rigging. Down the center the four main poles alternated with the three rings. At the sides of the oval tent were the reserved seats made up of individual folding chairs on wooden platforms and counting twelve or fifteen rows, each higher than its predecessor. Ushers stood at the base of each section and at the back of each was a huge letter sign designating the section as A, B, C, etc. Holders of the more expensive reserved seat tickets were ushered straight to their chairs on the front, or long side, of the big top. The back side of the reserved seats section was divided and consequently shortened by the placement of the bandstand, just back of the center ring. On each side were the entrances through which performers soon would come. At each rounded end of the tent were the "blues," those bleachers with narrow seat planks assembled in combinations of eight or ten or sixteen rows.

Usually the audience entered at one end of the tent and was directed to walk to the other. Those blues closest to the entrance were roped off. This meant that all holders of general admission seats must walk the full length of the tent, passing those sections of reserved seats and finding along the way two or three more salesmen who could convert their ticket into the reserved variety for an additional payment. On a few circuses the entrance itself was deliberately narrow and a ticket salesman was stationed there. More than a few patrons surmised that another ticket was necessary and reached into their purse for the additional price. Actually, of course, no additional purchase was necessary for anyone. Those with more expensive tickets were already entitled to reserved seats;

those with general admission tickets could proceed without further charge to the blues.

If one chose to sit in the bleachers and successfully passed the lineup of several ticket salesmen along the hippodrome track, he finally reached the far end of the tent where he occupied the seat of his choice. At those C-shaped bleachers the early-comers took the outside edges to be closest to reserved seat locations; latecomers filled in the far end. Occupying the blues, however, called for at least another point of circus-going expertise. After choosing where he would sit, the occupant also attempted to lay claim to the seat board in front of him. The blues usually had no footrest. Thus, as he sat on the eight-inch board he had the choice of placing his feet on the board ahead of him or dangling his legs below. For a two-hour circus, the latter could become uncomfortable. In fact, toward the end of the performance everyone in the blues was likely to be squirming and even the small folding chairs of reserved sections left something to be desired.

If the audience placed no particular demand upon the capacity of the blues, there was no problem. But the circus was determined to pack into the tent everyone who paid the price of admission. If the size of the crowd were such that all the seats were needed, then there was to be a row of people on each board and no room for feet. Even after a crowd became established on a two-row format, the circus was prepared to make a change before the show could start. In this case, a clown appeared and through humor and cleverness cajoled the audience into moving upwards and backwards to make room for more of their fellow townspeople. This process, called "raising the blues," could literally double the capacity. If one chanced to become impatient or uncomfortable, he was free to seek out those friendly ticket salesmen on the hippodrome track who would still have reserved seat tickets available. The next time one went to the circus, he might forget this whole process and again buy the low priced seats at the red wagon. However, if he remembered and could afford the difference, he was likely to patronize the white wagon with reserved tickets, when next he visited a midway.

Opposite: The phrase "step right up" originated with the sideshow talkers. {1892}

The Barnum & Bailey Greatest Show on Earth

GROUP OF NATURE'S MOST GIGANTIC, CURIOUS AND DIMINUTIVE LIVING SPECIMENS.

WONDERFUL HAIRLESS MARE WHOSE GLOSSY BODY IS DESTITUTE OF EVEN A SINGLE HAIR.

MOST WONDERFUL FREAK OF NATURE. A FINE HEALTHY **STEER** OF ORDINARY SIZE AND WEIGHT, BUT CURIOUSLY ENDOWED WITH 3 PERFECT **HORNS**, 3 DISTINCT **EYES** & 3 REGULAR **NOSTRILS**.

REMARKABLE **COLOSSAL OX** 6 FEET, 1 INCH, OR 18¼ HANDS HIGH. WEIGHING 3200 POUNDS. THE BIGGEST OF ITS SPECIES ON EARTH.

RARE DWARF CATTLE ONLY 32 INCHES HIGH THE CUTEST AND LITTLEST FEATHER-WEIGHT BOVINE PETS ALIVE.

TREMENDOUS **GIANT HORSE** 7 FEET, 6 INCHES or 22½ HANDS HIGH, WEIGHING 3600 POUNDS. TALLEST AND HEAVIEST IN EXISTENCE.

THE WORLD'S GRANDEST, LARGEST, BEST, AMUSEMENT INSTITUTION.

2-The Candy Pitch

During the come-in, members of the band took places in the center ring and played a preliminary concert of several pieces. Sometimes a clown worked among the newly arrived audience. A favorite trick was to spot a likely couple walking into the tent, then take the place of the husband just out of the wife's side vision. Perhaps the clown held her elbow and escorted her along the hippodrome track. When she turned and saw her husband's replacement, she screamed and the audience laughed.

With nearly everyone in their seats and only a few stragglers still coming from the menagerie into the big top, the ticket sellers and bandsmen disappeared. A hush fell over the audience, the show was about to start. Now an announcer stepped to the center. Wide-eyed, everyone anticipated the first thrill of the circus.

But that is not what the man proclaimed. Instead he explained that, "In a few weeks the Casey Candy Company of Chicago, Illinois, will place on the market a new confection." It would be available at your favorite candy, gift and department stores at two dollars per half-pound box. But as a special introductory offer, arranged through the generosity of the circus, the company was able to offer the candy here and now at a more favorable price.

Furthermore, each box would contain some gift of value. There was a wide range of gifts including "Mickey Mouse wristwatches, Kodak cameras, nylon hose for the ladies," and who knows what all. The circus had allowed just ten minutes for this introductory advertising offer, according to the announcer, and for this brief period agents "will pass among you, offering the prize candy at just twenty-five cents a box."

At that cue a battalion of white-coated concession men with bulky cases of candy moved toward the seats. Holding high a handful of candy boxes, they asked who would be first, and the man at the center again was saying, "Mickey Mouse wristwatches, Kodak cameras, nylons for the ladies . . . ."

Invariably the response to this candy pitch was tremendous. Children and adults alike clamored for the attention of the vendors. They pushed quarters at him as fast as he could take them, and the man at the center was saying: "There's a winner of a wristwatch. Hold it high, sir, so all can see; over there's a camera and here's a pocketknife; all you winners hold your prizes high." There were prizes, even some as described by the announcer, but more often they were paper novelties or plastic toys. The candy was not even very good.

It made no difference. The vendors soon exhausted their first supplies and went down to the center poles for new cases. Often people who had bought a box the first time now wanted a second. Still the man at the center kept up his patter, and still the audience bought. But as the time grew short and the edge was off the market, he had one more volley to fire. Excitedly he called to his vendors and breathlessly ordered them to "Stop the sales. Stop the sales. Come down out of the seats." Now, he explained to the

Opposite: Dog and pony drills were favorite fillers
between the star performances. {1914}

Every ring was so active under the Ringling-Barnum big top that circus patrons sometimes complained they were unable to see the whole show.

audience, because there still seemed to be a few doubters among his listeners, he had special instructions for his salesmen. "Set aside the cases you have now," he said loudly. "Take now those special cases, the ones with the heavy boxes, the ones with the bigger prizes." Then he explained to the audience that only three minutes remained. Now for the third time the vendors swarmed into the audience, nearly bending under the weight of those "heavier boxes." Again the audience bought. Again the boxes and the quarters flowed freely. Again there were more wristwatches, nylons, cameras, paper novelties and plastic toys. When it seemed the audience had been worked heavily enough and sales might slacken, the announcer declared the time was up, that unfortunately the circus management required the vendors to pull out. The candy pitch was over.

Now again a sort of noisy hush fell across the audience. The big top, rings and track were deserted. The audience and the generator each made their special kind of rumbling sounds that count as undertones, and all eyes turned nervously toward the entrance. Now, surely, the circus would start.

Opposite: The crowd was always thrilled by the danger of the mixed animal act. {1945}

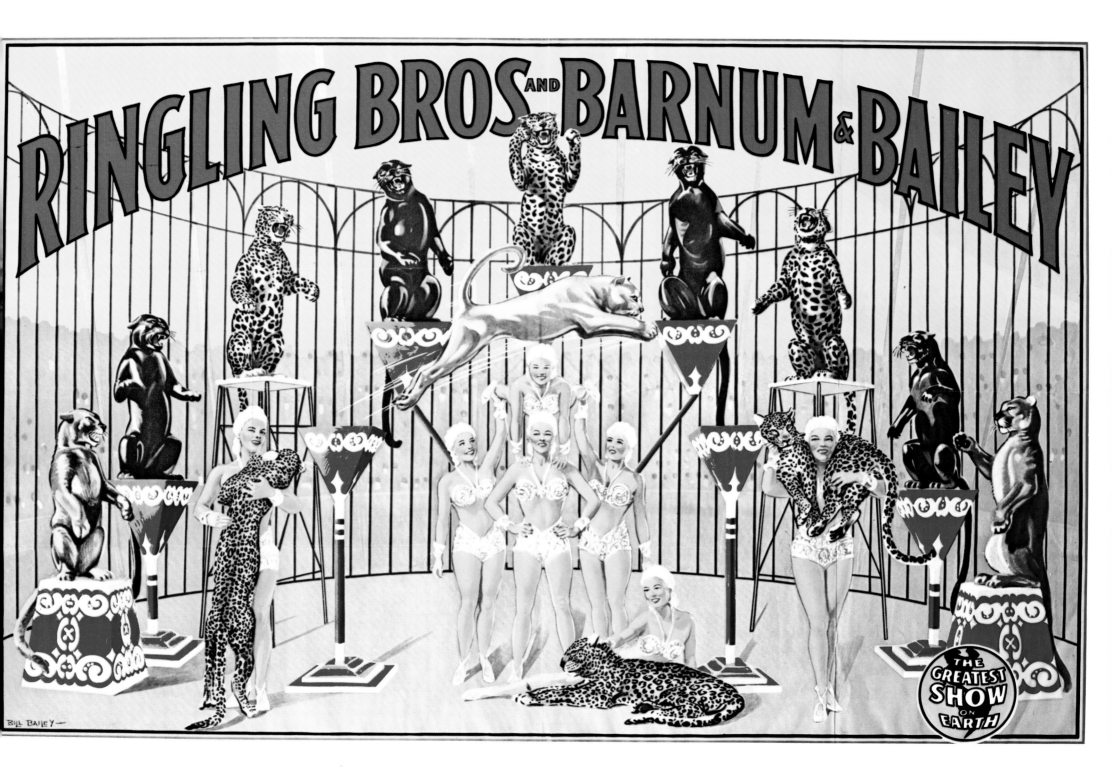

3-The Grand Entry

A ragged, brassy fanfare begins it all, then the back door curtain snaps open and the circus equestrian director announces a grand entry, "The Circus on Parade," or this year's grand historical pageant. With a blast of his whistle, the first of the spectacle, called "spec," steps into the tent.

Leading off are mounted riders with the national colors, followed by a pretty girl in a silky costume riding the head of a single swaying elephant. Next comes the band, stepping along to the tune of a circus march, and behind it in file is the varied procession. There are clowns in groups and interspersed throughout the lineup. Grooms lead Shetland ponies with monkeys as passengers. There are cowboys, cowgirls and Indians on horseback. Then comes a troupe of Chinese acrobats, followed by an Italian juggler and Arabian tumblers. Girls from the bareback troupe are perched daintily on the backs of their heavy dapple grays. Sometimes there are carriages with more girls or a mule pulling a clown police patrol. The show's camels and zebras are led along and next might be a troupe of knights in armor or a Roman in his racing chariot. As the first of the procession completes the circle of the big top track and nears the exit, the last of the spec is just coming in the other door. These are the rest of the elephants, caparisoned in their plush and spangled blankets, moving along trunk to tail, with attendants plodding alongside.

The band now steps out of the line of march and up onto its bandstand, and the equestrian director, immaculate in top hat and red coat, takes up his station from where he controls the myriad of cues and details for the next two hours of the performance.

Typically and traditionally, the grand entry marks the opening of a circus, but there have been exceptions. In the 1940's big Ringling-Barnum spectacles were postponed until a later spot in the program. During the same period indoor shows sometimes eliminated the grand entry entirely and simply got things started with a routine circus act. To do so was to abandon one of circusdom's most effective tools, because the drama and pageantry connected with such a grand opening greatly benefited circuses.

Circus spectacles have commemorated nearly every historical event of importance and some of little record. They have re-enacted Custer's last stand, the story of King Solomon, the raising of the flag at Iwo Jima, and the Whiskey Rebellion. Circus processional dramatists have pantomimed the story of Columbus, the glory of the Bengal Lancers and the happiness of nursery rhymes and holidays. In a dozen seasons starting with 1938, the Ringling-Barnum spectacles included new floats on the current year's theme, all unusual because of their one-sided design. Since circus spectacles always move counterclockwise, the audience would see only the right side of the float. It was designed with this in mind and the left side might be only a high background.

Opposite: The grand entry set the stage for the drama and pageantry to follow.

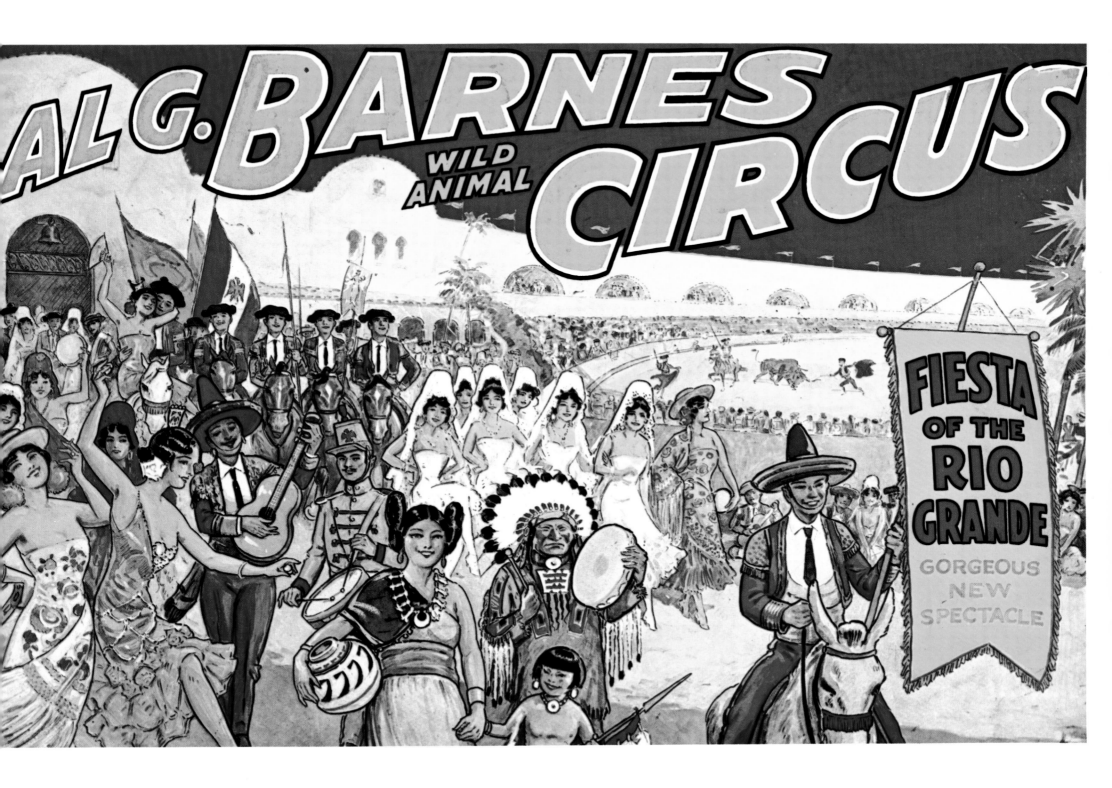

Spectacles on the biggest shows just after the turn of the century required elimination of seats on the back side of the tent and the installation of well-equipped stages. They displayed scenery and line after line of dancing girls, interspersed with knights or Crusaders or Biblical characters.

Often the spectacles moved from the hippodrome to the three rings, and there the principals might act out the rescue of John Smith by Pocahontas, the arrival of the Bengal Lancers or the making of peace with the Sioux or the Cheyennes.

One thing about circus spectacles has been the inevitable appearance of the elephants despite contradictions of history and geography. Call it "The Field of the Cloth of Gold" with a medieval French setting and there were the elephants. Label it "The Arrival of the Pony Express," and the ponies were followed by elephants. There often were Oriental themes that lent themselves well to the presence of the pachyderms; but so, also, could it be a spec about Darkest Africa which would include twelve Indian elephants. It has never seemed to bother the circus or its audience. The pageantry is all that counts. Now the equestrian director sounds a blast on his whistle to mark the end of the spec and the launching of the first act.

Until the 1950's, this was often the turn of the Lady Principal number, in which a single bareback rider appeared in each of the end rings. This was a picture act, designed to please the eye rather than to prove any startling feats of balance or prowess in somersaulting. Nevertheless, the pretty rider in a frilly, ruffled tutu displayed skill in the arts of posing, pirouetting and leaping. As her giant horse rocked around the ring, always a dependable understander, she posed on one foot and then another, leaped to and from the back of the horse, hopped over ribbons, and popped through paper hoops, always landing on the horse's back while continuing to circle the ring. The girls might be sisters and come from the show's big major riding act. The Lady Principal number demonstrated how beautiful, versatile and skillful were these riders. Then another hundred town boys fell madly in love with a bareback rider and considered the advisability of running away with the circus.

Another of the special kind of acts which often followed the spec was that of the aerial or horizontal bars. These performers came from the flying trapeze troupe but performed now on a separate aerial rigging. It involved several stationary bars, carefully spaced. A performer stood atop the first bar and stepped out into the void. His audience knew his foot would never reach the second bar and gasped for fear he would fall. But that second bar was placed just right for him to grasp by hand, and in a giant swing he came back up to the top side. Each trick he attempted seemed doomed to failure but always there was a bar for him to reach in an unexpected fashion.

Clowning quickly came into a routine like this. Two aerial comics met at the center bar and interlaced their legs so as a single unit they could rotate on the bar. When one was right side up the other was upside down. At the first stop the one on top swept off the other's seat with a broom that spewed wood shavings, and the audience laughed. Then after another revolution, the other clown was on top and he reached for a handy outsized hammer and walloped his partner with a blow that set off a firecracker inside the sledge. At that the victim kicked up his heels and fell into the safety net. But a surprise in the bar act was that the net bounced him right back up to within reaching distance of another bar. With a big show there would be two such acts, one over each end ring.

In either case, that of the Lady Principal or the aerial bar, the initial number was designed as a transition to get things started and as a filler to provide time for preparing the next act — the appearance of the wild animal trainer.

A star of any circus is the man who trains its lions and tigers, bears or leopards. His name is heavily advertised and the posters feature his picture amid a snarling pride of lions or leap of leopards. He is a major attraction of the show and full attention dwells upon him.

The act has to come very early in the performance because of its steel arena. This weighty cage is installed well before the audience arrives and stands in readiness. Outside the tent in the backyard are the several cages containing the trained animals as opposed to the display animals of the menagerie. These cages are fastened end to end and the last one is connected to the ring arena by a portable chute of wooden slats. Both the cages and the chute are equipped with several sliding gates that keep the animals apart while en route to the ring arena.

Attendants open the appropriate gates and the first lion jumps

Left: Defying geographical and historical accuracy, elephants effortlessly appeared in any setting, whether it be Roman or medieval French or Oriental.

Below: This is the grand entry of the 1938 Robbins Bros. Circus.

into the chute and races for the arena. Then the next gate is opened and the next cat moves. Some have to be prodded and some stop along the way to hiss and snarl or snap at the attendants who stay just out of reach. The audience can see little of this preparatory activity. But when that first black-maned Nubian lion pops into the arena, the audience gasps. There to meet the cat is the trainer.

American trainers favor safari suits and pith helmets. In their left hand they wield an old-fashioned kitchen chair and manage to grasp a pistol loaded with blanks and in their right hand is a bar or whip for cuing the act. European trainers sometimes enter the ring in the costume of a Roman gladiator or more often in formal attire including boiled shirt, black tie and tails. Nowhere is the difference between American and European circus artists so pointed as in the area of wild animal acts.

The philosophy of the American trainers seems to be that it is brave of them to be in the ring and that they battle these vicious beasts to gain control and require the performance of tricks. There is lots of noise and action. The blanks are fired repeatedly and the whiplashes resound with sharp cracks. Accompanying music is fast and furious, as the trainer progresses with his battle.

European wild animal trainers, while still recognizing that they are courting a gory death, nevertheless cue their animals quietly and give the impression that they have not subdued the animals but, instead, have tamed them and trained them to obey.

As the cats come into the arena each trots at once to his assigned station. Around the edge are pedestals of various heights and the cats sit atop them. As each animal enters the arena he is met by the trainer and ordered to his pedestal. Sometimes all the performers are lions, sometimes all of another species. But probably most exciting are the mixed acts. After the arrival of numerous lions there are new gasps as the first tiger slinks into the cage. The size and grace of tigers always win admiration. When these latecomers also have taken their pedestals, the performer goes on with the business at hand, cuing first one cat and then another to come forth and perform its special tricks.

There are roll-over tigers and lions that can walk on their hind legs. Four or five big cats lie down alongside each other, another leaps over them and then the trainer sits down among them. A lion leaps through a flaming hoop, and a tiger, balanced precariously atop a tall pedestal, springs through the air and lights gracefully atop another stand.

Above: These artful elegant props add an extra degree of grace to this tiger act.

Right: A tiger balancing on a ball is one of the more common features of a wild animal act.

Opposite: American trainers crack whips and fire blanks, supposedly to subdue the beasts.

Left: Clyde Beatty was a masterful trainer, equally adept in the art of timing and the psychology of handling an audience as well as an animal. Here he stares down one of his lions.

Below left: Terrell Jacobs, known as the Lion King, was a great wild animal trainer in the 1930's and 1940's.

Below: Mabel Stark, the Tiger Queen, appears unbelievably casual in the face of these snarling cats. The most famous female trainer of this century, she was a nurse before joining the circus.

There have been hundreds of trainers across the years, each more accomplished, each braver than the last. There were Terrell Jacobs, the Lion King, and Mabel Stark, the Tiger Queen; there were Pat Anthony, George Keller, Alfred Court, Rudolph Mathies, Eddie Kuhn and many more. None equalled or excelled the great Clyde Beatty, a lad who ran away from home to join the circus and began as cage boy, who grew up in the business to be the star of Hagenbeck-Wallace, then Cole Bros., and finally the show bearing his own name. Beatty was a masterful trainer, with parallel skills in the art of timing and the psychology of handling an audience as well as an animal.

In each wild animal act there is one cat that seems particularly vicious and desirous of eating the trainer alive. It roars and growls and snarls and claws at the trainer, but that brave fellow stands his ground, orders the cat to perform, and at one dramatic moment stares it down. The intrepid trainer holds his stare and finally the cat inevitably accedes and pads off as it has been ordered.

As the act comes to a close, the runway is opened again. Lions and tigers in their proper sequence run for their exit and head for home. But again there is one recalcitrant among them. The trainer has to prod him with the chair and the lion reaches out with vicious claws to knock that object from the trainer's grasp. But ultimately this lion, too, dashes for the runway that takes it back to its own cage. The trainer then runs to the safety door and out onto the hippodrome track to accept the applause of his admiring audience. Then he turns and trots to the back-side track and takes another bow. The equestrian director, fast with his whistle, gives it the toot that turns attention from the trainer to the next display. The wild animal man, sweaty and tired, walks out of the tent as the last of his cats is being prodded through the runway.

Already on deck are filler acts, often the show's pony drills, for the two end rings. Teams of six or eight Shetlands for each ring trot along, performing maneuvers and gyrations on cue from their trainers. These acts provide the necessary time for removing the cumbersome wild animal arena.

At the first possible moment a crew of property men swings into action. They remove the rope net that protects the top of the cage. Then they disassemble the numerous panels of bars that make up the circular arena. One man climbing the steel releases the fasteners and the panels fall to the hands of waiting property men. They lug them outside to a waiting wagon. If there is to be a second performance, the arena will have to be reassembled between shows.

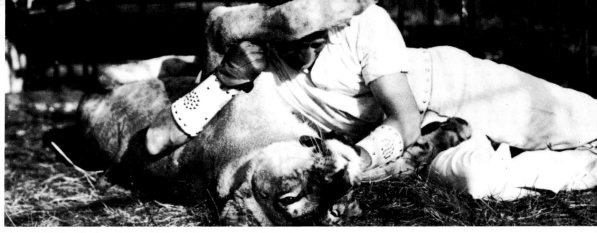

One of the highlights of Bert Nelson's lion act on Al G. Barnes Circus in 1936 was a wrestling match between trainer and cat.

But if this is the final performance, that wagon soon starts for the train. While the runway is being disassembled the cats either await the next performance or pace around their cages as workmen prepare to trundle them off.

In the earliest of years of animal acts, shows had large wheeled cages that were rolled into the arenas, and these provided adequate space for the limited acts of those times. By the 1890's wild animal acts had become big enough and circuses efficient enough to devise and operate the big steel arenas which caged in an entire forty-two-foot ring. For half a century circus men struggled manfully with the awkward and weighty panels of bars which constituted heavy steel arenas. Equestrian directors spent their winters pondering how they could best coordinate the filler act with work on the arena so that timing would be right. Only in late years have trainers and circuses developed lightweight arenas of alloys or chain net.

Meanwhile the pony drills go round and round. Each drill has its Shetlands trotting counterclockwise and countermarching single file, repeating with double ranks, wending in figure eights or other geometric formations. The little ponies sometimes form tableaux with the hooves of two at the hind quarters of a third.

If dogs and ponies are combined in the act, a favorite turn has the pony trotting under a bridge from which the dog leaps to its back. As the pony passes under a second bridge the first dog leaps from its back and another dog jumps from the bridge to start its ride. The ponies' routine is timed to last as long as there is dismantling to do at the center ring. When the equestrian director next blows his whistle, all three rings as well as the hippodrome track and aerial are available. The show is ready to proceed and the audience is prepared for anything.

Above and right: Every circus fan admires the size and grace of the cats. {1923, 1928}

224

4-The Eternal Clowns

Experts of the pratfall and the slapstick, practioners of hit-and-run comedy, those exponents of bizarre funny faces, the circus clowns work throughout the performance. The expert clown is as skilled as the television comic in pacing and timing his laugh-making. Clowns practice comedy at a lower — that is to say more basic — level than puns. Broad and blatantly drawn, their comedy is as plain as the noses on their faces. An expert clown is concerned with the nuances, gestures, the overall presentation of his small story. Occasionally there is a rare bit of sophistication, but much more often, the comedy of clowns is geared to gain the laughs of children and the less sophisticated. Sometimes their grotesque makeup and certainly their fireworks can frighten children. But more often they are on the same wavelength and a child laughs mightily at the antics of a clown who brings only a smile to the faces of some adults.

Circuses had clowns from the beginning and already their art was an ancient one, coming from medieval pantomimes and jesters. The first clowns in tiny American circuses could talk and sing to their modest-sized audiences. There were basic, aged gags like, "Why did the chicken cross the road?" "To get on the other side." There were jocular poems like, "Whether it's cold or whether it's hot, we shall have weather, whether or not." It was clowns who made popular some of our old favorite and standard songs — among them, "Turkey in the Straw," "Root Hog or Die" and "The Man on the Flying Trapeze." Clowns were the early-day equivalent of jukeboxes and disc jockeys, since it was they who were largely responsible for popularizing the music of the day. Leading clowns printed songbooks, and after they sang to the circus audience, they sold the books for customers to take home and try themselves. Several early clowns specialized in quotations from Shakespeare, and while neither that playwright nor his modern scholars might have recognized the doggerel, nevertheless, clowns carried on at length in what passed for quotations.

There are many specialized categories and types of clown makeup, but only a few are easily distinguishable today. Among the earliest was the whiteface clown wearing suits similar to leotards plus slippers and a pointed cap. Another style is the august, whose makeup usually includes an exaggerated mouth, over-stressed eyes and a huge nose, while his suit is comprised of baggy pantaloons, perhaps in a polka dot pattern, and his shoes are gigantic. Each clown creates his own facial makeup and a rule of the craft is that no one else may use the same design. If an audience cannot identify a man in his clown getup, it is not the same among clowns themselves. They may even know a fellow clown better by his makeup than by his natural appearance.

Early circuses carried only a single clown. He was one of the stars of the show. He worked closely with the riders, and the ringmaster was his straight man. In one of their most antique routines, a ringmaster asked where the clown came from, and he replied by giving the name of a little village near the town in which the circus was appearing. Sometimes this gag was used when the clown,

Opposite: The blatantly drawn humor of the clown is as plain as the nose on his face. {1934}

226

RINGLING BROS
AND
BARNUM
& BAILEY

Combined

CIRCUS

The
GREATEST
SHOW ON EARTH

acting like a local customer, came out of the circus seats to join the ringmaster and insist upon lifting the weights or riding the horse. Versions of this comedy, too, survive in today's show business.

When circuses necessarily increased the size of their tents and added rings, the days of the talking clown were ended. No one person could readily hold the attention of the larger audiences. Few voices could be heard throughout the big top. The single talking and singing clown survived for a few years with the smaller shows that continued the one-ring format for back-country territory and smaller villages.

But in the big shows clowning became a group activity. Clowns came on in big throngs, and the nature of their comedy changed accordingly. If they could not be heard or seen by the entire audience, then individual clowns would need to stop in front of each section of seats to repeat their gags. If a single clown no longer could dominate the entire audience, then a circus would have to offer five or ten or forty clowns.

With this came a great proliferation in style of clown costume and makeup. Now there came to be rube clowns, costumed as hayseeds that people in the audience could look down upon. There were midget clowns, others made up to resemble oversized kids and still others made up to look like grotesque women. Perhaps the biggest category was that of nationalities. For clowning developed its own versions of Swedish and German jokesters. There were monocled Englishmen of clowndom and little clowns with derbies and Hebrew humor as well as clowns made up as Chinese and Negroes and every other identifiable ethnic group. At the time, audiences thought each of these was hilarious, and they saw in the routines the humor (and only rarely any ridicule) of the Jewish neighborhoods in New York, the Negro worker in the cotton fields, the German immigrant at Cincinnati or St. Louis, and the awkward Swedish farm boy in North Dakota. Even at the peak of these clown depictions, there was greater than average care on the part of circus people to avoid clowning that would be offensive to any ethnic group. Clown versions of Jews and rubes and Germans were gentler than their counterparts in vaudeville and music halls.

A latecomer to this category was the hobo, or tramp clown. There were occasional clowns in this category through the 1920's when each circus's conclave of clowns might include one hobo. Apparently the Depression of the 1930's with its enlarged population of genuine hobos encouraged more clowns to adopt this makeup. Today they dominate clowning at the expense of the august and

The epitome of clowndom — a Shakespearian clown.

whiteface. Meanwhile the nationality clowns have disappeared, for it is no longer comic to portray minority groups.

In earlier decades circus clowns might occupy the same position as a movie or television comic of today. Dan Rice was the greatest of those who gained national reputations. He not only joked and bantered about the traditional topics of comedy, but also performed in the Shakespearean version of that form. Rice went on to comment on national affairs and crossed the comedian's forbidden barrier beyond which his commentary is partisan and no longer funny. Rice was too outspoken and too active in national politics and Presidential campaigns. His audiences became hostile and his popularity dropped. The lesson has been well learned by most clowns in succeeding generations, although some counterparts in space age television have confused the role of clown with that of political advocate.

In an age when clowns came on by the dozen, it was difficult for any one to rise above the average and gain wide fame. Some clowns complained that circus managers and equestrian directors held them back by disallowing space for carrying enough props. Management, on the other hand, bemoaned the lack of originality.

A few clowns, however, took the extra step to fame. One was Spader Johnson, whose pantomime of a one-man baseball team brought hilarity to audiences of Ringling Bros. and Barnum & Bailey. Another was an aerialist turned clown, Emmett Kelly, who perfected his comedy routines on Hagenbeck-Wallace and Cole Bros. Circus. With Ringling-Barnum he gained national stature and was featured in the billing as well as in the show's principal spectacle of one season, "Panto's Paradise." In hobo wardrobe, Kelly could stare mournfully at a lady in the audience in such a fashion that hundreds around her would disregard stars in the circus ring and laugh at Kelly instead. Then he would move on to repeat the process elsewhere in the crowd.

In the organization of clown contingents each circus names at least one to be producing clown. It is he who hires the others and selects the gags that will be used. He builds the props and develops ideas for new jokes. In all, he produces clown turns in whatever number and whatever style the equestrian director calls for. On the biggest shows there might be more than one producing clown, each coming up with his own materials and producing new ideas for clown comedy. Among the greatest innovators and builders of recent years has been Lou Jacobs. He has been building and clowning for Ringling-Barnum since 1924, except for only a brief

Above: One of the greatest production clowns ever, Lou Jacobs motorized a bathtub, a baby carriage and a tiny car in which he sped about.

Left: Long-necked Bumpsy Anthony clowned with Cole Bros. Circus in 1936.

229

A master of pantomime, hobo clown Emmett Kelly could stare mournfully at a lady in the audience until she began giggling and hundreds around her died laughing.

Below: Otto Griebling {on left} was also a great pantomimist. He is shown talking to friends in the Cole Bros. Circus backyard.

time with Sparks in the 1930's and with Polack Bros. Circus in the 1950's. Jacobs' clown makeup has become synonymous with the circus. It is used in Ringling posters and in the advertising artwork for many other shows . Among his greatest latter-day clown achievements was the creation of a midget car. Another producing clown was Paul Jung, who not only built original props for Ringling and other circuses, but also built comedy equipment and special effects for ice shows and other branches of show business.

Typical of other leading clowns in recent decades were Felix Adler, Joe Lewis, Earl Shipley, Otto Griebling, Arthur Borella and Paul Jerome. Each generation in the heyday of tented circuses produced scores of good clowns but now the number has dwindled to the point that the Ringling circus found it necessary to open a training school for new clowns.

A big part of clowning in modern circuses has been the walk-around. This is the gag, the funny bit, the comedy that can be performed as all of the clowns in the show walk around the hippodrome. It is in the walk-around that one sees clowns wearing big papier-mâché heads depicting Mickey Mouse or Clark Gable. There are stilt-walking clowns representing Uncle Sam. Others carry huge prop books and open them periodically so the audience can read the funny title or see the nonsense inside. Clowns lead tiny dogs leashed with giant four-inch hawsers, and another clown dog wears a head-like hat that makes it look like an elephant. Felix Adler did walk-arounds with a baby pig, which he bottle fed. Bluch Landolf walked along the track with a huge wooden beam balanced on his head; without warning he spun around and walked in the opposite direction — but the beam never changed position. A classic walk-around involves a frightened clown fleeing from a skeleton that chases him. There are clown gags which involve suit-like props that make it appear the clown is riding a horse or rowing a boat though he is simply walking.

Some walk-arounds require minimal production. One is the clown levitation in which one participant lies down to be mesmerized, then seemingly leaves the cot in a trance and floats through the air in a horizontal position. The trick is exposed when another clown pulls away the bed sheet to reveal the deception. The first clown is merely standing and the sheet shields two sticks he holds to support two shoes in the air in front. After performing this stunt for one section of the circus audience the clowns move down a few sections and repeat it.

Above: Felix Adler spent many years on Ringling-Barnum making people roar with laughter. His classic walk-around featured a little white pig which he cradled in his arms while feeding it from a bottle.

Below: The dissonant screeching of the musically disinclined clown band was a sound to be heard, but not listened to, on all the big circuses.

In a similar miniature production, one clown waves a magic cloak in front of another to transform him into a horse, a Negro mammy or some other character. The horse's head, for example, is affixed to the second clown's backside, and in the instant when he is hidden by the cloak, the clown quickly stoops over to bring the horse's head into place and hide his own identity underneath. Another flick of the magic cloak and the original clown is back. Then the pair moves on to repeat the gag elsewhere during the walk-around.

Clowns constantly try new walk-arounds. Many are connected with current events, so there might be timely jokes about Army rookies or Depression hobos or astronauts.

At least a couple of times in any circus worth its salt the center ring is turned over to the clowns for a major production. Now the comedy contingent has more time, and the full attention of the audience. In this spot they have benefit of special music, bigger props and help from the equestrian director. A basic production is the clown band in which each participant carries an instrument and together they make inane music, perhaps while bumping each other with a trombone or with drumsticks. The details and refinements are worked out by each producing clown.

It is the same with the clown wedding, but usually the biggest clown is the bride and a midget fills the groom's shoes. It ends in violent fashion — perhaps the bride's bouquet squirts water or she produces a rolling pin — at which point they all run out of the tent. A perennial is the clown boxing match in which the referee favors the bad guy while the good guy takes all of the punches and then reaches his corner just in time for the next starting bell. The boxers use huge elongated gloves that make a loud crack when slapped together. It seems that each is belaboring the other with mighty wallops, but in reality none is hurt and the audience never notices that the sound comes not from the aggressor's glove against the other's cheek, but rather from the defender's surreptitiously flapping his gloves together at the right moment.

A popular and hilarious clown production during wartime seasons consisted of a clown army, in which the comic squad would carry out an unbelievable close order drill, in which two files collided, the littlest draftee got the best of the sergeant, and finally

Opposite: The hilarious clown band was a standard of many street parades.

the underdog knocked the head off of a fellow rookie.

In a variation clowns would present a human cannonball. Sometimes the act was connected with the military misfit production and other times it recalled that the circus itself would present an actual human cannonball. In either case the clowns jammed a midget cohort into the barrel of a cannon, then fired a mighty charge, and from the far end of the big top a tiny parachute gently lowered what appeared to be the same midget cannonball.

A whole category of clown productions has been built around some devilish machine. In one version a bald clown pokes his head into a hair growing machine and comes out with a tremendous uncontrollable mop of curly hair. In another there is much shouting and hopping as many of the clowns chase and capture one of their number and jam him into the atom smashing machine — only this time it is spelled "Adam-smasher" because a huge clown is put in, there is a deafening explosion, and a half-dozen miniature copies of the original clown emerge in identical costumes.

Still another category of clown productions has the center ring given over to a horde of clowns depicting women at an automatic laundry or at a bargain counter. Invariably they get into a squabble and pelt each other with laundry or merchandise. In a similar affair, the clowns are painters who have a calamitous time with ladders and scaffolding. First one and then another spills some paint until ultimately they are flipping a loaded brush at each other's face or pouring a fresh can of red paint over each other's head.

Automobiles account for at least three principal clown productions. In one, an ordinary sedan pulls into the ring where it is met by a single clown. He opens a door to let a passenger out. After the door slams shut, there is a honk so he opens it again and another passenger hops out. There is another and another and another, until a fantastic number of clowns has come out of the car. When the group seems to be complete there is a tumult as the clowns greet each other. But suddenly the horn sounds and everyone knows there is yet another inside. They open the door and out comes not just a clown, but one with a live pony or bass drum or some other giant prop that makes the car's original load seem all the more impossible.

In another, Lou Jacobs has a tiny car that enters the tent with horns tooting and engine roaring. When it pulls to a stop beside a gas pump attended by a midget at the center ring the audience expects another midget to hop out. Instead, tall and lanky Lou Jacobs comes forth. First he waves a giant shoe and then eases a knee out of the car. Little by little he unwinds his tall frame to stand unbelievably tall beside his tiny car. Jacobs' early circus years as a contortionist make it possible. As the act proceeds the radiator cap explodes and squirts water into the clown's face, and a dozen other gimmicks go off.

In a class by itself was the clown car or the Phunny Phord. During the early 1930's nearly every principal circus had one. Each was built out of a Model T, but Ford and Detroit never saw one like this. Step on the running board and it gave way. Sit in the back seat and the front wheels reared into the air. Turn a corner and the steering wheel came off in the clown driver's hand. Raise the hood and there was a horrible explosion. Check the water and a six-foot snake jumped out. The horn sounded constantly and the engine raced and backfired. Then as the driver sought to crank his car, it backed up, got away and turned on him, with the driverless car finally chasing the hapless driver out of the tent.

One more production looms large in circus lore — the clown firehouse. In the center ring there is a prop cottage and suddenly it is ablaze. Someone turns in an alarm, and here comes the clown fire department, with tiny trucks or pony-drawn fire wagons circling the hippodrome. There are bells and sirens everywhere. The clown firemen trip each other with their hose, narrowly avert disaster with the ax, and upset each other on the ladders. There is a shout from the rooftop and a lady clown passes a baby clown out to the heroic firemen. Just then a new blast of fire charges up her spine. The heavy lady leaps and all but squashes the little fireman holding the safety net.

There are clowns in the bareback act, clowns with the aerial bars, clowns nearly everywhere and anywhere as the big show of the circus progresses.

Left above: The feather is attached to the clown's false nose, but his facial contortions seem to indicate the difficulties of balancing it.

Above: This is the clown troupe that was on the 1943 Cole Bros. Circus. At lower left is Otto Griebling.

Left: A classic walk-around features a clown leading a tiny dog around on a four-inch hawser. Here it is performed by a clown on Dailey Bros. Circus in 1946.

235

5-Acrobats and Jugglers

Circus acrobats and jugglers have developed a fantastic assortment of feats performed in all manner of ways from a variety of starting points. It is part of the game for their achievements to seem to go beyond the possible, because by their very nature circus acrobats seek to amaze their audiences by performing the difficult, the illogical, the impossible-till-now.

In this neighborhood of the circus, balance and timing are deified. Somersaults and pirouettes are the epitome of beauty. Bravado and the bizarre are commonplace. Juggling and acrobatics are the basic arts to which are added elements of posing, contortion and ballet.

If one acrobat balances on his hands, another will do it with a single hand. If one juggles on the ground, the next will juggle from horseback or from aerial rigging. When one does a stunt suspended by his arm, others will follow to equal the trick while suspended by their teeth or hair or while standing on a forefinger. If one acrobat stands atop another's head, the next duo will balance themselves head to head. Acrobats will do their stunts from swaypoles and teeterboards, roller skates and bicycles, Roman ladders and Roman rings and giant globes. Altogether they demonstrate the most amazing adaptations and skills to which the human body may be trained or subjected.

The fundamental acts are those of the juggler and acrobat. Jugglers working alone or in pairs can keep surprising numbers of objects in the air while acrobats can project themselves and their fellow performers into the air. Arabian acrobats in companies of six or eight or twelve, work amazing flipflaps, somersaults and tumbling feats from the sawdust ring, just as their forefathers performed on rugs in the Middle East. And the same company can assemble in a human pyramid that places the weight and balance of the entire group on a single sturdy under-stander.

Another kind of under-stander may hold a tall perch pole on his shoulder, or even his forehead, then one or two girls of his troupe climb the pole. From the top spot they perform gyrations of posing, balancing and revolving. Bicycle acts come along with many of the formations of the Arabian under-stander, but with the added complication of bicycles. Small portable stages are assembled in or between the circus rings so that bicycle troupes will have a smooth place on which to work.

The basic juggler is upstaged by other performers who lie on their backs and perform duplicate juggling accomplishments with their feet. Then along comes an acrobat who lies on his back and juggles other members of his troupe on his feet. In the Risley act, the under-stander supports a second acrobat on his feet. The second man is spun rapidly with two and then a single foot; finally he is thrown upwards, caught on his back, then thrown again and balanced in a foot-to-foot catch.

Whole families or large troupes appear in teeterboard acts. Here one man jumps on the teeterboard to catapult another into the air. The second dives or somersaults and lands on the shoulders of a third performer or in a huge wicker chair held aloft by fellow

Opposite: Circus acrobats seek ever more difficult feats to amaze their audience.

Far right: The Antalek troupe performs a graceful and difficult perch pole act.

Right: Acrobats and jugglers seem to go beyond the possible.

Below right: One under-stander is balancing eleven men in this act by the sensational Abadualla Homido troupe. A 1916 photo.

Below: This 1940 photo taken at Madison Square Garden shows an Oriental troupe performing a beautiful balancing act.

acrobats. For a climax trick, a teeterboard performer jumps from a pedestal to the first teeterboard, thus tossing a second man to another teeterboard and casting a third far into the air to perform somersaults and twists before straightening out to land as the top mounter in a three-high combination of fellow performers.

Similar aerial catapulting is part of the antique circus art and act called simply "The Leaps." In this, performers line up to take turns in running along a ramp, bounding upon a springboard and flying forward over an ever increasing number of elephants or horses. Landing on a huge mat, the acrobat goes back to the end of the line and waits his turn again to hit the springboard and swan dive over the growing array of obstacles. In pioneer circus times leaps were such a basic part of the performance that all acrobats signed for any type of act were required to double as leapers.

In a later variation of The Leaps' springboard, circus performers used the trampoline to bound into the air and to catch them after their pirouettes and somersaults.

Balance, so important to acrobats and jugglers, is stressed in such circus stunts as the Roman ladders, rolling globe and rolla bolla. In a Roman ladders act, two tall parallel ladders of ordinary design are perpendicular to the earth, supported by people standing between them. Other performers pose not only between the two ladders but atop them and at the sides of each. Rolling globe performers utilize a ball of about three feet in diameter. Standing atop it, they maintain their balance while propelling the ball up and down a ramp. Rolla bolla performers balance themselves on a board which in turn is on a tube or cylinder. Another performer may work as a top mounter and the ultimate feat is a head-to-head stand while balanced on a rolla bolla.

Whether he uses Roman rings, the bounding rope or other concoctions, the ambitious acrobat is continually adding to the repertoire new feats of contortion, new points of balance, new kinds of somersaults and new forms of pirouettes. Jugglers work while in a teeth suspension, and others revive the old aerial trick of hair suspension, and still others go into a forefinger stand and juggle hoops and balls on their feet in the air. As if the more familiar and traditional starting points are not enough, there are acrobats in novelty upside-down walking. Usually it is a clown who assembles a tower of six or eight tables and then rocks them precariously until finally they go over the brink and clatter to the ground. He rides them down and goes into a somersault at the last minute. Circus performers came to think the table-rock people were a little soft in the head after so many falls.

Above: Juggling and acrobatics are basic arts to which are added elements of posing, contortion and ballet.

Right: Truzzi was a juggler on the Ringling Circus in the late 1940's and early 1950's. For the climax of his act he juggled six flaming torches in the dark.

Jugglers balance twelve plates simultaneously on as many poles or snap a cigarette from the mouth of an assistant ten paces away with a giant Australian bull whip. Another is not satisfied merely to outline his partner with knives he has thrown, but rather he straps the partner to a revolving board and throws the knives while the partner is spinning.

In a class by themselves are the variations of aerial ballet acts. While the accomplishments of acrobats and jugglers require endless practice plus great discipline and strong desire, the aerial ballets of most circuses have been fill-in affairs, utilizing available people and enhancing their sometimes marginal benefit to the show. One such display is the Spanish Web number in which the aerial rigging supports a dozen or more suspended ropes that are encased in canvas. Girls in silken capes and bikini-like costumes march in, and each goes to one of the ropes in company with a clown or other male performer. While the man holds down the end of the rope, each girl climbs hand-over-hand to a point about twenty feet high. There, holding to a hand loop, she and the others in unison go into a routine of poses and acrobatics. With an ankle in the loop and the opposite foot against the rope, each girl supports herself in a horizontal position. Then she reverses, with hands to the rope and body at 90 degrees to it. At this point the man at the ground end of each rope begins to turn it in giant swings, thus spinning the girls in unison.

In a similar turn, the same aerial ballet girls may go to aerial ladders and again pose while holding on with various combinations of hands or feet. Third in the category is the iron jaw number in which each girl places a teeth suspension device in her mouth. The device is then attached to a rope, and it and the hanging girl are drawn upwards. Often the iron jaw girls wear airy scarves of silk and these are moved in kaleidoscopic gyrations, giving the act its name of "Butterflies."

The web, ladder and iron jaw numbers have the unique distinction of making a strong impression on the audience but requiring a minimum in skill and training from the performers. A capable trainer can convert novices into an attractive aerial ballet in a matter of only a few weeks' training in winter quarters, and then win rave reviews and strong applause from suave New York critics.

The wire artists constitute an outstanding set of specialists among acrobats. Divided into three categories, they often consider themselves expert in sharply varying skills, and while they all depend first on highly developed senses of balance, each of the

240

An Oriental high wire walker balances precariously beneath his colorful parasol.

Far left: Con Colleano performed miracles on the tight wire. In addition to being a highly accomplished wire walker, he had a superb sense of showmanship.

Left: Unus startled the show world with his one-finger balancing act. He is shown here in 1948 in Madison Square Garden on the Ringling Circus.

Below: The Niatto sisters, Nio and Ala, were center ring stars on the Ringling Circus in the 1940's. They performed astounding feats on the tight wire.

Elly Ardelty was perfection in balance: high over the center ring she balanced on one foot while swinging on a trapeze.

three — performing on tight wire, slack wire or high wire — is indeed in a category of his own.

The tight wire artist generally works alone and performs on a taut cable strung between two A-frames about five feet above the ground. In the costume of a toreador he might dart from one end of the wire to the other, or as an inebriated reveler in top hat, he might stagger and sway at midpoint on the wire. A tight wire performer takes a chair to the midpoint, balances its two opposite legs on the wire, then sits on the chair, perfectly balanced. As a clincher he moves to a standing position atop the chair, still maintaining that delicate balance. Tight wire performers turn somersaults — both forward and backward and sometimes with huge wicker baskets strapped to their feet. Girls on the tight wire, dancing daintily, carrying a parasol and wearing a ballet costume, might leap over a ribbon or through a paper hoop.

Slack wire artists, as their name implies, make use of a wire that is slack. It hangs loose from end supports but even at the center is a few feet above the ground. A slack wire artist performs many stunts similar to those of the tight wire artist, but his specialty is balancing at the midpoint while his feet on the slack wire move exceedingly rapidly from side to side.

The royalty of wire walkers is the high wire troupe. They work on rigidly guyed cables strung between two towers at a point approximately twenty feet high. From tiny platforms atop the towers, they slide one slippered foot and then another out on the cable, stepping gingerly into their straight and narrow professional world. High wire artists generally carry long and heavy balancing poles to help maintain their equilibrium. At midpoint on the cable the high wire performer might turn about or sit down and then roll over in a somersault. Working in troupes, two high wire artists become under-standers, one behind another. A shoulder bar is placed between them and a third performer balances himself on it. Other high wire performers ride bicycles or motorcycles along the cable.

The Great Wallendas, a large troupe whose principal accomplishment was the sensational seven-person pyramid, are probably the most famous among high wire acts. When this feature was presented everything in the big top would become quiet. The audience was spellbound. Karl and Herman Wallenda shouted cues and signals in German as their precarious pyramid took shape. Four members mounted bicycles and rode out onto the wire. Shoulder bars connected them in pairs, and another performer stood on the bar above each pair. These second-story combinations were connected with yet another bar and one of the Wallenda girls then stepped onto it. At its midpoint she sat on a chair as the pyramid of pyramids slowly edged its way out onto the cable. When it stopped the balancing poles wigwagged. Then in silence, the girl on the chair, slowly moving with great care, found her way to a standing position atop the balanced pyramid.

That was the peak of the act, but with the Wallendas, there could be no sudden finale. Great care had to be taken in disassembling the seven-person pyramid. Slowly the pyramid moved forward until one after the other of the troupe reached the safety of the opposite platform. Not until the seventh person came in off of the cable and swung his bicycle to a hook at the side could the audience express its relief and admiration with great rounds of applause. There have been many great circus acts, many great high wire performers, many who accomplished unbelievable feats at great heights and without safety devices. Brave as they are, however, none has surpassed the Great Wallendas.

These acrobats are often expected to participate in more than one act. {1912}

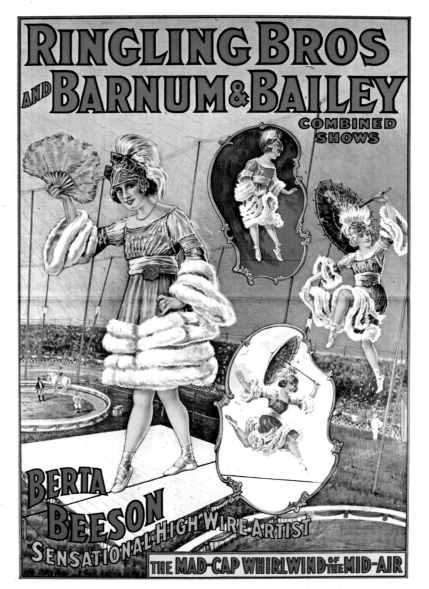

Among wire specialists, the high wire artist reigns supreme. {1928}

6-Wild West Stars and the Aftershow

About midway through the performance there was an interruption. Excitedly the equestrian director demanded that the hippodrome track be cleared to make way for cowboys and Indians. It was the concert announcement, a circus feature which has all but died. However, until the 1960's, most shows carried an aftershow — a variety program, minstrel show or, more often, a Wild West demonstration. It was here that the circus displayed its cowboys and Indians, and here in the heyday of the movies that the circus exhibited its motion picture superstars.

The circus has developed stars and celebrities of its own, and for most of its two centuries of activities, the circus has featured its own current equivalents of Emmett Kelly, Poodles Hanneford, Alfredo Codona, Lillian Leitzel and Clyde Beatty. But there came a time when celebrities of the Western films inhabited circusdom as well. Greatest of these was Tom Mix, a pioneer in Western movies and one of the most powerful drawing cards in that business. He joined Sells-Floto for 1929 and 1930 and performed in the concert.

At a particular time during the big show, these famous personalities and other cowboys and Indians in the show came galloping into the tent. The equestrian director introduced them and announced that agents would pass among those in the audience selling tickets to the aftershow, when the roughriders, sharpshooters, whip crackers and lariat artists would do their stuff.

Mix proved to be such a powerful force at the box office that other cowboys followed him into featured circus spots. Hoot Gibson was with Wallace Bros. and Hagenbeck-Wallace. Buck Jones survived the financial disaster of his own Buck Jones Wild West Show to join Robbins Bros. Circus as a concert feature. Ken Maynard was with Cole Bros. and later with Biller Bros. Circus. Tim McCoy was a concert feature with Ringling Bros. and Barnum & Bailey through 1937, when the circus discontinued that adjunct, and Tim McCoy launched his own, short-lived Tim McCoy's Real Wild West Show.

Sometimes shows featured second echelon actors like Reb Russell on Russell Circus, or even unknowns like Juan Lobo on Cole Bros. Circus. Lee Powell, "The Original Lone Ranger," of the radio serial, joined Wallace Bros. Circus. Then, when television revived the old Western films, some cowboys attained even greater popularity, so Hopalong Cassidy joined Cole Bros. Circus, and the Cisco Kid toured briefly with the Clyde Beatty Show and with the Tom Packs Circus.

Among other major concert features over the years were three heavyweight boxing champions of the world. Jess Willard came to the Miller & Arlington 101 Ranch Real Wild West Show and ultimately bought it. Jack Dempsey was with Cole Bros. Circus and Joe Louis made the Canadian route of Dailey Bros. Circus in 1950.

Concert stars presented sharpshooting, roughriding or roping on the one hand and sparring with boxing partners on the other. Such personalities were well paid by the circus and they were worth it, for they proved to be powerful ticket-selling forces. A lot of people came to see Sells-Floto because Tom Mix was there.

Opposite: Tim McCoy launched his show during the heyday of Western film stars. {1938}

244

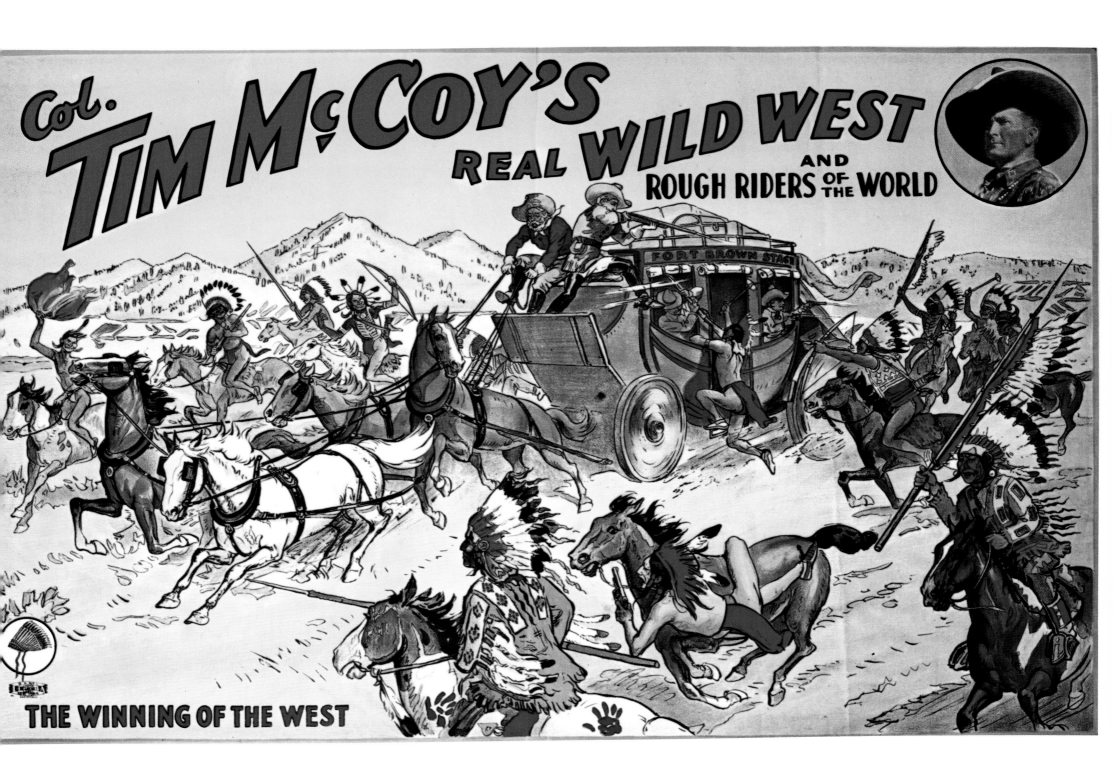

Left: Tom Mix was a Hollywood star of Western films when he joined Sells-Floto for 1929 and 1930. He went on to start his own successful truck show which lasted until 1938.

Below left: The 101 Ranch show, while not held under a big top, was generally considered as circus. Wild West shows produced many stars who later became concert features.

Opposite: Trick-riding and sharpshooting, once a circus in itself, eventually became part of the aftershow on most circuses. {1889}

Below: In 1938, Tim McCoy launched his own Tim McCoy's Real Wild West Show. Prior to that he had been one of Ringling Bros. and Barnum & Bailey's star concert attractions.

ADAM FOREPAUGH'S NEW AND GREATEST ALL FEATURE SHOW.

A STREET SCENE IN MEXICO.

WOODWORKERS OF MEXICO.

MEXICAN PULQUE VENDOR.

MEXICAN HOME LIFE.

MEXICAN HUNTERS ON THE FRONTIER.

ANTONIO AND JOE ESQUEVEL
THE GREATEST LASSO THROWERS AND
ROUGH RIDERS IN THE WORLD.

ANTONIO ESQUEVEL, THE CHAMPION ROUGH RIDER OF MEXICO.

AT HOME IN THE SADDLE.

MEXICAN STREET MERCHANT.

EARLY TRAINING OF THE BROTHERS ESQUEVEL.

MEXICAN VAQUEROS.

Entirely New and Sensational Exhibition MEXICO AND THE MEXICANS, Just Added to the Enormous Enterprise

7-Performing Horses

For 180 seasons of circusing the horse clearly was king. From the time of the earliest performances of trick riding at livery stable yards, the rider was a principal star of the performance, if not its sole participant. With the early trick riders came the trainers of "learned" horses and ponies. And, of course, from its earliest times the circus was moved from town to town by baggage horses, then hauled from train to lot by baggage horses. Shows prided themselves on their stud of horses to the extent that some, like Hagenbeck-Wallace and William P. Hall circuses, advertised specifically that they had the finest horses in the world.

From this standpoint the horse and buggy era lasted longest at the circus. Ultimately, even the circus gave way. By the 1940's there were no baggage horses on American shows, and for some seasons in the 1950's the Clyde Beatty Circus could not claim a single performing horse, a situation akin to having the cone without the ice cream.

Despite this fact, horses are still a major factor in circus performances. There are bareback acts, liberty horses, high school horses and trained ponies.

Bareback riders are the elite of circus society, a situation dating back to the origin of the circus itself. Often the leading riders appear as families, but this was not always true in the early American circus. Famous riders such as Levi J. North worked alone. However, in more recent decades the bareback act was one of those often presented by a distinguished family with generations of circus prominence behind them. Bareback riding families such as the Hannefords came from Ireland, while the Davenports were native Americans. The Cristianis were Italian and the Loyal-Repenskys traced their circusing back to Napoleon giving some horses to one of their ancestors.

The very size of circus rings is credited to the riders. The earliest among them discovered that for a man standing on a horse's back, a forty-two-foot diameter provided the maximum advantage of centrifugal force and related factors of physics which contributed to balance and posturing. In the early days trick riders worked with saddle horses, and later the first somersaulting riders performed on broad fabric pads harnessed to the horse's back. After a somersault it was easier to come in for a landing on a flat pad than on the irregular back of a horse. But that is precisely what brought about the next innovation in trick riding. In order to demonstrate greater skill and daring, star riders of the circus gave up the pad and began to work strictly on the broad back of a Percheron horse. The idea of the pad survives now only among older circus performers who refer to the dressing room as the pad room, which dates from the time when such a tent was both stable for ring horses and dressing room for riders. Both the horses and pads have moved out but dressing tents still are called pad rooms.

The typical bareback act incorporates several types of riding, among them principal riding, the jockey act, somersault riding and the big pyramid displays. The principal riding features the pretty young daughters of the bareback family. Their pirouettes and

Opposite: Poodles Hanneford delighted the crowds with his antics on horseback. {1916}

posing are presented in a graceful fashion befitting an equine ballerina. Then come the young men of the family in the somersaulting phase. There are forward and backward somersaults, and the best acts bring on a second mount for horse-to-horse somersaults. It was in this that the great Davenports and the Cristianis excelled.

For the next step three rosin-back horses are brought to the ring, and slower than before, they circle the ring at their familiar, nodding pace while riders leap up to form a high-riding pyramid. It was in this bareback acrobatic display that the Loyal-Repenskys excelled. Eight or nine people work together with the five horses to create the human pyramid that circles the ring aboard its mounts.

Such riding spectaculars are relative latecomers in the history of bareback riding troupes, but incorporated in them was one of the oldest elements of the act — a comedy rider. Poodles Hanneford was the master of this and the creator of many bits of business still used by bareback clowns. He swept into the ring in a coonskin coat and then leaped and stumbled, wobbled and rode in an uproarious fashion. At one point he got on the horse backwards holding the tail, a laughable bit during the days when all the customers had horses at home. He gained the strange effect of suddenly eliminating speed when he casually stepped off the back end of a horse. When one after another of the family of riders each jumped to the horse's back, Poodles was last, and seemingly had to hold up the tail to find a place to sit on the crowded horse.

Poodles' mantle has been picked up by his nephew, Tommy Hanneford, and by one of history's most accomplished riders, Lucio Cristiani. Each has perfected the comedy; each is at his laughable best when he makes a run for the horse, dives but goes clear over it and collides catastrophically with a popcorn vendor. And each uses the stunt of jumping from a horse, rolling over his coat and coming up with the garment on, then somersaulting again to come up wearing his hat.

After the comedy comes the finale of the bareback display. Now the slowly paced horses are removed in favor of the jockey act in which the horse runs around the track at a much greater speed, while the rider leaps to and from its back. The fast act is pepped up further by the ringing of silver bells on the horse's halter. The jump-ups and bareback riding at this stepped-up pace build audience interest to a desirable climax at the end. Riders take their bows and grooms trot the horses back to the stables.

250   The bareback act, carrying impressive credentials and pedigree

Comical he was, but Poodles Hanneford was also a superb bareback rider. Brought from Ireland during World War I, he was on Barnum & Bailey.

A member of the Loyal-Repensky troupe somersaults from the back of one galloping horse to the back of another {left}. The famous Davenports share standing room only on the backs of four trotting horses {below left}. The Hodgini troupe worked with Sells-Floto in 1925 {below right}. The size of the circus ring itself is attributed to the earliest of bareback riders who discovered that a forty-two-foot diameter gave the best centrifugal force needed for balance and posturing.

Left: The safety and success of this act depends almost entirely on the training and ability of the horse.

Below: The Cristiani family of bareback riders is one of the finest of the twentieth century.

for its place in circus history, retains that prominent spot even today. For bareback riding is one of the high spots of any circus performance, along with the wild animal act, flying trapeze and performing elephants.

But bareback riding is not the only example of equestrianism at the circus. Another feature is the high school display, in which gaited horses perform on the hippodrome track. The three- and five-gaited mounts are put through their paces one by one. Circuses also display *haute école,* in which even more highly trained horses perform their intricate maneuvers, and the riders win featured billing on the show for the excellence in which they demonstrate points of dressage.

A standard with circuses has been the liberty act. In this display a trainer brings eight horses to the ring and they trot around the circle. Then, according to his cues, they circle back, countermarch, form columns and files, move in even more elaborate formations, all without riders and all by remote cue, thus the name "liberty act." As an old standard, each horse carried a number on its harness and the trainer mixed them up, keeping them out of numerical sequence. Then the horses were turned loose in the ring and one by one they found their proper places until the big numerals read 1 through 8 again.

Bringing up the rear in the equine department are the pony drills. These are miniature copies of the liberty acts, with eight or more Shetland ponies circling the ring and following their trainer's cues into one new formation after another.

Across most of the years that horses have been performing in circuses, most of the audience was highly informed about such animals. Many were good judges of a horse's quality and, also, they knew from their own experience that it would be difficult and demanding to teach a horse some of the routines that were performed at the circus. Appreciation for the trainers, the stock and their combined accomplishment was great in earlier days, but one wonders, now when children rarely see horses away from riding stables, if many onlookers are aware of the effort and patience required on the part of the trainer.

In days when farmers were more numerous and livestock was a field of general knowledge, circuses presented other trained domestic animals. In one variety of act, trained pigs climbed stairsteps,

Opposite: During 180 seasons of circusing, the horse was clearly the king. {1894}

Bareback riders, the elite of circus society, usually appear as a family troupe.

Left: Rudy Rudynoff, who once worked with the John Robinson and Ringling shows, was a thirty-year veteran of the liberty act. He never forced a horse and used his whip only for cues and to add excitement to the act.

Below: A typical act of Gentry Bros. Dog & Pony Show featured a monkey dressed as Ben Hur in a miniature chariot pulled by two collies; a third dog leaped over them.

scooted down slides and otherwise completed a series of stunts. There were goat acts that featured similar tricks, but soon the presence of trained goats was restricted to the smaller shows playing the smaller towns. For, regardless of what the public thought of it, a circus was discredited in the eyes of performers if it carried a goat act.

In quite a different category were the trained dogs. Big shows often presented displays of racing and leaping greyhounds. Frequently there were general dog acts as well. But it was on the small circus that trained dogs came into their own. Outfits such as Gentry Bros. Dog & Pony Show included hundreds of pedigrees and mongrels. There were little dogs that climbed ladders and jumped off into safety nets. There were other dogs that stepped between the trainer's legs each time he took a step. There were poodles that walked on their hind legs and jumped the rope. There were dogs of all kinds which wore little costumes in keeping with their tricks. Sometimes dogs and ponies worked together in a single act, and dogs often were an integral part of a clown's routine.

8-High Acts and Thrill Acts

For an instant the performance became terrifying. High acts and thrill acts carried the clear possibility of instant death. Circus programs dwelt mostly upon skills and arts. The trainers, the riders, the clowns and acrobats performed their acts with skill and ability, but usually there was only limited threat to life and limb. Of course, the lion trainer's business life was one of jeopardy, but even that bloody threat seemed slightly less imminent, possibly less permanent, than that facing the high wire performer and his cohorts at high hazard. A good high wire act was one of the exceptions with which a circus scared its audience. A so-called thrill act was basic in the thinking of many who organized circus performances.

There was a variety from which to choose in this world of ziippp — boom, dive and crash, drum rolls and altitude.

In the past, perhaps the tamest was the well named but over-sold slide for life. In this a cable was stretched at an angle from high on a center pole to a distant point on the ground. A wire walker stood on the cable and rapidly slid downwards and backwards. Or a girl hung by her hair from a wheeled device and rode the wire to the ground.

More to the point of stopping the hearts of the audience was the man who "hangs himself and lives." From atop an aerial perch he fitted the noose to his neck and then dived off. It was a true thrill act, built up strongly with preliminary preparations and conversation. It scared the beejeebers out of audiences twice a day for several seasons. It did, at least, until the day it broke the neck of the Great Peters.

Of a similar nature were the circus versions of the fairgrounds' high dive from a tower to a tank or pad. In other seasons long gone one mechanical device fired a human arrow and another catapulted a man across the big top.

Just after the turn of the century — dawn of the motor car age and peak of the bicycle fad — circus goers were deluged with loop-the-loop devices. One man did it on a bicycle, but more often a performer climbed into a tiny car at the peak of a tracked ramp. At the climax of the equestrian director's buildup, the car rolled forward. It plummeted down the ramp and into an arc that both cast it through the air and twisted it into a somersault. The little coaster car plopped heavily into a net or onto a second ramp that slowed it down. When the rider regained his addled balance, he stood to accept the relieved applause of his audience. Soon, however, looping cars were relegated to history.

The new thriller was circusdom's classic, the human cannonball. Actually, cannon acts had a prior history of sorts. The billing was the same, but the nineteenth-century version of the mechanism left something to be desired. If some of the posters were accurate and

Opposite: Foreign commands were followed by a violent explosion as the human cannonball hurled into space. {1930}

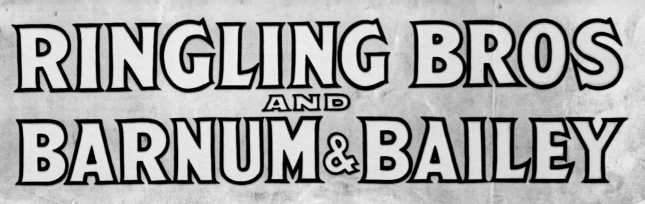

RINGLING BROS
AND
BARNUM & BAILEY

THE HUMAN PROJECTILE
HUGO ZACCHINI
A LIVING PERSON SHOT THROUGH SPACE WITH VIOLENT VELOCITY FROM THE MOUTH OF A MONSTER CANNON
THE SENSATION OF THE CENTURY!

RINGLING BROS AND BARNUM & BAILEY COMBINED
DANVILLE
SAT. JULY 26

THE
WORLD'S
GREATEST
CIRCUS
ALL NEW
THIS YEAR

TWO PERFORMANCES DAILY AFTERNOON AND NIGHT

Left: There is a great variety of aerial acts, all thrilling and most carrying the clear possibility of instant death. Jenny Rooney is shown swinging out over the crowd in a "cloud swing" act.

Opposite: Loop-the-loop acts were soon relegated to history. {1908}

Below: The Great Peters dove off a platform with a noose around his neck. The material that held the noose was elastic enough to keep him from getting hurt — except for the last time he did the act.

the girl fired from such a pioneer cannon actually grasped a trapeze in mid-air, they were remarkable indeed. But indications are that the facts were somewhat less amazing.

The act of the human cannonball reached its peak with arrival on the scene of the Zacchinis, Fearless Gregg and the Great Wilno. Sells-Floto, Robbins Bros. were among those with cannon acts. But as usual it was the Ringling-Barnum aggregation which topped them all.

Hugo Zacchini, in white leather coveralls and aviator's helmet, walked up the slope of the barrel, then eased himself into the mouth of the cannon. The audience became still and some held their ears. There were commands shouted in a foreign tongue and then an outlandish explosion. Recovering from its blink, the audience watched for that micro-time that the cannonball completed his trajectory and hit the landing net. If that was a tough act to follow, the Zacchinis found a way. Next they came up with Hugo and Mario Zacchini in "The Monster Repeating Cannon." Now the tension was magnified. Now there were two deafening explosions, and two Zacchinis bolting through the air.

When war came the Zacchini men were replaced by Zacchini girls and still their cannons roared on the home front.

Above: In 1947 the Alzanas performed on the Ringling Circus, astounding crowds with their death-defying act.

Above left: The Wallenda troupe is unsurpassed in the annals of circus history. Their name was a household word for thirty years.

The automotive age ushered in such thrill acts as this sphere which rolled up and down a spiral track with no visible motor. {1902}

9-Rare and Exotic Animals

All the strange extremes of the animal kingdom have been brought together on the circus. There are to be found not only domestic animals, but all manner of unusual and weird birds and beasts. The wild ones are exhibited in cages and arenas, the tame ones on tethers. But virtually all species at some time have been with the circus, sometimes as exhibits of viciousness or rarity, sometimes as examples of man's cleverness and the animal's ability to learn.

Some animals are expected to learn tricks and perform acts, while others are not. The typical circus goer expects to see horses and dogs or other domestic animals in performing combinations. Trained ponies may execute some complicated formation which astounds the audience, but the basic fact that these animals are in the ring is not surprising. However, no one expects to see a hippopotamus there. With the notable exceptions of elephants, the major cats and minor members of the monkey family, few of nature's strangest creatures have been trained successfully enough to appear in the circus ring. Other exceptions have been infrequent.

Among the rare animals which have appeared with the circus generally as non-performers are the enormous ones, such as the sea elephants; the exotic, such as giraffes; or the most ferocious, such as gorillas. Others are the stupid or languid, among them tortoises and crocodiles.

Some of the most exotic are those trained least and exhibited least. Thus, giraffes have been seen, but not often, around circuses. The Ringling-Barnum show carried giraffes for many decades, and some giraffe families could boast of several generations with the circus. Yet they always were merely menagerie exhibits, and they never appeared in the ring, never performed any routines. The same was true with giraffes of other shows, although there is some evidence that the Montgomery Queen Circus of the early 1870's and another occasional outfit in those times not only exhibited giraffes but made modest performers of them. European trainers have had minor success in training giraffes to harness.

Another reluctant trouper and non-performer is the gorilla. The number of genuine gorillas that have appeared with circuses can be counted on one's fingers. The superstar among them was Gargantua the Great, exhibited on Ringling-Barnum and then Barnes-Sells-Floto in 1938 and with Ringling for several years thereafter. Whether it was a case of ferocity or not knowing its strength is immaterial, the fact remains that Gargantua never was the subject of a trainer's serious efforts. In his first year of circusing, the cage in which he rode was driven around the hippodrome track so that all in the seats could see while the lecturer described gorillas in general and Gargantua in particular. Except for this season of twice-daily rides, Gargantua spent his show business career as a menagerie exhibit. Bob Noell of Noell's Ark Gorilla Show has had considerable success in not only exhibiting but also manhandling gorillas, and he has had several with the show he takes on carnivals. Ringling-Barnum also exhibited a female gorilla and bought several very young specimens, all for exhibition. But no gorilla has yet been trained to a routine for presentation in the circus ring.

A similar example is that of sea elephants. These blubbery giants are amazing merely to view, and their conformation precludes much in the way of stunts, even if they could be trained. Circuses exhibited these giants, however; both Ringling-Barnum and Sells-Floto displayed a sea elephant. In each case it was merely coaxed

Opposite: The superstar of gorillas spent his career in an air-conditioned cage. {1938}

onto a flat wagon and towed around the hippodrome track.

Rhinoceroses, including some of the species now exceedingly rare, have been exhibited from time to time on circuses. Back in Dan Rice's day there were claims of a trained rhino on his show. A hundred years later, the little Cole & Walters Circus joined the small number of outfits which has exhibited a rhinoceros, notable for the fact the public was allowed to touch it, but nobody else has come even that close to domesticating a rhino. Some shows have exhibited ostriches hitched to carts, and many have shown snake charmers at work with giant constrictors. But snake charmers usually have been relegated to the sideshow and none has taught reptiles to perform stunts.

Like snakes, both alligators and crocodiles have seen limited service with circuses. Only two performers in recent times have brought them into the ring. One was a girl, Tanit Ikao, who generally appeared with Hunt Bros. Circus; the other was Blackaman, Hindu animal hypnotist, who was featured for a year with Hagenbeck-Wallace. In both cases the gist of the feat was that the trainers dared to be in contact with the 'gators. They wrestled the animals and tranquilized them by rubbing their undersides, but in neither case did the alligators themselves become more than props in the act.

It has been a different story with another set of animals that includes camels, zebras, llamas and hippos. In a few cases, notably on the Al G. Barnes Circus and later on Al G. Kelly & Miller Bros. Circus, hippos have made arena appearances. In each case, the hippopotamus was taken out of its cage and encouraged to walk unleashed around the track. Circus trainers considered it startling enough that these unfamiliar animals were to be seen at liberty. And they were correct. Circus audiences looked on in amazement and with at least a little apprehension as Lotus on the Barnes Show, or Miss Oklahoma with Kelly-Miller, came lumbering along. These river hogs would drift to a stop and then break into a trot, and customers never could be quite certain the animal would not charge into the seats. There were efforts to tie a hippo to a two-wheeled cart with a single arcing shaft that connected with a collar on the animal. Such attempts at training hippos rarely got off the ground and never lasted.

Circuses, especially Sells-Floto and Hagenbeck-Wallace, tried to train zebras both for harness work and for liberty acts, but this species is just mule enough to refuse to learn. While there have been performances with zebras and occasionally zebras have

264

Above: Various circuses, expecially Sells-Floto and Hagenbeck-Wallace, tried to train zebras for liberty acts, but they are too mulish to learn much.

Below: Attempts to train camels have been largely unsuccessful, although in the 1950's Jack Joyce succeeded in training five camels to a liberty act.

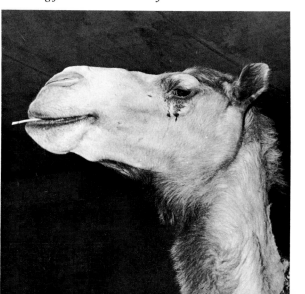

Because of his fragility, the exotic giraffe is a rare circus exhibit. {1928}

The De Jonghes Chimp Act on the Ringling Circus in 1955. Chimps rather quickly reach an age when they can be dangerous.

appeared in mixed acts, liberty turns using several are virtually unheard of. Attempts to train camels have been similarly unsuccessful. The humped species that seemed so domesticated and useful in North Africa turned out to be considerably less cooperative on circuses. There have been numerous teams of camels for drawing parade wagons, yet these efforts often ended in disaster. Attempts at training camels for ring routines have been successful even less frequently.

The magnificent exception was the Jack Joyce Camel Act. The successful trainer of many circus horses, Joyce was schooled in the ways of cowboys and the Wild West and he used his savvy to break five camels. He introduced his act in the 1950's on Polack Bros. Circus, dressing the animals in ornate Oriental blankets. They loped and lumbered through an elaborate routine with the turn-abouts, countermarches and other attributes of equine liberty acts.

Another of the exceptions was a combination of exotic animals trained by Hugo Schmitt. In one of his rare seasons away from Ringling, Schmitt presented a guanaco, zebra and elephant in a meticulously executed liberty act. The llama-like guanaco was particularly captivating for an audience when it made soaring leaps over barricades in a seemingly effortless manner. This was a feature of Leonard Bros. Circus until Schmitt, like Joyce, returned to the Ringling banner, where both of their highly unusual acts appeared simultaneously.

Now the latest newcomer among mixed exotic acts is that of John Herriott of the Circus World Museum. He has successfully

trained a combination that includes camel, llama, horse, mule and pony and presented it at the Museum, then moved to Ringling.

When Van Amburgh began working with lions, it was act enough merely to be in the cage with a wild animal. Little by little trainers led the public to expect more until the lions and tigers were expected to perform dexterous feats on call. For some ferocious species, like the gorillas mentioned previously, it would always be enough for a performer merely to join them. But there are other cases in which animals once considered too vicious to show now have been exhibited successfully outside of any cage. Trained bear acts predate the modern circus and its acts, but still only certain types of bears were used in such open ring acts. The Pallenbergs, Klausers and others kept their bears on leashes while the animals performed, even to the extent of riding motorcycles. While brown bears and black bears have been worked without cages, this was thought to be impossible to achieve with polar bears until John Cuneo successfully trained such an animal. Similarly, Robert and Charlotte Baudy had a turn with leashed leopards.

Chimpanzees comprise species which frequently perform in the open ring. Their cute and comic expressions sometimes belie their true nature, because, although they are exhibited in little suits and shoes like children and they ride scooters or pogo sticks, the chimps quickly reach an age when they are dangerous. Old chimpanzees are responsible for more than a few nine-fingered trainers.

Less mobile and less vicious but equally out of their natural element are the trained seals or sea lions. Relative latecomers to circus performances, seals quickly became a favorite and nearly every big show carried them for about twenty years. They are born jugglers and so trainers generally worked them in routines of ball catching. Seal trainers also discovered they could put to use their charges' forceful exhaling. A set of tuned horns was procured and on cue the seals could blow specific notes. Then the most breathy among them, if not the most musical, could snort a recognizable version of "My Country 'Tis of Thee." When trainers broke the seals to slap their giant front flappers together, audiences took it for applause and the combination made seals among the most lovable comic animals in the circus. In recent seasons the big acts with four and six animals have disappeared and only a few single seals remain with circuses.

Opinions and results change with the generations. Once it was thought that camels would never be successful performers, but circus people keep striving for the impossible. Who can say there never will be a steel arena full of trained gorillas, and who can be sure some circus will not perfect a liberty act of giraffes?

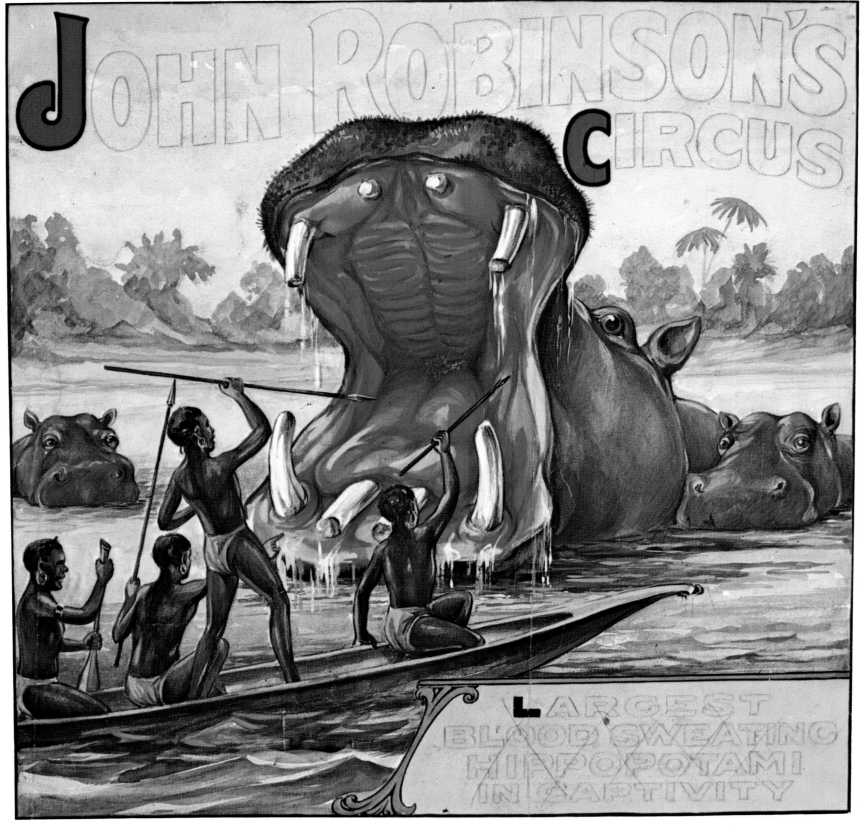

Circus audiences were startled and a little apprehensive when the hippopotamus was unleashed to lumber around the track.

Opposite: Because of his shapelessness, the blubbery sea elephant was never trained to perform. {1932} Right: Bears were worked on leashes outside their cages. {1916}

10-Elephants: The Circus's Favorite Animal

Wagons may roll, bands play and lions roar. But until an elephant shuffles onto the scene you don't know for sure that you have a circus. If any single element sets off a circus from other kinds of shows, it is the elephant. Barnum is supposed to have said that elephants and clowns are the pegs that circuses are hung upon. These strangest and largest of land animals are born troupers, great ham actors and a quadruped version of circus people themselves. Rain or shine the elephants are with it and for it.

As circuses grew, so did the elephant herds. Once the biggest circuses were fortunate to exhibit a single elephant. Ultimately the Ringling Bros. and Barnum & Bailey Circus of 1955 and 1956 exhibited a herd of fifty and more elephants. Often circuses of principal dimensions carry from five to fifteen elephants and occasionally herds are increased to twenty-five or thirty.

During the show, elephants make appearances in the spec and perhaps in single acts, but the big elephant display comes late in the program. With the trunk of one holding the tail of another, the herd trots into the big top and immediately splits into three groups, one for each ring. For convenience in making formations there usually are three or five to a ring. An elephant man works with the animals, cuing them and making sure that they do not get away with leaving out parts of the act or cutting corners. Usually a girl fronts the act. Knowing the routine, she is always in the right place to pose prettily when the animals form the next trick. Once in the ring the animals circle it at a trot and go into their act. The elephants might carry out a military drill; they form large, ponderous pyramids. In one routine the elephants put a foot on a pedestal and then move in a circle while the band plays merry-go-round music. While one makes a bridge another walks or crawls under it and the band plays "London Bridge Is Falling Down." Some elephants can walk a narrow plank and others, balanced precariously on a large cylinder, can walk it from point to point.

Some elephant trainers prefer for their giant charges to play diminutive scenes. Thus, in one routine the elephants act as if they are in a band, ringing bells, shaking cymbals, beating drums and faking the trombone and cornet parts. Another routine is set in a barber shop and one elephant ministers to another. There was an elephant baseball act and one involving an elephant which supposedly had imbibed too freely and was run in by the elephant which wore a police hat and carried a billy club in its trunk. In still another routine, one elephant sat on a tub alongside a giant table and rang a bell to summon another as waiter, then seemed to enjoy all the amenities of eating out.

The barber shop and dining table style of routine has been more suited to the small circuses, while large outfits have offered more of the pyramids, merry-go-rounds and London Bridge type of act.

In the past, a hind-leg stand or a foreleg stand appeared in most acts and others performed a hind-leg walk or foreleg walk. In recent seasons, a very few elephants have been trained to balance on one foot, the climax of their act.

Among the larger herds the finale is sure to be the long mount. In this, all of the elephants come out of the rings, gather around the hippodrome track in single file and move at once to the front side.

Opposite: The circus is often measured by the number of elephants it claims. {1927}

There, each stands on its hind legs and puts its forelegs on the back of the elephant in front. Sometimes they then walk along for a few elephant paces. It is an awesome thing to be sitting in the front row and have a dozen elephants tower over you in the long mount. With the act over, trainers and animals run out the back door.

It just might have been hippos instead of elephants that became the favorite circus animal. For size and strangeness, perhaps hippopotamuses might have done as well. But elephants are the animals that have come to be the circus favorite. For a time it appeared that camels had the edge. Once, shows had more camels than elephants and featured them in about the same way. But it is the elephant that captured the affection of the showmen and the public. Now the size of a circus often is measured by the number of elephants it can claim. Audiences murmur excitedly and even applaud when the elephant act appears.

Only the elephant serves a circus in so many ways. Mankind works in each department, but while many different men fill these jobs, elephants serve everywhere and the same few meet all those needs. A show may have a hundred horses, but some are liberty, some baggage, some high school, and some saddle (including one assigned to the elephant department). But the versatile elephants are not categorized. Although Hannibal had a huge army of men and horses, he is remembered for his thirty-three elephants. Ringling Bros. had up to a hundred cars, a thousand people, four

Above: Mac and Peggy MacDonald presented Baby Opal doing the one-leg stand in 1960 on Polack Bros. Circus, a feat accomplished by few elephants because of its unnaturalness.

Left: Elephants are natural-born hams and are thought of as quadruped versions of circus people: they have indomitable spirits, they are tireless and they invariably perform their hearts out.

The most famous elephant of all time, Jumbo was purchased by Barnum from the London Zoo and was billed in the 1880's as the largest brute on earth.

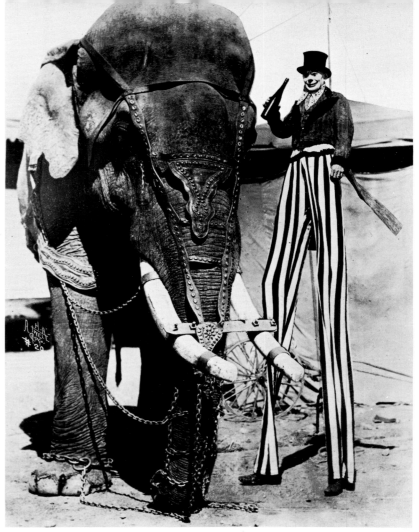

Above: Black Diamond was a gigantic bull Indian elephant on the Al G. Barnes Circus. In 1929 the animal killed a woman and the circus ordered it destroyed.

Left: A girl usually fronts the elephant act. "Trunk up!" is the call and the elephant lifts the girl high in the air.

hundred horses, but its elephants had an importance out of proportion to their number, whether it was four or forty.

On several circuses, the Barnes show in particular, the elephants helped unload the train and pulled wagons to the lot. Elephants might pull the stake driver wagon to its scores of stops and then lean into work harness to pull the center poles up into position. Elephants powered the rigging to raise the canvas itself. Then elephants made the march — the grand free street parade at noon. Next it was time for the afternoon performance in which elephants were dressed in spangled blankets for the spec and later came back for the featured elephant display. They might also be brought in for The Leaps or for single elephant numbers. All of this was duplicated at the night performance, after which the elephants pulled the stakes, hauled the wagons, loaded the train and then rode to the next town to repeat the whole process.

But that was not all. If the lot was muddy, elephants had the extra chore of helping teams drag wagons through the mire to reach firm ground. A recent development is that elephants tow private autos from the muddy show grounds — first the cars of customers and then the cars and house trailers of show people. The elephant handlers get extra tips for this service, but for the animals it is merely more tugging to do.

The public partiality for elephants just might be linked to the fact that for practical purposes and expressions, the elephant has no face. The big trunk fills the space where most animals have their faces. A lion can look sleepy or ferocious. A tiger's temperament can be measured by the way it snarls or bares its teeth. Sacred cattle and zebras have faces by which even an inexperienced human thinks he can gauge whether the animal is wild or dull, mean or friendly. But an elephant has no face — at least none that hints of

Most people consider the faceless elephant a lovable beast.

275

its mood to the untrained observer. Of course, elephant trainers disagree, because they know their animals, but the public cannot. Moreover, since the elephant is uncaged, circus goers have come to feel that it is a big, lovable friend. People, without their usual ways of gauging, assume the best of the beast. Children are awed by their size but not frightened by their countenance. The public looks upon elephants about like a Walt Disney creation — jolly and docile. That is hardly an accurate appraisal, however, for elephant men declare that elephants are like most wild animals: They sometimes are trained but never tamed for certain. Let down your guard and the friendliest of the herd may uncoil its trunk to slap his "friend" with a deadly blow.

However, because circus elephants usually are close enough for popular appraisal and enigmatic enough to hide any animosity, the public continues in its illusion. So the faceless elephant — not the hippo and not the camel — is the creature that the public likes best among the wild animals on a circus. A dog or a horse may be man's best friend at home, but not on a circus.

276

Above: Bill Woodcock, Sr., one of the top elephant trainers of this century, knew nearly every elephant in every circus herd — the bad ones, the hard workers, the leaders.

Above left: Because of their intelligence and tremendous strength, elephants were broken to harness and taught to push and pull. They were especially useful to free wagons mired in mud.

Opposite: Since they are always a hit, the elephants appear late in the program. {1909}

11-Flying Acts and the Finale

The circus holds the best until last. The elephants are late in the show and traditionally the flying trapeze is the finale. Show business, with all its Hamlets and its concertos, holds no more artistic moment than that in the performance of a flying return act. Here is grace and beauty, tone and form — here is that extra fillip of a true master as the flyer seems now to float, now to catapult through the air. It is as if he takes wing for that second to hover, flutter his pointed toes and then gently soar away. The best flyers and catchers are true artists. They are athletes, like a ballet dancer is an athlete.

It is a summer's matinee. The white top filters the sunshine and the audience's attention turns upward. A whistle sounds followed by a chord as the band eases into the delicate tones of ''The Crimson Petal Waltz''; the performers, graceful in their pink tights, bow to the audience and turn to their work.

There are at least three of them, often a man and a girl on the tiny aerial platform and another man swinging on a distant trapeze. The girl flies first. Poised and awaiting the critical point of timing, she drops something — a bit of paper, or was it a crimson petal? — to emphasize the height. Swinging out on the trapeze, hers is a simple trick to open the act. Sometimes it seems that as she and her fellow flyer alternate with more tricks there is superfluous swinging and stalling between stunts. She touches a cable as she steps to the edge of their tiny elevated world and he steps to the flybar. Barely crouched, holding the trapeze, he goes to his tiptoes and waits, counts, waits — and leaps into the sky. His lightning-like action slices the proper second. His launching power swings him high and wide, far above the center ring. Two, maybe three times he completes the giant arc. And then, timed to a semi-quaver, he throws his trick to the catcher.

Meanwhile, on the far end of the rigging, a big heavy-shouldered man with taped wrists has been sitting sideways on the bar of a short-rigged trapeze. He swings out the stalling time, then powerfully moves to the upside down position, wraps his legs around the canvased ropes of his trapeze. He is the catcher. The swings of those trapezes determine time in the flyer's world, just as if they were pendulums. On that timing, honed to an artist's sharpness, he claps his hands — and his flyer leaps.

It may be a somersault or a pirouette or a twister that swimmers call gainers. Then the flyer's wrists sock hard into the hands of the catcher. They swing to the far limits of the rigging and back again. Like the preview of an astronaut's rendezvous, the flyer leaves his catcher and turns to grasp what at first seems to be only air but suddenly becomes the other trapeze that transports him back to the starting platform.

Opposite: Men soar through the air as the breathtaking grand finale begins. {1892}

The Barnum & Bailey Greatest Show on Earth

NEW, GRACEFUL AND MOST FEARLESS FEATS PERFORMED IN MID-AIR UPON HORIZONTAL BARS, WITH REMARKABLE DIVES, TREMENDOUS AERIAL FLIGHTS AND THRILLING CATCHES. DOUBLE AND TRIPLE SOMERSAULTS BY THE LA MOYNE BROTHERS, THE ONLY ARTISTS IN THE WORLD EVER ATTEMPTING THESE PERILOUS PERFORMANCES.

THE WORLD'S GRANDEST, LARGEST, BEST, AMUSEMENT INSTITUTION.

The lights fade and all faces turn to the drama being enacted above them.
The success of the passing leap lies primarily in the hands of the catcher.

There are dozens of ways for the flyer to get to the catcher and back. Some are the simple maneuvers seen also on backyard swing sets. Some are difficult achievements, such as the double somersault, the two-and-a-half and the elusive triple.

Perhaps these same people early in the show performed on the horizontal bars. Their artistic cousins perform an act called "casting," which utilizes a ground-based rigging for stunts quite similar to those of the trapeze. Historically their own act once concerned a flyer's leaping from bar to bar and back; there was no catcher. Today, there are other kinds of trapeze performances, the single traps and double traps acts that entail the great skills of aerial acrobats.

But those who perform the flying return are the kings among aerialists, the supreme artists among daredevils. This particular kind of variation of aerial activity is French in origin. Americans perfected the art and thrived on its presentation. Now, accomplished Mexican artists predominate in the field, undoubtedly inspired by their countryman, Alfredo Codona. In the 1920's, an age of heroes and superstars in every field, Codona was the master among flyers. From his family's modest circus in Mexico he moved upward to the center ring of Ringling Bros. and Barnum & Bailey Circus. He, with his brother as catcher, mastered the speed and force of the triple somersault. That feat also was accomplished by the capable Flying Wards and then by the Flying Concellos. More recently, it was performed with regularity by the Flying Malkos, the Flying Gaonas and the Flying Valentines. Today others are doing the triple as well and there is talk of an unbelievable quadruple.

Sometimes big circuses have presented two flying acts simultaneously, or even one over each ring. There have been criss-cross flying acts which placed some flyers in a trajectory bisecting that of others. The Ward-Bell Flyers had a three-in-one rigging and nine people. Their most spectacular stunt was a three-way passing leap. Three flyers went simultaneously to three catchers. Three more flyers leaped out with the three intermediate trapezes. Each catcher tossed a flyer away and almost instantly caught another. At that moment there were six people flying in mid-air. The audience was aghast at the spectacular confusion. Then catchers and trapezes sorted out the soaring humans and wafted them off to safety.

At the end of a flying act, each flyer in turn takes the trapeze to mid-point and then dives into the safety net. The girls perform a simple and graceful free fall, the catcher a more elaborate drop.

Lalo Codona {right} was catcher for his brother Alfredo {left}. The Flying Codonas were outstanding aerialists who mastered the triple somersault.

Then the star flyer swings the trapeze to its peak, his back touching the very top of the tent. Pressing the trapeze for speed, he rides it out and then plummets in a graceful swan dive. At the last instant, he cuts back to save his neck. Upon impact, the net bounces him back into the air and then accepts him again as a groundling. The trio steps to the ring curb to take its bows.

More often than not this closes a circus performance. As the equestrian director thanks the audience, prop hands and riggers attack the flyers' net, ushers slam shut the first of the thousands of folding chairs. The flyers, mere humans again, head for the pad room, now dodge the riggers and the avalanche of customers coming down out of the seats. As the crowd walks toward the exit, an army of circus roustabouts moves in behind them, seemingly devouring the tonnage of rigging, seats and props, then spewing it into the baggage wagons.

The rest of the circus gear has already been packed away, thus bewildering the audience as it steps out to where the menagerie was and discovers only the ordinary pasture remains. The cookhouse and cotton candy are gone. The cages and ticket wagons have disappeared. Still, the generator wagon rumbles and trucks and teams and tractors move their loads on the first step of their journey to the next town.

The circus is all out and over. It is almost down and almost gone. By just after midnight this will be yesterday's town, and today is waiting a hundred miles ahead.

Spectacular aerial acts never fail to stupefy the crowds below.

Adam Forepaugh's New and Greatest All-Feature Show. {1890}

THE GRANDEST OUTPOURING OF MAGNIFICENT SURPRISES EVER SEEN ON EARTH

As presented in the Stupendous Highway Parade of this Great Show; introducing 50 Cages of Wild Beasts, 12 Gorgeous Golden Tableau Cars, Wonderfully Constructed and Ornamented Chariots, Steam Musical Instruments, 10 Bands of Music, Highland Bagpipers, Continental Martial Bands, 9 Teams of Elephants, 3 Teams of Camels drawing Chariot Cages, Congress of Nations Grouped on Floats, Jubilee Singers, a Whole Army of Led Animals, 500 Men, Women and Children.

Sells Bros. Circus. {1884}

Bibliography

There are known to exist approximately 1,100 books on the specific subject of the circus that have been printed in English. This bibliography of 160 titles deals with those books pertaining to the American circus (with very few exceptions) that are historical and factual. The novels *Chad Hanna* and *Toby Tyler* are exceptions and are listed because they have become classics in this field. Library of Congress press marks have been included where known.

— — The Authors

Alden, W. L. *Among the Freaks.* Longmans Green & Co., 1896.

Allen, Edward, and Kelley, F. Beverly. *Fun by the Ton.* New York: Hastings House, 1948.

American Heritage. *Great Days of the Circus* (LC 62-12907). American Heritage Publishing Company, 1962.

Bailey, Olga. *Mollie Bailey* (LC GV 1811. B23B3). Harben-Spotts Co., 1943.

Ballentine, Bill. *Wild Tigers & Tame Fleas.* Rinehart & Co., 1958.

Banks, G. L. *Blondin, His Life and Performances.* Routledge, Warne & Routledge, 1862.

Barnum, P. T. *An Autobiography* (LC GV 1811. B3A3). 3d ed. Redfield, 1885.

———. *Barnum's Own Story.* New York: Dover Publications, 1961.

Barton, Bob. *Old Covered Wagon Show Days as told to G. Ernest Thomas* (LC PZ7. B284701). New York: E. P. Dutton & Co., 1939.

Beal, George Brinton. *Through the Back Door of the Circus* (LC GV 1815. B32). McLaughlin Bros., 1938.

Beatty, Clyde. *The Big Cage* (LC GV 1829. B4). New York: The Century Co., 1933.

Bernard, Charles. *Half Century Reviews and Red Wagon Stories* (LC GV 1815. B4). The Author, 1931.

Bodin, Walter, and Burnet, Hershey. *It's a Small World, Story of Midgets.* New York: Coward-McCann, 1934.

Bostock, E. H. *Menageries, Circuses and Theatres.* New York: F. A. Stokes, 1928.

Bostock, Frank. *The Training of Wild Animals* (LC GV 1829. B74). New York: The Century Co., 1903.

Bowman, Harry P. *As Told on a Sunday Run.* Flint, Michigan: Circus Research Foundation, 1942.

Bradna, Fred. *The Big Top* (LC GV 1815. B7). New York: Simon & Schuster, 1952.

Brick, Hans. *The Nature of the Beast.* New York: Crown Publishers, 1962.

Brown, Maria Ward. *The Life of Dan Rice.* London Branch, New Jersey: The Author, 1901.

Burroughs, W. H. *The Art of Training Animals.* Excelsior Pub. Co., 1869.

Carrington, Hereward. *Side Show & Animal Tricks.* Sphinx, 1913.

Cavin, Lee. *There were Giants on the Earth.* Seville, Ohio *Chronicle,* 1959.

Chindahl, George L. *A History of the Circus in America* (LC GV 1803. C47). Caldwell, Idaho: The Caxton Printers, Ltd., 1959.

Chipman, Bert. *Hey Rube* (LC GV 1815 C5). Hollywood Print Shop, 1933.

Cochran, Charles Blake. *The Secrets of a Showman.* New York: Henry Holt, 1926.

Cody, Louisa F. *Memories of Buffalo Bill.* New York: Appleton, 1919.

Collier, Edmund. *The Story of Annie Oakley* (LC PZ 7. C6777SR). New York: Grosset & Dunlap, 1956.

Collings, Ellsworth, and Miller, Alma. *The 101 Ranch.* Norman: University of Oklahoma Press, 1937.

Conklin, George. *The Ways of the Circus* (LC GV 1811. C6A3). New York: Harper & Brothers, 1921.

Conover, R. E. *Telescoping Tableaux.* Xenia, Ohio: The Author, 1956.

———. *The Life and Times of James A. Bailey.* Xenia, Ohio: The Author, 1957.

———. *The Great Forepaugh Show.* Xenia, Ohio: The Author, 1959.

———. *Allegorical Pony-Drawn Parade Floats.* Xenia, Ohio: The Author, 1960.

———. *European Influence on the American Circus Parade.* Xenia, Ohio: The Author, 1961.

———. *Give 'em a John Robinson.* Xenia, Ohio: The Author, 1965.

———. *The Circus, Wisconsin's Unique Heritage.* Baraboo: Circus World Museum, 1967.

———. *The Fielding Bandchariots.* Xenia, Ohio: The Author, 1969.

Cooper, Courtney Riley. *Annie Oakley, Woman at Arms* (LC GV 1157. 03C6). New York: Duffield & Brothers, 1927.

———. *Circus Day* (LC GV 1815. C77). New York: Farrar & Rinehart, 1931.

———. *Lions 'n' Tigers 'n' Everything* (LC GV 1815. C78). Boston: Little, Brown and Company, 1924.

———. *Under the Big Top* (LC GV 1815. C8). Boston: Little, Brown and Company, 1923.

———. *With the Circus.* Boston: Little, Brown and Company, 1924.

Cooper, Frank C. *The Stirring Lives of Buffalo Bill and Pawnee Bill.* New York: S. L. Parsons & Co., 1912.

Coplan, Maxwell Frederick, and Kelley, F. Beverly. *Pink Lemonade.* New York: McGraw-Hill Book Company, Inc., 1945.

Coup, W. C. *Sawdust & Spangles; Stories & Secrets of the Circus* (LC GV 1815. C85). Henry S. Stone & Co., 1901.

Court, Alfred. *My Life with the Big Cats* (LC GV 1829. C615). New York: Simon & Schuster, Inc., 1955.

Day, Charles E. *Show Life Illustrated* (LC PN 6231. C4D3). S. Booth, 1873.

Delavoye, Will. *Show Life in America.* The Author, 1925.

Denier, Tony. *How to Join a Circus.* New York: Dick & Fitzgerald Co., 1877.

DeWolff, J. H. *Pawnee Bill's True History of the Great West.* Pawnee Bill's Historic Wild West Co., 1902.

Dhotre, Damoo G. *Wild Animal Man.* Boston: Little, Brown and Company, 1961.

Dickens, Charles. *Memories of Joseph Grimaldi.* T. B. Peterson, 1875.

Driesbach, Dan. *Musician's Secrets of Circus Business.* DeGroot, 1880.

Durant, John and Alice. *Pictorial History of the American Circus.* Cranbury, New Jersey: A. S. Barnes & Co., Inc.. 1957.

Edmonds, Walter D. *Chad Hanna,* Boston: Little, Brown and Company, 1940.

Edwards, W. F. L. *Story of Jumbo.* Sutherland Press Ltd., 1935.

Fawcett, Claire H. *We Fell in Love with the Circus.* Lindquist, 1949.

Fellows, Dexter W. *This Way to the Big Show* (LC GV 1811. F4A3). New York: Viking Press, 1936.

Ferguson, O. J. *Biographical Sketch of Van Amburgh.* Booth & Co., 1865.

Fillis, James. *Principes de Dressage* (LC SF 287. F5). C. Marpon et E. Flammarion, 1890.

Fox, C. P. *Circus Parades-A Pictorial History* (LC GV 1801. F68). New York: Century House, 1953.

———. *Circus Trains.* Kalmbach Publishing Company, 1947.

———. *Pictorial History of Performing Horses.* Seattle: Superior Publishing Company, 1960.

———. *A Ticket to the Circus.* Seattle: Superior Publishing Company, 1959.

Frost, Thomas. *Circus Life and Celebrities.* Chalto & Windus, 1881.

Gipson, Fred. *Fabulous Empire; Colonel Zack Miller's Story.* Boston: Houghton Mifflin, 1946.

Glenroy, John H. *Ins & Outs of Circus Life.* M. M. Wing, 1885.

Gollmar, Robert H. *My Father Owned a Circus* (LC 65-13651 GV1821. G6G6). Caldwell, Idaho: The Caxton Printers, Ltd., 1965.

Gould, Geo. M., AM and MD, and Pyle, Walter, LMD. *Anomalies & Curiosities of Medicine,* 2 vols. W. B. Saunders, 1900.

Graham, Philip. *Showboats, A History of an American Institution.* Austin: University of Texas Press, 1951.

The Great American Circus. McLaughlin, 1889.

Greenwood, Isaac J. *The Circus; Its Origin and Growth Prior to 1835* (LC GV 1801. G8). Dunlap Society, 1898.

Griffin, C. E. *A Circus Man's Diary & Route Book.* Petland Press, 1908.

———. *Four Years in Europe with Buffalo Bill* (LC GV 1821. B93). Stage Publishing Company, 1908.

———. *How to Become a Contortionist.* New York: The Author, 1908.

———. *Juggling & Balancing.* New York: The Author, 1908.

———. *Rope & Wire Walking Made Easy.* New York: The Author, 1908.

Griswold, Larry. *Trampoline Tumbling.* Cranbury, New Jersey: A. S. Barnes & Co., Inc., 1948.

Hacker, Fred A., and Eames, P. W. *How to Put On an Amateur Circus.* Chicago: T. S. Denison, 1923.

Haines, G. W. *P. T. Barnum & His Museum.* New York: The Author, 1874.

Hamid, George A. *Circus, as told to his Son.* New York: Sterling Publishing Co., Inc., 1950.

Hamilton, Harry. *All their Children were Acrobats.* Indianapolis: The Bobbs-Merrill Co., Inc., 1936.

Harlow, Alvin F. *The Ringlings — Wizards of the Circus.* New York: Messner, 1951.

Henderson, J. Y. *Circus Doctor* (LC SF 613. H4A3). Boston: Little, Brown and Company, 1951.

Hubler, Richard G. *The Cristianis.* Boston: Little, Brown and Company, 1966.

Hudgins, Mary. *What and How of the Amateur Circus.* Chicago: Dramatic Publishing Company, 1928.

Hunt, Charles T. *The Story of Mr. Circus.* The Record Press, 1954.

Jennings, John J. *Theatrical & Circus Life.* Barney & Deland, 1884.

Keller, George. *Here Keller, Train This* (LC GV 1829. K38). New York: Random House, Inc., 1961.

Kelley, F. Beverly. *Denver Brown and the Traveling Town.* Exposition Press, 1966.

Kelly, Emmett, with Kelley, F. Beverly. *Clown*. New York: Prentice-Hall, Inc., 1954.

Kern, Alfred. *The Clown*. Translated by Gerard Hopkins. New York: Pantheon Books, 1960.

Kerr, Alex. *No Bars Between*. New York: Appleton-Century-Crofts, 1957.

Kober, Auguste H. *Circus Nights and Circus Days*. New York: Morrow, 1931.

Kunzog, John. *The One Horse Show (Life of Dan Rice)*. The Author, 1962.

Lambert, Wm. *Show Life in America*. W. Delavoye, 1925.

Lano, David. *A Wandering Showman*. East Lansing: Michigan State University Press, 1957.

Lathrop, West. *River Circus*. New York: Random House, 1953.

Leighton, Peter. *Memoirs of a Tattooist*. New York: Crown Publishers, Inc., 1958.

Lewis, George. *Elephant Tramp*. Boston: Little, Brown and Company, 1955.

Liederman, E. *Secrets of Strength, Strong Men*. New York: The Author, 1925.

Maloney, Tom. *Circus Days and What Goes On Back of the Big Top*. Philadelphia: Edward Stern, 1934.

Mannix, Dan. *Memoirs of a Sword Swallower*. Hamish-Hamilton, 1951.

Marcosson, Isaac F. *Autobiography of a Clown (Jules Turnour)*. New York: Moffatt, Yard and Company, 1910.

May, Earl Chaplin. *The Circus from Rome to Ringling* (LC GV 1801. M3). New York: Duffield & Green, 1932.

Metcalf, Francis. *Side Show Studies*. Outing Publishing Co., 1906.

Middleton, George. *Circus Memories*. Geo. Rice & Sons, 1913.

Mix, Olive Stokes. *The Fabulous Tom Mix* (LC PN 2287. M65M5). Englewood Cliffs, New Jersey: Prentice-Hall, 1957.

Moffett, Cleveland. *Careers of Danger and Daring*. Century Co., 1906.

Moll, Henry. *The Art of Juggling*. Henry Moll Co., 1949.

Moss, Arthur, and Harzberg, Hiler. *Slapstick & Dumbbell*. Jos. Lauren, 1924.

Newton, Douglas. *Clowns — History of Clowning*. Franklin Watts, Inc., 1957.

North, Henry Ringling. *The Circus Kings* (LC GV 1821. R5N6). Garden City, New York: Doubleday & Company, Inc., 1960.

Norwood, E. P. *The Circus Menagerie* (LC GV 1815. N55). Garden City, New York: Doubleday & Page, 1929.

——. *The Other Side of the Circus*. Garden City, New York: Doubleday & Page, 1926.

Orr, G. *Here Come the Elephants*. Caldwell, Idaho: The Caxton Printers, Ltd., 1943.

Otis, James. *Toby Tyler* (LC P27. K124-T021). New York: Harper Bros., 1880.

Pancoast, C. L. *Trail Blazers of Advertising*. The Grafton Press, 1924.

Parry, Albert. *Tattoo*. New York: Simon & Schuster, Inc., 1933.

Paulinette, P. H. *The True Art of Hand Balancing* (LC GV 553. P3). Geo. D. Lamb, 1931.

Posey, Jake. *Last of the Forty Horse Drivers* (LC GV 1811. P65A3). New York: Vantage Press, 1959.

Proske, Roman. *Lions, Tigers and Me* (LC GV 1829. P7). New York: Holt, 1956.

Proulx, Zotique. *How to Become a Wire Walker* (LC GV 553. P96). Roylance Printing, 1896.

Reichmann, William D. *Arthur Konyot, My 60 Years as a Circus Equestrian*. Barrington, Illinois: Hill & Dale Press, 1961.

Reynolds, Chang. *Pioneer Circuses of the West*. Los Angeles: Westernlore Press, 1966.

Rigney, Wm. J. *The Great American Circus*. McLaughlin Bros., 1889.

Ringling, Alf. T. *Life of the Ringling Bros.* (LC GV 1811. R5A3). R. R. Donnelley & Sons, 1900.

Ripley, Wm. Z. *Professional Gymnast & Acrobat* (LC GV 551. R57). Peck & Snyder, 1879.

Robeson, Dave. *Louis Roth; 40 Years with Jungle Killers*. Caldwell, Idaho: The Caxton Printers, Ltd., 1941.

——. *Al G. Barnes, Master Showman* (LC GV 1811. B27R6). Caldwell, Idaho: The Caxton Printers, Ltd., 1935.

Robinson, Gil. *Old Wagon Show Days* (LC GV 1815. R57). Cincinnati: Brockwell Publishers, 1925.

Robinson, Josephine DeMott. *The Circus Lady*. New York: Thomas Y. Crowell Company, 1926.

Rosenberg, C. G. *Jenny Lind in America and Cuba*. New York: Stringer and Townsend, 1851.

Rowe, J. A. *California's Pioneer Circus* (LC GV 1821. R6). H. S. Crocker Co., 1926.

Russell, Donald B. *The Lives and Legends of Buffalo Bill*. Norman: University of Oklahoma Press, 1960.

Scott, Matthew. *Autobiography of Jumbo's Keeper* (LC QL-795. E454). Trows Printing & Booking Co., 1885.

Sell, H. B., and Weybright, Victor. *Buffalo Bill and the Wild West*. New York: Oxford University Press, 1955.

Sherwood, R. E. *Here We Are Again* (LC GV 1811. S5A3). Indianapolis: The Bobbs-Merrill Co., Inc., 1926.

——. *Hold yer Hosses! The Elephants are Coming!* New York: The Macmillan Company, 1932.

Shirley, Glenn. *Pawnee Bill; A Biography of Major Gordon Lillie*. Albuquerque: University of New Mexico Press, 1958.

Stark, Mabel. *Hold that Tiger*. Caldwell, Idaho: The Caxton Printers, Ltd., 1938.

——. *Tiger Lady* (LC GV 1829. S7). Caldwell, Idaho: The Caxton Printers, Ltd., 1938.

Stott, R. Toole. *Circus & Allied Arts; A World Bibliography*. 4 vols. Derby, England: Harpur & Sons, Ltd., 1958.

Taylor, Robert Lewis. *Center Ring*. Garden City, New York: Doubleday, 1956.

Thomas, Lowell. *Men of Daring*. New York: Grosset & Dunlap, 1937.

Thomas, Richard. *John Ringling*. Pageant Press Inc., 1960.

Thompson, Wm. C. *On the Road with a Circus* (LC GV 1815. T46). Goldmann, 1903.

Tyron, John. *The Old Clown's History* (LC GV 1815. T87). Torrey Bros., 1872.

Upton, George P. *Musical Memories* (LC ML 423. U61). Chicago: A. M. McClurg & Co., 1908.

Vail, R. W. G. *History of Early American Circus* (LC E172. A35). American Antiquarian Society, 1934.

Walston, E. C. *Secrets of Circus and Theatrical Business*. J. W. Pepper, 1887.

Ware, James A. *Gargantua the Great*. New York: William Morrow & Co., Inc., 1959.

Webber, Malcolm. *Medicine Show* (LC GV 1815. W4). Caldwell, Idaho: The Caxton Printers, Ltd., 1941.

Werner, M. R. *"Barnum"*. New York: Harcourt, Brace & World, Inc., 1923.

Willson, Dixie. *Where the World Folds Up at Night*. D. Appleton & Co., 1932.

Wood, Ed. J. *Giants and Dwarfs*. Richard Bentley, 1868.

Xenophon. *The Art of Horsemanship* (LC SF 309. X5). Boston: Little, Brown and Company, 1893.

Zora, Lucia. *Sawdust and Solitude* (LC GV 1811. 26A3). Boston: Little, Brown and Company, 1928.

Zucker, Hal. *Tattooed Women and Their Mates*. Andre Levy, 1955.